Classical and Modern Cryptography for Beginners

Rajkumar Banoth • Rekha Regar

Classical and Modern Cryptography for Beginners

 Springer

Rajkumar Banoth
Department of Computer Science
The University of Texas at San Antonio
San Antonio, TX, USA

Rekha Regar
Indian Institute of Technology (IIT)
Kharagpur, India

ISBN 978-3-031-32961-6   ISBN 978-3-031-32959-3   (eBook)
https://doi.org/10.1007/978-3-031-32959-3

This Springer imprint is published by the registered company Springer Nature Switzerland AG
The registered company address is: Gewerbestrasse 11, 6330 Cham, Switzerland

Preface

Both the transmission of information and its security are aspects of the same tapestry, with the protection aspect having more twisted and complex strands. The more specialized field of classical cryptography, which prevents a communication's content from being understood by uninvited recipients but does not else secure the message, is at the center of the topic of information protection. This book devotes a good deal of its time to discussing cryptography in the traditional sense, but it does it in a highly advanced manner. This book's content reflects the interesting intersection of computer science, engineering, informatics, and mathematics that characterizes the present fields of cryptography and information protection in general.

Information security is quickly becoming into a topic that extends much beyond the traditional ideas of point-to-point cryptography. Security and confidentiality are becoming essential components of huge public networks. Many other critical concerns, such as those related to authorization, certification, and authentication that bring many delicate considerations into the discussion, are significant within this wider context of public networked communication. The book focuses on these other subjects even though cryptography is its main focus. Our focus is on the formal, and hopefully timeless, parts of the topic rather than the specifics of systems that are already in use.

San Antonio, TX, USA
Kharagpur, India

Rajkumar Banoth
Rekha Regar

Acknowledgments

Writing this book, entitled as *Classical and Modern Cryptography for Beginners*, is not soft to touch than we thought and is more important than we could have ever imagined.

I Dr. Rajkumar would say, None of this would have been possible without my best friend.

Mr. Praveen Choudhary, Staff Software Engineer—SONiC at LinkedIn, USA. He was the first friend I made when I moved to National Institute of Technology, Hamirpur, India, for my graduate studies. He stood by me during every struggle and all my successes. That is true friendship.

I'm eternally grateful to Professor and Chair of Computer Science and ACM Distinguished Scientist Dr. Sushil K. Prasad who took in an extra interest to motivate me to write this book where he didn't have to. He taught me discipline, manners, respect, and so much more that has helped me succeed in the current tenure at the University of Texas San Antonio.

Dr. Rajkumar Banoth:

To my mother (Ulli) and brother (Cheenya), thank you for letting me know that you have nothing but great memories of me; special thanks to Aruna Kranti for designing the images of this book on time. So thankful to have you in my life. To Aunt and Uncle Subhashini (a school teacher) and Dr. Hanamantah Rao: for always being the persons I could turn to during those dark and tough years. They sustained me in ways that I never knew that I needed.

Finally, to all those who have been a part of my journey to write this book.

Rekha Regar:

Special thanks to my mother (Laxmi Devi), father (Bhagwan Lal), brother (Devkishan), and sisters (Tara, Sangeeta), who have always been with me and strongly supported to follow my insights for the betterment of family and friends.

Contents

List of Figures

List of Tables

About the Authors

Rajkumar Banoth, B.Tech, M.Tech, Ph.D. is Associate Professor at the University of Texas San Antonio, USA. He is IEEE senior member and Cyber Security Operations Certified Trainer. He has published eight books comprising domains such as Networking, Computer Organization and Architecture, and Computer Forensic, published 27 Hi-indexed SCI and Scopus journals, and presented nine conference papers. He is a member of "The Institution of Engineers (India)" and so on.

ORCID: https://orcid.org/my-orcid?orcid=0000-00 02-0398-2754

Rekha Regar, B.Tech, M.Tech, (Ph.D.) is a PhD Scholar at the Centre of Excellence in Artificial Intelligence, Indian Institute of Technology, Kharagpur, India. She has done Master of Technology in Information Security from the National Institute of Technology, Jalandhar, India. She has done Bachelor of Engineering in Computer Science and Engineering from M. B. M. Engineering College, Jodhpur, India.

ORCID: https://orcid.org/0000-0003-1791-125X

Abbreviations

3DES	Triple Data Encryption Standard
AE	Authenticated Encryption
AEAD	Authenticated Encryption with Associated Data
AES	Advanced Encryption Standard
ALPN	Application-Layer Protocol Negotiation
ANSI	American National Standards Institute
ARP	Address Resolution Protocol
BEAST	Browser Exploit Against SSL/TLS
CBC	Cipher Block Chaining
CCM	Counter with CBC-MAC
CCMP	CTR Mode with CBC-MAC Protocol
CFB	Cipher Feedback
CMAC	Cipher-based Message Authentication Code
CMC	CBC-Mask-CBC
CRC	Cyclic Redundancy Check
CRL	Certificate Revocation List
CTR	Counter
CWC	Carter-Wegman + CTR mode
DES	Data Encryption Standard
DH	Diffie-Hellman
DNS	Domain Name System
DSA	Digital Signature Algorithm
DSS	Digital Signature Standard
EAP	Extensible Authentication Protocol
ECB	Electronic Codebook
ECC	Elliptic Curve Cryptography
ECDSA	Elliptical Curve Digital Signature Algorithm
EME	ECB-Mask-ECB
HMAC	Keyed-Hash Message Authentication Code
HTTPS	Hyper Text Transfer Protocol Secure
IAPM	Integrity Aware Parallelizable Mode

ICM	Integer Counter Mode
IDEA	International Data Encryption Algorithm
IEC	International Electrotechnical Commission
IEEE	Institute of Electrical and Electronics Engineers
IETF	Internet Engineering Task Force
ISO	International Organization for Standardization
IV	Initialization Vector
KEK	Key Encryption Key
KPK	Key Production Key
KSA	Key-Scheduling Algorithm
LSB	Least Significant Bit
MAC	Message Authentication Code
MD	Message Digest
MD5	Message Digest 5
MEK	Message Encryption Key
MITM	Meet In the Middle
MPDU	MAC Protocol Data Unit
MSB	Most Significant Bit
NIST	National Institute of Standards and Technology
NPN	Next Protocol Negotiation
OCB	Offset Code Book
OFB	Output Feedback
OMAC	One-key MAC
OTP	One-Time Pad
PCBC	Propagating Cipher Block Chaining
PGP	Pretty Good Privacy
PIN	Personal Identification Number
PKC	Public Key Cryptography
PKCS	Public Key Cryptography Standards
PKI	Public Key Infrastructure
PKIX	Public Key Infrastructure X.509
PRG	Pseudo-random Generator
PRGA	Pseudo-random Generation Algorithm
RC4	Rivest Cipher 4
RFC	Request For Comments
RSA	Rivest, Shamir, Adleman
SHA	Secure Hash Algorithm
SIC	Segmented Integer Counter
SISWG	Security in Storage Working Group
SRTP	Secure Real-time Transport Protocol
SSH	Secure Shell
SSL	Secure Socket Layer
SSPI	Security Support Provider Interface
SV	Starting Variable
TDEA	Triple Data Encryption Algorithm

TEA	Tiny Encryption Algorithm
TEK	Traffic Encryption Key
TKIP	Temporal Key Integrity Protocol
TLS	Transport Layer Security
TSK	Transmission Security Key
UDP	User Datagram Protocol
VMPC	Variably Modified Permutation Composition
VPN	Virtual Private Network
WEP	Wired Equivalent Privacy
WPA	Wi-Fi Protected Access
WPA2	Wi-Fi Protected Access II
WPS	Wi-Fi Protected Setup
XOR	Exclusive OR
XTS	XEX Tweakable Block Cipher with Ciphertext Stealing

Chapter 1
An Introduction to Classical and Modern Cryptography

1.1 Overview

Securing Communications

One must provide support to secure data as it travels across links. There are four elements of secure communications:

1. *Data Integrity*
2. *Origin Authentication*
3. *Data Confidentiality*
4. *Data Non-Repudiation*

Cryptography can be used almost anywhere that there is data communication. Hashes are used to verify and ensure data integrity. Hashing is based on a one-way mathematical function that is relatively easy to compute, but significantly harder to reverse. The cryptographic hashing function can also be used to verify integrity. A hash function takes a variable block of binary data, called the message, and produces a fixed-length, condensed representation, called the hash.

There are four well-known hash functions:

1. *MD5 with 128-bit digest,*
2. *SHA-1*
3. *SHA-2*
4. *SHA-3*

While hashing can be used to detect accidental changes, it cannot be used to guard against deliberate changes that are made by a threat actor. Hashing is vulnerable to man-in-the-middle attacks. To provide integrity and origin authentication, something more is required. To add authentication to integrity assurance, use a keyed-has message code (HMAC). HMAC uses an additional secret key as input to the hash function.

R. Banoth, R. Regar, *Classical and Modern Cryptography for Beginners*,
https://doi.org/10.1007/978-3-031-32959-3_1

Data Confidentiality
There are two classes of encryption that are used to provide data confidentiality:

1. Asymmetric
2. Symmetric.

These two classes differ in how they use keys.

Symmetric encryption algorithms, such as DES, 3 DES, and AES are based on the premise that each communicating party knows the pre-shared key. Data confidentiality can also be ensured using asymmetric algorithms, including Rivest, Shamir, and Adleman (RSA) and PKI. **Symmetric algorithms** are commonly used with VPN traffic because they use less CPU resources than asymmetric encryption algorithms. Symmetric encryption algorithms are sometimes classified as either block cipher or stream ciphers.

Asymmetric algorithms (public key algorithms) are designed so that the key that is used for encryption is different from the key used for decryption. Asymmetric algorithms use a public and private key. Examples of protocols that use asymmetric key algorithms included IKE, SSL, SSH, and PGP. Common examples of asymmetric encryption algorithms include DSS, DSA, RSA, ElGamal, and elliptic curve techniques.

Asymmetric algorithms are used to provide confidentiality without pre-sharing a password. The process is summarized using this formula: *Public key (Encrypt) + Private Key (Decrypt) = Confidentiality*. The authentication objective of an asymmetric algorithm is initiated when the encryption process is started with the private key. The process can be summarized with this formula: *Private Key (Encrypt) + Public Key (Decrypt) = Authentication*. Combining the two asymmetric encryption processes provides message confidentiality, authentication, and integrity. Diffie-Hellman (DH) is an asymmetric mathematical equation algorithm that allows two computers to generate an identical shared secret key without having communicate before. Two examples of instances when DH is used are when data is exchanges using an IPsec VPN, and when SSH data is exchanged.

Public Key Cryptography
Digital signatures are a mathematical technique used to provide three basic security services:

1. Authenticity
2. Integrity
3. Nonrepudiation

Properties of digital signature are that they are authentic, unalterable, not reusable, and non-repudiated. Digital signatures are commonly used in the following two situations:

1. Code Signing
2. Digital Certificates

There are three Digital Signature Standard (DSS) algorithms that are used for generating and verifying digital signatures:

1. Digital Signature Algorithm (DSA)
2. Rivet-Shamir Adelman Algorithm (RSA)
3. Elliptical Curve Digital Signature Algorithm (ECDSA)

Digitally signing code provides assurances about the software code: the code is authentic and is actually sourced by the publisher, the code has not been modified since it left the software publisher, and the publisher undeniably published the code. A digital certificate is equivalent to an electronic passport. It enables users, hosts, and organizations to securely exchanges information over the internet. Specifically, a digital certificate is used to authenticate and verify that a user who is sending a message is who they claim to be.

Authorities and the PKI Trust System
When establishing secure connection between two hosts, the hosts will exchange their public key information. There are trusted third parties on the internet that validate the authenticity of these public keys using digital certificates. The Public Key Infrastructure (PKI) consists of specifications, systems, and tools that are used to create, manage, distribute, use, store, and revoke digital certificates. PKI is needed to support large-scale distribution of public encryption keys.

The PKI framework facilitates a highly scalable trust relationship. Many vendors provide CA servers as a managed service or as an end-user product. Some of these vendors include Symantec Group (VeriSign), Comodo, Go Daddy Group, GlobalSign, and DigiCert among others. The class number (0 thorough 5) is determined by how rigorous the procedure was that verified the identity of the holder when the certificate was issued, with five being the highest. PKIs can form different topologies of trust. The simplest is the single-root PKI topology. Interoperability between PKI and its supporting services is a concern because many CA vendors have proposed and implemented proprietary solution instead of waiting for standards to develop. To address the interoperability concern, the IETF published the Internet X > 509 Public Key Infrastructure Certificate Policy and Certification Framework (RFC 2527).

Applications and Impacts of Cryptography
There are many common uses of PKIs including a few listed here:

1. SSL/TLS Certificate-Based Peer Authentication
2. HTTPS Web Traffic,
3. Secure Instant Message
4. Securing USB Storage Devices

A security analyst must be able to recognize and solve potential problems related to permitting PHI-related solutions on the enterprise network. For example, threat actors can use SSL/TSL to introduce regulatory compliance violations, viruses, malware, data loss, and intrusion attempts in the network.

Other SSL/TSL related issues may be associated with validating the certificate of the web server. PKI-related issues that are associated with security warnings include validity date range and signature validation. Some of these issues can be avoided due to the fact that the SSL/TSL protocols are extensible and modular. This is known as the *cipher suite*.

The key components of the *cipher suite* are the

1. Message Authentication Code Algorithm (MAC)
2. The Encryption Algorithm
3. The Key Exchange Algorithm
4. The Authentication Algorithm.

Cryptography is dynamic and always changing. One must maintain a good understanding of algorithms and operations to be able to investigate cryptography-related security incidents. Encrypted communications can make network security data payloads unreadable by cybersecurity analysts. Encryption can be used to hide malware command and control traffic between infected hosts and the command and control servers. In addition, malware can be hidden by encryption and data can be encrypted during exfiltration, making it hard to detect.

Therefore, this chapter gives basic understanding of cryptography along with substitution, transposition, symmetric-key and asymmetric-key algorithms. Some basic terms of cryptography like Plaintext, Ciphertext, Cryptology, Cryptanalysis, Symmetric key and Asymmetric key. It gives knowledge of the cryptography ciphers like Ceaser cipher which is most basic cipher for encryption and decryption, Substitution cipher, Vigenere cipher, Transposition and Permutation cipher, Frequency analysis for an algorithm, Playfair cipher, Block cipher.

1.2   Introduction to Cryptography

Cryptography can be powerful or vulnerable. The amount of time and resources needed to decrypt plaintext is a measure of the strength of a cryptographic system. Strong cryptography produces ciphertext that is incredibly difficult to crack without the right decoding software. How hard is it? It is impossible to decipher the outcome of strong cryptography until the end of the universe, even with all the processing power and time available today—even a billion computers performing a billion checks every second.

Therefore, it stands to reason that robust cryptography will withstand even the most tenacious cryptanalyst. Who can truly say? No one has demonstrated that the best encryption now available will remain effective in the face of future computational capability. However, PGP uses the strongest cryptography that is currently accessible. But rather than boasting about being impenetrable, practise caution and restraint. An encryption and decryption process uses a mathematical function known as a cryptographic algorithm, sometimes known as a cypher. The plaintext is encrypted using a cryptographic technique and a key, which might be a word, number, or phrase.

With different keys, the same plaintext can be encrypted to produce distinct ciphertext. Both the strength of the cryptographic algorithm and the confidentiality of the key determine how secure encrypted data is.

A cryptosystem is made up of a cryptographic algorithm, all conceivable keys, and all the protocols that enable it to function. Cryptosystems include PGP.

As internet commerce and communication technologies have gained in popularity and penetration and become a potential conduit for security concerns, information security has grown in importance in the modern world. Modern data communications use cryptography, an efficient, effective, and crucial component for secure information transfer, to overcome these security concerns by applying security parameters including Confidentiality, Authentication, Accountability, and Accuracy. Various definition came into consideration for cryptography some are as follows:

Definition 1 The practice of utilizing mathematics to protect data and foster a high level of confidence in electronic systems.

Definition 2 Art or science that deals with the concepts, techniques, and procedures for obfuscating plain text and decrypting encrypted data, respectively.

Definition 3 The discipline that embodies the principles, means, and methods for the transformation of data in order to hide their semantic content, prevent their unauthorized use, or prevent their undetected modification.

1.3 Cryptography Terminologies

- **Plain-Text:** original message, often denoted as m in cryptography and security. If you can make sense of what is written, then it is in plaintext. Not all data inputted into or outputted by cryptography algorithms is plaintext. The majority of applications prefer plaintext. Plaintext should be visible in a browser, word processor, or email client, for instance.
- **Cipher-Text:** ciphertext is what encryption algorithms, or ciphers, transform an original message into. Data is said to be encrypted when a person or device lacking to read it. They, would need the decipher to decrypt the information.
- **Encryption:** to prevent unwanted parties from reading a message, a readable message is transformed into an unreadable form through the process of encryption. The encryption is depicted in fig. 1.1.
- **Decryption:** the process of restoring an encrypted message to its original (readable) format is known as decryption, presented in fig. 1.2. The plaintext message is the original communication. The ciphertext message is the name given to the encrypted message.

- **Key:** if only the sender and recipient have access to the key, then communication between them can be done safely. An encryption algorithm uses a key, which is a string of characters, to change data so that it appears random. It locks (encrypts) data, just like a real key, so that only someone with the proper key may unlock (decrypt) it.

  Private Key: the private key uses the same secret key for both encryption and decryption. The sole key used to decipher the encrypted text is copied or shared by another party, which makes this key *symmetric*. Compared to public-key cryptography, it is faster.

  Public Key: a public key contains two keys. For encryption and decryption, separate keys are employed. The plain text is encrypted using a public key to create cypher text, and the recipient decrypts the cypher text with a private key to read the message.

- **Cryptography:** The discipline that embodies the principles, means, and methods for the transformation of data in order to hide their semantic content, prevent their unauthorized use, or prevent their undetected modification.

- **Cryptanalysis:** cryptanalysis is the study of techniques for deciphering encrypted data without having access to the secret data generally needed to do so. Knowing how the system operates and locating a secret key are typically required. Another name for cryptanalysis is codebreaking or cracking the code.

- **Cryptology:** mathematics that support cryptography and cryptanalysis are known as cryptology. These include number theory, the use of formulas, and the use of algorithms.

- **Attack:** an attack is an attempt to take down computers, steal data, or utilise a computer system that has been compromised to launch more assaults. Cybercriminals launch attacks using a variety of techniques, such as malware, phishing, ransomware, man-in-the-middle attacks, and other techniques. Generally, there are two types of attacks – *passive attack* and *active attack*, further they also divided into two categories called – web-based attacks and system-based attacks.

- **Passive attack:** A Passive attack attempts to learn or make use of information from the system, but does not affect system resources. Two types of Passive Attack:

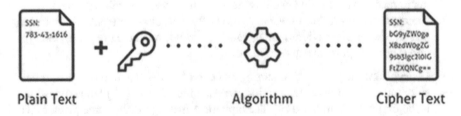

Plain Text   Algorithm   Cipher Text

Fig. 1.1 Encryption

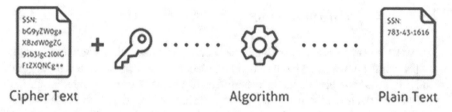

Fig. 1.2 Decryption

1. **Release of message content:** it may be desirable to prevent the opponent from learning the contents (i.e., sensitive or confidential info) of the transmission.
2. **Traffic analysis:** a more subtle technique where the opponent could determine the location and identity of communicating hosts and could observe the frequency & length of encrypted messages being exchanged there by guessing the nature of communication taking place.

- Passive attacks are very difficult to detect because they do not involve any alternation of the data. As the communications take place in a very normal fashion, neither the sender nor receiver is aware that a third party has read the messages or observed the traffic pattern. So, the emphasis in dealing with passive attacks is on prevention rather than detection.

- **Active Attacks:** active attacks involve some modification of the data stream or creation of a false stream. An active attack attempts to alter system resources or affect their operation. Four types of Active attack as follows:

   1. **Masquerade:** Here, an entity pretends to be some other entity. It usually includes one of the other forms of active attack.
   2. **Replay:** It involves the passive capture of a data unit and its subsequent retransmission to produce an unauthorized effect.
   3. **Modification of messages:** It means that some portion of a legitimate message is altered, or that messages are delayed to produce an unauthorized effect.
      Ex: "John's acc no is 2346" is modified as "John's acc no is 7892".
   4. **Denial of service:** This attack prevents or inhibits the normal use or management of communication facilities.

I. Ex: a: Disruption of entire network by disabling it, b: Suppression of all messages to a particular destination by a third party.
   Active attacks present the opposite characteristics of passive attacks. Whereas passive attacks are difficult to detect, measures are available to prevent their success. On the other hand, it is quite difficult to prevent active attacks absolutely, because of the wide variety of potential physical, software and network vulnerabilities. Instead, the goal is to detect active attacks and to recover.

1.4   Goals of Cryptography

The study and application of methods for secure communication when third parties are present is known as cryptography. In a broader sense, it involves developing and studying protocols that counteract the effect of attackers or other external parties and that are connected to many aspects of information security, such as ***data confidentiality, data integrity, authentication, and non-repudiation***. These aspects are main goal of cryptography.

1.4.1   Data Confidentiality

There are two classes of encryption used to provide data confidentiality; asymmetric and symmetric. These two classes differ in how they use keys.

Symmetric encryption algorithms such as Data Encryption Standard (DES), 3DES, and Advanced Encryption Standard (AES) are based on the premise that each communicating party knows the pre-shared key. Data confidentiality can also be ensured using asymmetric algorithms, including Rivest, Shamir, and Adleman (RSA) and the public key infrastructure (PKI). The figure highlights some differences between symmetric and asymmetric encryption (Fig. 1.3).

Symmetric Encryption Symmetric algorithms use the same pre-shared key to encrypt and decrypt data. A pre-shared key, also called a secret key, is known by the sender and receiver before any encrypted communications can take place.

Consider an example where Alice and Bob live in different locations and want to exchange secret messages with one another through the mail system. In this example, Alice wants to send a secret message to Bob.

In the figure, Alice and Bob have identical keys to a single padlock. These keys were exchanged prior to sending any secret messages.

- Alice writes a secret message and puts it in a small box that she locks using the padlock with her key.
- She mails the box to Bob.

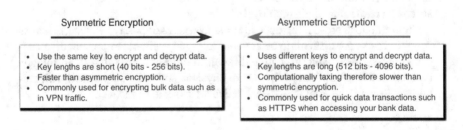

Fig. 1.3 Symmetric and asymmetric encryption

- The message is safely locked inside the box as the box makes its way through the post office system.
- When Bob receives the box, he uses his key to unlock the padlock and retrieve the message. Bob can use the same box and padlock to send a secret reply back to Alice (Fig. 1.4).

Symmetric encryption algorithms are commonly used with VPN traffic. This is because symmetric algorithms use less CPU resources than asymmetric encryption algorithms. This allows the encryption and decryption of data to be fast when using a VPN. When using symmetric encryption algorithms, like any other type of encryption, the longer the key, the longer it will take for someone to discover the key. Most encryption keys are between 112 and 256 bits. To ensure that the encryption is safe, a minimum key length of 128 bits should be used. Use a longer key for more secure communications.

Symmetric encryption algorithms are sometimes classified as either

1. A Block Cipher
2. A Stream Cipher

Block ciphers transform a fixed-length block of plaintext into a common block of ciphertext of 64 or 128 bits. Common block ciphers include DES with a 64-bit block size and AES with a 128-bit block size (Fig. 1.5).

Stream ciphers encrypt plaintext one byte or one bit at a time. Stream ciphers are basically a block cipher with a block size of one byte or bit. Stream ciphers are typically faster than block ciphers because data is continuously encrypted (Fig. 1.6).

Examples of stream ciphers include RC4 and A5 which is used to encrypt GSM cell phone communications. Well-known symmetric encryption algorithms are described in the table 1.1.

Asymmetric Encryption Asymmetric algorithms, also called public-key algorithms, are designed so that the key that is used for encryption is different from the key that is used for decryption, as shown in the figure. The decryption key cannot, in any reasonable amount of time, be calculated from the encryption key and vice versa (Fig. 1.7).

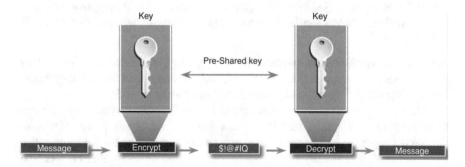

Fig. 1.4 Symmetric key

Fig. 1.5 Block Cipher

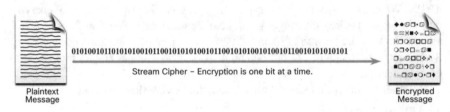

Fig. 1.6 Stream Cipher

Asymmetric algorithms use a public key and a private key. Both keys are capable of the encryption process, but the complementary paired key is required for decryption. The process is also reversible. Data that is encrypted with the public key requires the private key to decrypt. Asymmetric algorithms achieve confidentiality and authenticity by using this process. Because neither party has a shared secret, very long key lengths must be used.

Asymmetric encryption can use key lengths between 512 to 4096 bits. Key lengths greater than or equal to 2048 bits can be trusted, while key lengths of 1024 or shorter are considered insufficient.

Examples of protocols that use asymmetric key algorithms include:

Internet Key Exchange (IKE) - This is a fundamental component of IPsec VPNs.
Secure Socket Layer (SSL) - This is now implemented as IETF standard Transport
   Layer Security (TLS).
Secure Shell (SSH) - This protocol provides a secure remote access connection to
   network devices.
Pretty Good Privacy (PGP) - This computer program provides cryptographic pri-
   vacy and authentication. It is often used to increase the security of email
   communications.

Asymmetric algorithms are substantially slower than symmetric algorithms. Their design is based on computational problems, such as factoring extremely large numbers or computing discrete logarithms of extremely large numbers.

Because they are slow, asymmetric algorithms are typically used in low-volume cryptographic mechanisms, such as digital signatures and key exchange. However, the key management of asymmetric algorithms tends to be simpler than symmetric algorithms, because usually one of the two encryption or decryption keys can be made public.

Table 1.1 Symmetric encryption algorithms

Symmetric Encryption Algorithms	Description
Data Encryption Standard (DES)	This is a legacy symmetric encryption algorithm. It uses a short key length that makes it insecure for most current uses.
3DES (Triple DES)	The is the replacement for DES and repeats the DES algorithm process three times. It should be avoided if possible as it is scheduled to be retired in 2023. If implemented, use very short key lifetimes.
Advanced Encryption Standard (AES)	AES is a popular and recommended symmetric encryption algorithm. It offers combinations of 128-, 192-, or 256-bit keys to encrypt 128, 192, or 256 bit-long data blocks.
Software-Optimized Encryption Algorithm (SEAL)	SEAL is a faster alternative symmetric encryption algorithm to AES. SEAL is a stream cypher that uses a 160-bit encryption key and has a lower impact on the CPU compared to other software-based algorithms.
Rivest ciphers (RC) series algorithms	This algorithm was developed by Ron Rivest. Several variations have been developed, but RC4 was the most prevalent in use. RC4 is a stream cipher that was used to secure web traffic. It has been found to have multiple vulnerabilities which have made it insecure. RC4 should not be used.

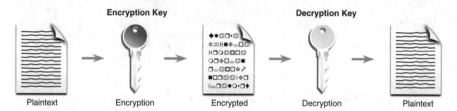

Fig. 1.7 Asymmetric Encryption

Common examples of asymmetric encryption algorithms are described in the table 1.2.

Asymmetric Encryption – Confidentiality Asymmetric algorithms are used to provide confidentiality without pre-sharing a password. The confidentiality objective of asymmetric algorithms is initiated when the encryption process is started with the public key.

The process can be summarized using the formula:

$$\textbf{Public Key}\left(\textbf{Encrypt}\right) + \textbf{Private Key}\left(\textbf{Decrypt}\right) = \textbf{Confidentiality}$$

When the public key is used to encrypt the data, the private key must be used to decrypt the data. Only one host has the private key; therefore, confidentiality is achieved.

If the private key is compromised, another key pair must be generated to replace the compromised key.

Example: The private and public keys can be used to provide confidentiality to the data exchange between Bob and Alice.

Step1: Alice acquires Bob's public key.

Table 1.2 Asymmetric encryption algorithms

Asymmetric Encryption Algorithm	Key Length	Description
Diffie–Hellman (DH)	512, 1024, 2048, 3072, 4096	The Diffie–Hellman algorithm allows two parties to agree on a key that they can use to encrypt messages they want to send to each other. The security of this algorithm depends on the assumption that it is easy to raise a number to a certain power, but difficult to compute which power was used given the number and the outcome.
Digital Signature Standard (DSS) and Digital Signature Algorithm (DSA)	512 - 1024	DSS specifies DSA as the algorithm for digital signatures. DSA is a public key algorithm based on the ElGamal signature scheme. Signature creation speed is similar to RSA, but is 10 to 40 times slower for verification.
Rivest, Shamir, and Adleman encryption algorithms (RSA)	512 to 2048	RSA is for public-key cryptography that is based on the current difficulty of factoring very large numbers. It is the first algorithm known to be suitable for signing, as well as encryption. It is widely used in electronic commerce protocols and is believed to be secure given sufficiently long keys and the use of up-to-date implementations.
ElGamal	512 - 1024	An asymmetric key encryption algorithm for public-key cryptography which is based on the Diffie–Hellman key agreement. A disadvantage of the ElGamal system is that the encrypted message becomes very big, about twice the size of the original message and for this reason it is only used for small messages such as secret keys.
Elliptic curve techniques	224 or higher	Elliptic curve cryptography can be used to adapt many cryptographic algorithms, such as Diffie–Hellman or ElGamal. The main advantage of elliptic curve cryptography is that the keys can be much smaller.

Alice requests and obtains Bob's public key (Fig. 1.8).

Step2: Alice uses Bob's public key.

Alice uses Bob's public key to encrypt a message using an agreed-upon algorithm. Alice sends the encrypted message to Bob (Fig. 1.9).

Step3: Bob decrypts message with his private key.

Bob then uses his private key to decrypt the message. Since Bob is the only one with the private key, Alice's message can only be decrypted by Bob and thus confidentiality is achieved (Fig. 1.10).

1.4.2   Data Integrity

Hashes are used to verify and ensure data integrity. Hashing is based on a one-way mathematical function that is relatively easy to compute, but significantly harder to reverse. Grinding coffee is a good analogy of a one-way function. It is easy to grind coffee beans, but it is almost impossible to put all of the tiny pieces back together to rebuild the original beans. The cryptographic hashing function can also be used to verify authentication.

As shown in the figure, a hash function takes a variable block of binary data, called the message, and produces a fixed-length, condensed representation, called the hash. The resulting hash is also sometimes called the message digest, digest, or digital fingerprint (Fig. 1.11).

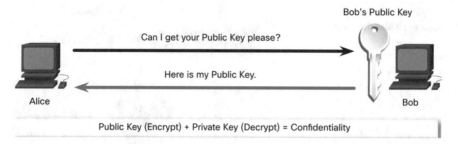

Fig. 1.8 Alice requests

Fig. 1.9 Alice uses
public key

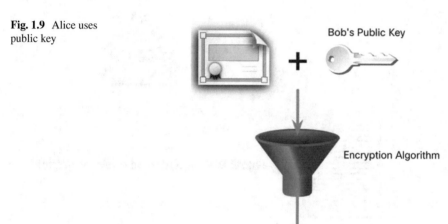

With hash functions, it is computationally infeasible for two different sets of data to come up with the same hash output. Every time the data is changed or altered, the hash value also changes. Because of this, cryptographic hash values are often called digital fingerprints. They can be used to detect duplicate data files, file version changes, and similar applications. These values are used to guard against an accidental or intentional change to the data, or accidental data corruption.

The cryptographic hash function is applied in many different situations for entity authentication, data integrity, and data authenticity purposes.

Cryptographic Hash Operation   Mathematically, the equation $h = H(x)$ is used to explain how a hash algorithm operates. As shown in the figure, a hash function H takes an input x and returns a fixed-size string hash value h.

The example in the figure summarizes the mathematical process. A cryptographic hash function should have the following properties (Fig. 1.12):

- The input can be any length.

Fig. 1.10 Bob decrypts
message with private key

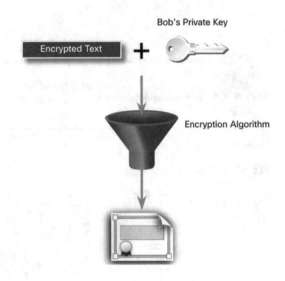

Fig. 1.11 Cryptographic hash functions

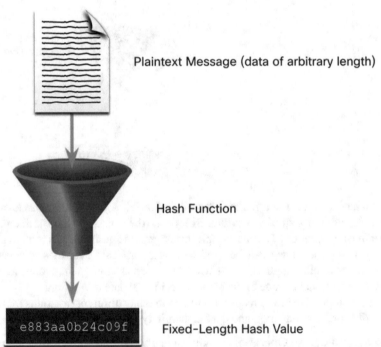

- The output has a fixed length.
- H(x) is relatively easy to compute for any given x.
- H(x) is one way and not reversible.

- H(x) is collision free, meaning that two different input values will result in different hash values.

If a hash function is hard to invert, it is considered a one-way hash. Hard to invert means that given a hash value of **h**, it is computationally infeasible to find an input for **x** such that **h = H(x)**.

Example: Hash functions are used to ensure the integrity of a message. They ensure data has not changed accidentally or intentionally. In the figure, the sender is sending a $100 money transfer to Alex. The sender wants to ensure that the message is not accidentally altered on its way to the receiver. Deliberate changes that are made by a threat actor are still possible (Fig. 1.13).

The hash algorithm works as follows:

1. The sending device inputs the message into a hashing algorithm and computes its fixed-length hash of **4ehiDx67NMop9**.
2. This hash is then attached to the message and sent to the receiver. Both the message and the hash are in plaintext.
3. The receiving device removes the hash from the message and inputs the message into the same hashing algorithm. If the computed hash is equal to the one that is attached to the message, the message has not been altered during transit. If the hashes are not equal, as shown in the figure, then the integrity of the message can no longer be trusted.

There are four well-known hash functions:

- **MD5 with 128-bit digest** - Developed by Ron Rivest and used in a variety of internet applications, MD5 is a one-way function that produces a 128-bit hashed message. MD5 is considered to be a legacy algorithm and should be avoided and

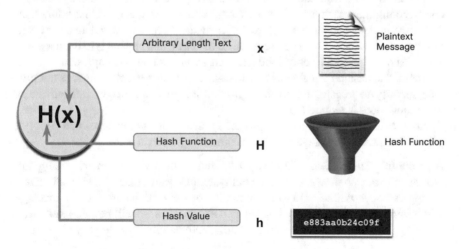

Fig. 1.12 Cryptographic Hash Operation

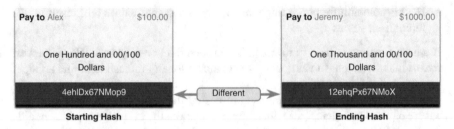

Fig. 1.13 MD5 and SHA hash functions

used only when no better alternatives are available. It is recommended that SHA-2 or SHA-3 be used instead.

- **SHA-1 –** Developed by the U.S. National Security Agency (NSA) in 1995. It is very similar to the MD5 hash functions. Several versions exist. SHA-1 creates a 160-bit hashed message and is slightly slower than MD5. SHA-1 has known flaws and is a legacy algorithm.
- **SHA-2 –** Developed by the NSA. It includes SHA-224 (224 bit), SHA-256 (256 bit), SHA-384 (384 bit), and SHA-512 (512 bit). If you are using SHA-2, then the SHA-256, SHA-384, and SHA-512 algorithms should be used whenever possible.
- **SHA-3 -** SHA-3 is the newest hashing algorithm and was introduced by NIST as an alternative and eventual replacement for the SHA-2 family of hashing algorithms. SHA-3 includes SHA3–224 (224 bit), SHA3–256 (256 bit), SHA3–384 (384 bit), and SHA3–512 (512 bit). The SHA-3 family are next-generation algorithms and should be used whenever possible.

While hashing can be used to detect accidental changes, it cannot be used to guard against deliberate changes that are made by a threat actor. There is no unique identifying information from the sender in the hashing procedure. This means that anyone can compute a hash for any data, as long as they have the correct hash function.

For example, when the message traverses the network, a potential attacker could intercept the message, change it, recalculate the hash, and append it to the message. The receiving device will only validate against whatever hash is appended.

Therefore, hashing is vulnerable to man-in-the-middle attacks and does not provide security to transmitted data. To provide integrity and origin authentication, something more is required.

Note: Hashing algorithms only protect against accidental changes and does not protect the data from changes deliberately made by a threat actor.

Asymmetric Encryption – Integrity Combining the two asymmetric encryption processes provides message confidentiality, authentication, and integrity. The following example will be used to illustrate this process. In this example, a message will be ciphered using Bob's public key and a ciphered hash will be encrypted using Alice's private key to provide confidentiality, authenticity, and integrity.

Step 1: Alice wants to send a message to Bob ensuring that only Bob can read the document. In other words, Alice wants to ensure message confidentiality.

Alice uses the public key of Bob to cipher the message.

Only Bob will be able to decipher it using his private key (Fig. 1.14).

Step 2: Alice also wants to ensure message authentication and integrity.

Authentication ensures Bob that the document was sent by Alice, and integrity ensures that it was not modified Alice uses her private key to cipher a hash of the message.

Alice sends the encrypted message with its encrypted hash to Bob (Fig. 1.15).

Step 3: Bob uses Alice's public key to verify that the message was not modified.

The received hash is equal to the locally determined hash based on Alice's public key. Additionally, this verifies that Alice is definitely the sender of the message because nobody else has Alice's private key (Fig. 1.16).

Step 4: Bob uses his private key to decipher the message (Fig. 1.17).

1.4.3   Authentication

Authentication guarantees that the message is not a forgery and does actually come from whom it states. Many modern networks ensure authentication with protocols, such as hash message authentication code (HMAC).

Fig. 1.14 Alice uses the public key of Bob

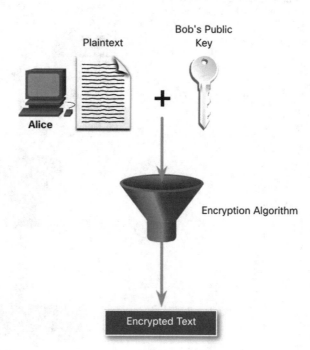

To add authentication to integrity assurance, use a keyed-hash message authentication code (HMAC). HMAC uses an additional secret key as input to the hash function.

Step 1: As shown in the figure, an HMAC is calculated using any cryptographic algorithm that combines a cryptographic hash function with a secret key. Hash functions are the basis of the protection mechanism of HMACs (Fig. 1.18).

Only the sender and the receiver know the secret key, and the output of the hash function now depends on the input data and the secret key. Only parties who have access to that secret key can compute the digest of an HMAC function. This defeats man-in-the-middle attacks and provides authentication of the data origin.

If two parties share a secret key and use HMAC functions for authentication, a properly constructed HMAC digest of a message that a party has received indicates that the other party was the originator of the message. This is because the other party possesses the secret key.

Step 2: As shown in the figure, the sending device inputs data (such as Terry Smith's pay of $100 and the secret key) into the hashing algorithm and calculates the fixed-length HMAC digest. This authenticated digest is then attached to the message and sent to the receiver (Fig. 1.19).

Step 3: In the figure, the receiving device removes the digest from the message and uses the plaintext message with its secret key as input into the same hashing

Fig. 1.15 Alice encrypts a hash using her private key

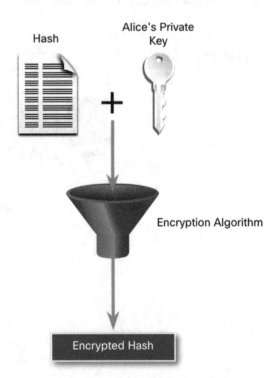

Fig. 1.16 Bob uses Alice's
public key to decrypt
the hash

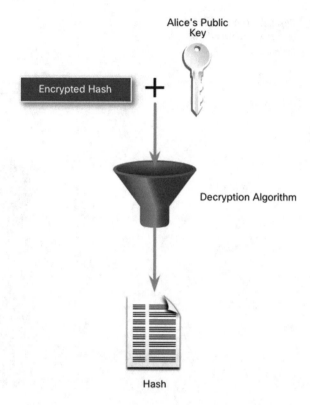

function. If the digest that is calculated by the receiving device is equal to the digest
that was sent, the message has not been altered (Fig. 1.20).

Additionally, the origin of the message is authenticated because only the sender
possesses a copy of the shared secret key. The HMAC function has ensured the
authenticity of the message.

Example: The figure shows how HMACs are used by a routers that are configured to use Open Shortest Path First (OSPF) routing authentication.

R1 is sending a link state update (LSU) regarding a route to network 10.2.0.0/16:

- R1 calculates the hash value using the LSU message and the secret key.
- The resulting hash value is sent with the LSU to R2.
- R2 calculates the hash value using the LSU and its secret key. R2 accepts the
  update if the hash values match. If they do not match, R2 discards the update
  (Fig. 1.21).

Asymmetric Encryption – Authentication The authentication objective of asymmetric algorithms is initiated when the encryption process is started with the private key.

The process can be summarized using the formula:

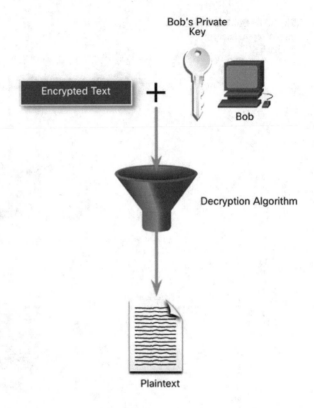

Fig. 1.17 Bob uses his private key to decrypt the message

Private Key (Encrypt) + Public Key (Decrypt) = Authentication

When the private key is used to encrypt the data, the corresponding public key must be used to decrypt the data. Because only one host has the private key, only that host could have encrypted the message, providing authentication of the sender. Typically, no attempt is made to preserve the secrecy of the public key, so any number of hosts can decrypt the message. When a host successfully decrypts a message using a public key, it is trusted that the private key encrypted the message, which verifies who the sender is. This is a form of authentication.

Example: The private and public keys can be used to provide authentication to the data exchange between Bob and Alice.

Step 1: Alice use her private key.

Alice encrypts a message using her private key. Alice sends the encrypted message to Bob. Bob needs to authenticate that the message did indeed come from Alice (Fig. 1.22).

Step 2: Bob requests Alice's public key.

In order to authenticate the message, Bob requests Alice's public key (Fig. 1.23).

Step 3: Bob uses Alice's public key to decrypt the message (Fig. 1.24).

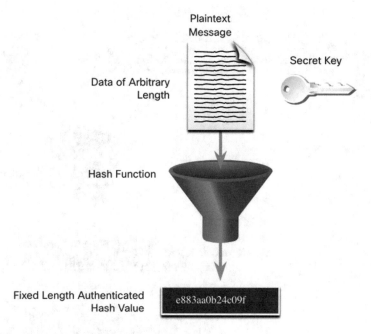

Plaintext
Message

Secret Key

Data of Arbitrary
Length

Hash Function

Fixed Length Authenticated
Hash Value   e883aa0b24c09f

Fig. 1.18 HMAC hashing algorithm

Non-Repudiation
Ensures the inability of an author of a statement resp. a piece of information to deny it.

Cryptography can either be strong or weak considering the intensity of secrecy demanded by your job and the sensitivity of the piece of information that you carry. If you want to hide a specific document from your sibling or friend, you might need weak cryptography with no serious rituals to hide your information. Basic cryptographic knowledge would do. However, if the concern is intercommunication between large organizations and even governments, the cryptographic practices involved should be strictly strong observing all the principles of modern encryptions. Therefore, these goals are main concerning points for any system to provide level of security or cryptography.

1.5   Analysis Criteria of Cryptography Algorithms

- **Architecture:** explains the components, properties, and methods used to implement an algorithm's structure and actions. Additionally, it establishes whether the technique is symmetric or asymmetric and uses a secret key or a public key for encryption and decryption.

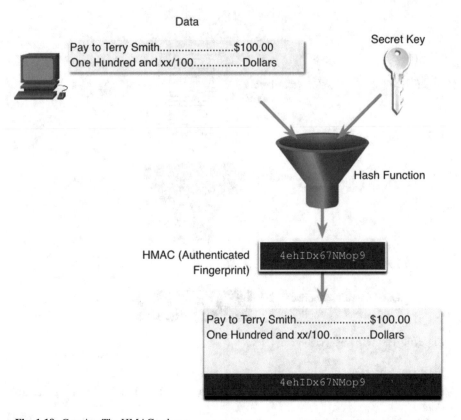

Fig. 1.19 Creating The HMAC value

- **Security:** Any encryption technique that has the attribute of distinguishability (made by repeatedly mixing substitution with transposition) is desirable and should include a positive indicator of the system's resilience to attacks. The strength of an encryption depends on the size of the keys used to carry out the encryption; in general, the stronger the encryption, the more secure the algorithm. Key length is expressed in bits.
- **Flexibility:** determines whether the algorithm can withstand modest changes in accordance with the criteria.
- **Scalability:** It is one of the key components that can be used to examine encryption methods. A number of factors, including memory usage, encryption rate, software hardware performance, and computational efficiency, affect scalability.
- **Limitations (Attack):** defines how well the algorithm performs by utilizing the computing resources at its disposal. Additionally, how frequently is susceptible to certain attacks.

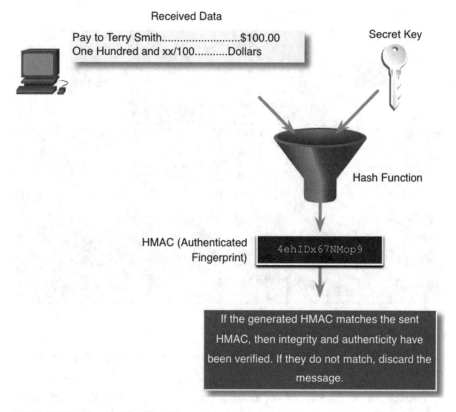

Fig. 1.20 Verifying the HMAC value

1.6 Classical Cryptography

The classical encryption and decryption algorithms are sometimes used to refer to historical pen and paper cyphers that were once in use. Due to their vulnerability to attack, historical cyphers are rarely employed as a stand-alone encryption solution. Numerous traditional cyphers are susceptible to brute force attacks or analysis of the sole ciphertext other than the one-time pad. They consist of following techniques for encryption/decryption:

• **Substitution:** Any character of plain text from the predetermined fixed set of characters is replaced by another character from the same set according to a key in a substitution cypher. *As an illustration in* fig. 1.25, if there was a shift of 1, A would be replaced by B, B by C, and so on.

By spelling down the alphabet in some order to indicate the substitution, simple substitution can be shown. When the cypher alphabet is complexly shifted, reversed, or jumbled, it is referred to as a mixed alphabet or disturbed alphabet. Traditionally, mixed alphabets are made by writing out a keyword first, then eliminating any

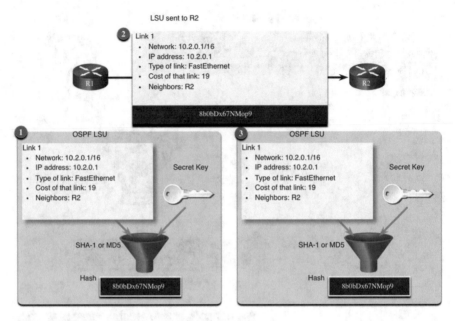

Fig. 1.21 Router HMAC

duplicate letters from it before writing the other letters in the alphabet in the normal order.

- **Transposition:** An encryption technique known as a transposition cypher in cryptography involves shifting the positions of plaintext units, which are often characters or groups of characters, in accordance with a regular system so that the ciphertext is a permutation of the plaintext. In other words, the units' order is altered (Fig. 1.26).

A bijective function is used to the positions of the characters in mathematics to encrypt, and an inverse function is applied to decrypt.

- **Polyalphabetic substitution Cipher**: a substitution cypher (Vigenère cypher and Enigma machine) that employs several substitution alphabets.
- **Permutation Cipher:** a transposition cipher in which the key is a permutation.

Substitution and transposition are the two overarching ideas on which all encryption algorithms are built. The fundamental criterion is that no data be lost. Numerous levels of replacements and transpositions are present in the majority of systems referred to as product systems. Therefore, in this chapter substitution and transposition algorithms covered in following sections.

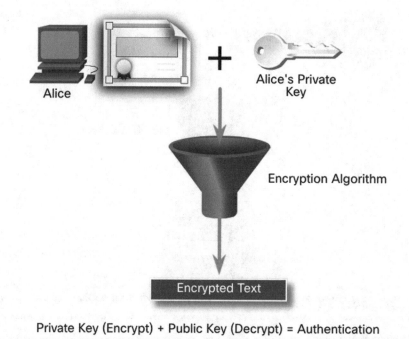

Private Key (Encrypt) + Public Key (Decrypt) = Authentication

Fig. 1.22 Alice uses her private key

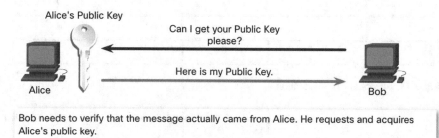

Bob needs to verify that the message actually came from Alice. He requests and acquires Alice's public key.

Fig. 1.23 Bob requests Alice's public key

1.6.1 Substitution Algorithms

It is one in which different letters, numerals, or symbols are used in place of the plaintext's letters. The substitution cipher comes in a variety of forms. An encryption is referred to be a simple substitution cypher if it just works with single letters; a poly-graphic cipher is one that works with larger groups of letters. A unit from the plaintext is mapped to one of several possibilities in the ciphertext in a polyalphabetic cipher, and vice versa. A monoalphabetic cipher uses fixed substitution over

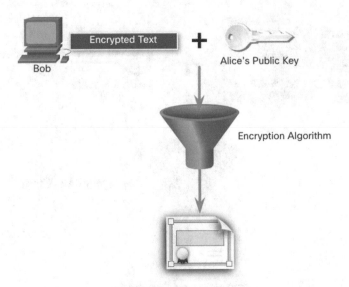

Bob uses the public key to successfully decrypt the message and authenticate that the message did, indeed, come from Alice.

Fig. 1.24 Bob decrypts the message

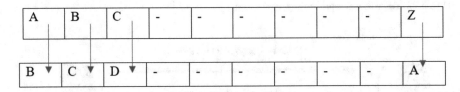

Fig. 1.25 Illustration of Substitution

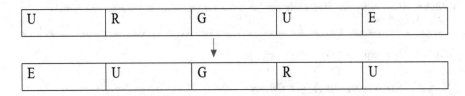

Fig. 1.26 Illustration of Transposition (The order of characters is reversed)

the entire message, whereas a polyalphabetic cipher uses several substitutions at different positions in the message.

As per Sir Arthur Conan Doyle's Adventure of the Dancing Men (1903), where Sherlock Holmes cracks a monoalphabetic substitution cypher with stick figures of a human in various dance-like poses as the ciphertext symbols, the ciphertext symbols in a substitution cipher need not be the same as the plaintext characters. The most straightforward substitution ciphers are those where the cipher alphabet is just a cyclical shift of the plaintext alphabet. The Caesar cipher, used by Julius Caesar, is the most well-known of them. In it, letters A and B are encoded as the letters D and E, respectively. Cyclic-shift substitution ciphers are not secure, nor are any other monoalphabetic substitution ciphers in which a given plaintext symbol is always encrypted into the same ciphertext symbol, as many a schoolboy has found to his embarrassment. Monoalphabetic substitution ciphers are frequently used as a source for amusing cryptograms due to the English language's inherent redundancy, which only necessitates roughly 25 symbols of ciphertext to allow for cryptanalysis. The reason for this flaw is that, other from the symbols' new labels, the frequency distributions of the symbols in the plaintext and the ciphertext are identical. The duty of the cryptanalyst is made simple since any structure or pattern in the plaintext is kept intact in the ciphertext. With substitution ciphers, there have primarily been two methods used. One method is to encrypt plaintext components made up of two or more symbols, such as trigraphs and digraphs. Utilizing many cipher alphabets is the alternative. One-time keys or pads are produced when the polyalphabetic substitution method is taken to its logical conclusion. With these not it is clear that various types of substitution ciphers came into consideration among them some are as follows:

- Caesar cipher
- Monoalphabetic Substitution Cipher
- Playfair Cipher
- Hill Cipher
- The Vigenère cipher
- One-Time Pad

1.6.1.1 Caesar Cipher

The encryption rule is straightforward: swap out each letter for the one that is three positions lower in the alphabet. The alphabet is twisted so that Z comes after A. Different substitution will result from using a different key. Caesar cypher is a mathematical operation that can be expressed as:

$$\text{Encryption with Caesar cipher}: E(p) = (p+k)\bmod(26).$$

$$\text{Decryption with Caesar cipher}: D(C) = (C-k)\bmod(26).$$

The example is as follows considering key as 2:
Plaintext is: Raj Kumar

$$Encryption: E(p) = (p+k)\bmod(26).$$

$$\text{Encrypted text of } R : E(R) = (R+2) \bmod (26) = T$$

$$\text{Encrypted text of } a : E(a) = (a+2) \bmod (26) = c$$

$$\text{Encrypted text of } R : E(j) = (j+2) \bmod (26) = l$$

$$\text{Encrypted text of } K : E(K) = (K+2) \bmod (26) = M$$

$$\text{Encrypted text of } u : E(u) = (u+2) \bmod (26) = w$$

$$\text{Encrypted text of } m : E(m) = (m+2) \bmod (26) = o$$

$$\text{Encrypted text of } R : E(a) = (a+2) \bmod (26) = c$$

$$\text{Encrypted text of } R : E(r) = (r+2) \bmod (26) = t$$

$$\text{Decryption} : D(C) = (C-k) \bmod (26).$$

$$\text{Decrypted text of } T : D(T) = (T-2) \bmod (26) = R$$

$$\text{Decrypted text of } T : D(c) = (c-2) \bmod (26) = a$$

$$\text{Decrypted text of } T : D(l) = (l-2) \bmod (26) = j$$

$$\text{Decrypted text of } T : D(M) = (M-2) \bmod (26) = K$$

$$\text{Decrypted text of } T : D(w) = (w-2) \bmod (26) = u$$

$$\text{Decrypted text of } T : D(o) = (o-2) \bmod (26) = m$$

$$\text{Decrypted text of } T : D(c) = (c-2) \bmod (26) = a$$

$$\text{Decrypted text of } T : D(t) = (t-2) \bmod (26) = r$$

Despite being incredibly simple, it can still be easily exploited. It implies that it is simple to decrypt a message encrypted using this technique. It offers very little protection. The complete message can be decoded by examining the letter arrangement in it.

Advantages of Caesar Cipher Use of merely a small key throughout the entire process makes it one of the simplest methods for using cryptography and can offer the least amount of protection for the information.

- If the system is unable to employ any difficult coding techniques, one of the finest approaches to use
- Few computational resources are needed

Disadvantages of Caesar Cipher Utilisation of a simple structure

- May only offer the information the bare minimum of security
- A key indicator for interpreting the complete message is the frequency of the letter pattern.

Analysis of Caesar Cipher Even in a ciphertext-only environment, the Caesar cypher is easily cracked. There are two scenarios that can be considered:

1. where an attacker is aware that a simple substitution cypher has been used, but not specifically that it is a Caesar scheme; and.
2. where an attacker is aware that a Caesar cypher has been used, but is unaware of the shift value.

The **first scenario** allows for the use of frequency analysis or pattern words to decipher the cypher using the same methods as for a general simple substitution cypher. An attacker is likely to rapidly recognise the regularity in the solution while the problem is being solved and conclude that the method being used is a Caesar cypher.

The **second situation** makes it considerably simpler to foil the plan. A brute force approach may test each conceivable shift in turn because there are only a finite number of them (26 in English). Writing down a portion of the ciphertext in a table of all feasible shifts is one approach to accomplish this; this method is referred to as "completing the plain component." The complete alphabet is spelled out in reverse starting at each letter of the ciphertext, which is another way to look at this procedure.

Matching the frequency distribution of the letters is another **brute force** method. A human can quickly determine the value of the shift by examining the displacement of specific graph features after graphing the frequencies of the letters in the ciphertext and knowing the predicted distribution of those letters in the original language of the plaintext. The term for this is **frequency analysis**. For instance, the plaintext frequencies of the letters E, T (generally most frequent) and Q, Z (often least frequent) in the English language are highly recognisable. The actual frequency distribution's congruence with the predicted distribution can also be determined by computers; one tool for this is the chi-square statistic.

Even if several alternatives are conceivable for extremely brief plaintexts, there will most likely only be one decryption that makes sense for plaintext in natural language.

1.6.1.2   Monoalphabetic Substitution Cipher

The alphabets are **given any random permutation** as opposed to the fixed Caesar cipher shift of an amount. Monoalphabetic substitution cipher is the term used to describe this kind of encryption. When letters like A, B, D, and C are swapped out for others like Q, T, and so on, the Caesar cipher becomes significantly more robust.

With this change, there are now a total of **26!** alternative keys. As a result, in this situation, a **brute force attack** is not viable. One more assault, though, might occur. Certain characters are used more frequently than others in human languages because they are redundant. One can take use of this fact.

English's most frequent letter is "e," which is followed by "t," "r," "n," "o," "a," etc. Less commonly used letters include 'q', 'x', and 'j'. Additionally, trigrams like "the" and di-grams like "th" are more common. These letters' frequency can be calculated. If the plaintext is in uncompressed English, then these can be used to guess the plaintext. Di-grams are the most popular two-letter pairings, such as the letters th, in, er, re, and an. Trigrams are the most typical three-letter pairings. For instance, the, ing, and, and ion.

Advantages of Monoalphabetic Cipher   Simple to comprehend and use.

- A random permutation of all 26 letters of the alphabet is supported by the replacement characters and symbols. 26! The number of possible alphabet permutations is $4*10^{26}$. This makes it difficult for the hacker to obtain the key without using a **brute force approach.**

Disadvantages of Monoalphabetic Cipher The main drawback is that *longer messages and longer transmission times arise from using more than one character of ciphertext to replace each value of plaintext.*

- The need for *extra training and discipline* to benefit from the increased security is a second disadvantage.

1.6.1.3   Playfair Cipher

The **Playfair cypher** is a well-known digraph substitution cipher. Information is mathematically secured by encrypting a message using a key. Information intended for sender and receiver is shielded from prying eyes.

This method encrypts **two or more** letters simultaneously and makes use of a **5 x 5 matrix**, often known as a key matrix. Two letters at a time are used to encrypt the plaintext, the detailed procedure is as follows where the considered key is **monarchy**:

M	O	N	A	R
C	H	Y	B	D
E	F	G	I/J	K
L	P	Q	S	T
U	V	W	X	Z

1. Make **pairings of two consecutive letter** pairs in the plaintext.
2. In the plaintext, add a **filler character like "X"** if a pair consists of repeated letters, such as "Balloon" is handled as "ba lx lo on."
3. Replace each letter with the letter to its right (wrapping back to start from finish), for example, "**AR**," if both letters are in the same row of the key matrix "as "**RM**" encryption
4. Replace each letter with the letter below it if they are in the same column (again, wrapping from bottom to top); for example, "**MU**" encrypts to "**CM**." ".
5. In the absence of that, each letter is changed to the one in its row in the column of the other letter in the pair, for instance, "**HS**" becomes "**BP**" and "**EA**" becomes "**IM**" or "**JM**".

Since two letters are encrypted at a time, there are 26 X 26 = 676 diagrams, making the security significantly better than monoalphabetic. This means that a 676 entry is required for frequency computation. It's a somewhat weak encryption that only uses digraphs rather than monographs to make it better than a straightforward substitution cipher.

The fact that a digraph in the ciphertext (AB) and its reverse (BA) will have equivalent plaintexts like UR and RU is an intriguing weakness (and ciphertext UR and RU will correspond to plaintext AB and BA, i.e., the substitution is self-inverse).

If the language of the plaintext is known, that can be simply taken advantage of with the help of frequency analysis.

Advantages of Playfair Cipher Since the frequency analysis method used to crack simple substitution cyphers is challenging, it can only be applied to (25*25) = 625 digraphs rather than 25 monographs, which makes it *substantially more challenging to crack*.

- *Frequency analysis needs more cypher text to decrypt the data.*

Disadvantages of Playfair Cipher The fact that a digraph in the ciphertext (AB) and its reverse (BA) will have equivalent plaintexts like UR and RU is an intriguing

weakness (and ciphertext UR and RU will correspond to plaintext AB and BA, i.e., the substitution is self-inverse).

- The fact that the Playfair cypher uses the same key for both encryption and decryption because it is a **symmetric cypher is another drawback**.

Analysis of Playfair Cipher The Playfair cypher can be easily broken if there is enough text, just as most classical cyphers. If the plaintext and ciphertext are both known, getting the key is rather simple. **Brute force** is used when just the ciphertext is known. In order to decipher the cypher, cryptanalysts must search the key space for correspondences between the frequency of diagrams (pairs of letters) and the known frequency of diagrams in the presumed language of the original message.

Playfair's cryptanalysis is comparable to that of the four-square and two-square cyphers, but because of its relative simplicity, it is simpler to find potential plaintext strings.

The fact that a Playfair digraph and its opposite (for instance, AB and BA) will decode to the same letter pattern in the plaintext is most notable (e.g., RE and ER). Many English words, including REceiver and DEpartED, contain these reversible digraphs. It is simple to produce potential plaintext strings with which to start building the key by identifying nearby inverted digraphs in the ciphertext and matching the pattern to a list of known plaintext terms bearing the pattern.

The **shotgun hill climbing** method is an alternative strategy for cracking a Playfair cypher. A square of random letters appears to start this. Then, little adjustments are made to see if the candidate plaintext resembles standard plaintext more than it did before the alteration (such as altering letters, rows, or reflecting the entire square) (perhaps by comparing the diagrams to a known frequency chart). The new square is adopted and then further mutated to locate an even better contender if it is judged to be an improvement. Eventually, the plaintext or something quite similar is discovered to receive the highest grade possible under the given grading scheme. Although clearly beyond the capabilities of the average human patient, computers may use this procedure to decipher Playfair cyphers.

The fact that Playfair never contains a double-letter diagram, such as EE, is another feature that sets it apart from four-square and two-square cyphers. It is quite likely that the cypher used is Playfair if the ciphertext contains no double letter diagrams and the message's size is sufficient to make this statistically relevant.

1.6.1.4 Hill Cipher

A poly-graphic substitution cipher built on linear algebra is the Hill cipher. A number modulo 26 represents each letter. It is common to employ the straightforward formula A = 0, B = 1,..., Z = 25, however this is not a necessary component of the encryption. Each block of n letters, which is thought of as an n-component vector, is multiplied by an invertible **n by n matrix** against modulo 26 to encrypt a message. Each block is multiplied by the inverse of the encryption matrix to decrypt the message. The set of invertible n by n matrices should contain the cipher key, which is the matrix used for encryption (modulo 26).

The Hill cipher's strength is its perfect concealment of single-letter frequencies. The Hill cipher can be quickly cracked using a known plaintext attack, yet being robust against cipher text-only attacks.

Advantages of Hill Cipher It works incredibly well at hiding single-letter frequencies.

- 3x3 hill cyphers are quite effective for hiding both single-letter and two-letter frequency information.
- Cipher offers excellent protection against attacks performed using cypher text.

Disadvantages of Hill Cipher The Hill cypher, which is based on matrix multiplication and is one of the most well-known symmetric-key encryption algorithms, has some intriguing structural characteristics that, for example, can be used to teach both cryptology and linear algebra. However, because of these characteristics, it is now susceptible to certain types of attacks, such as the known-plaintext assault, and is therefore useless in situations where it would actually be used.

1.6.1.5   Vigenère Cipher

This kind of substitution cipher uses **numerous replacements**, depending on the key, and is **polyalphabetic**. The key in this kind of cipher chooses which specific substitution to employ. A key that is the same length as the message is required to encrypt it. The key is typically a term that repeats itself. For instance, the message "we are discovered save yourself" is encrypted as follows if the **keyword is deceptive**:

Key: deceptivedecept
Plaintext: wearediscovered
Ciphertext: ZICVTWQNGRZGVTW

The Vigenere Table, where ciphertext is the letter key's row and plaintext's column, or the following formula can be used to perform encryption and decryption respectively:

$$\textbf{Encryption} : \mathbf{E_i} = \left(\mathbf{P_i} + \mathbf{K_i} \right) \bmod \mathbf{26}$$

$$\textbf{Decryption} : \mathbf{D_i} = \left(\mathbf{E_i} - \mathbf{K_i} + \mathbf{26} \right) \bmod \mathbf{26}$$

Decryption is also straightforward. The row is again identified by the key letter. The column is determined by the location of the cypher text letter in that row, and the plaintext letter is at the top of that column. The advantage of this encryption is that it conceals the letter frequency information while retaining some knowledge of the plaintext structure by using multiple ciphertext letters for each plaintext letter, one for each unique letter of the keyword.

Advantages of Vigenère Cipher   The cypher hides the letter frequency in plaintext.

- The fundamental goal of this cypher, like that of the majority of earlier poly alphabetic substitution cyphers, was to mask letter frequency so as to hinder frequency analysis techniques.
- largely impossible to break without method knowledge.
- It is exceedingly impossible to find the key using anything other than brute force techniques if you don't know the Kasiski method or the Friedman test.
- literally unbroken for three centuries.
- a sizable important area.
- The key space has a size of 26 k, where k is the key's length.
- The number of keys you could reach with simply a key of length 10 is 141,167,095,653,376.

Disadvantages of Vigenère Cipher   One of the oldest cryptographic methods, Vigenère Cipher is a symmetric key algorithm that uses the same key for both encryption and decryption. The downside of the Vigenère Cipher is that the key is repeated until it is equal to the length of the plaintext, which of course enables cryptanalysts to perform the cryptanalysis process. The security of key distribution is another shortcoming of the symmetric key cryptographic technique; if others know the key, then the purpose of cryptography itself is rendered meaningless.

- The repetition of the key (largest weakness that leads to other weaknesses).
- It is considerably simpler to estimate the length of the key because it repeats. The length of the key can be determined significantly more quickly using Kasiski inspection and the Friedman test than with brute force techniques.
- Just a little bit more could be done by using a one-time pad or a running key cypher, which is essentially a Vigenère cypher with a key that is longer than the message and typically consists of a passage from a book or something similar.

Analysis of Vigenère Cipher   The Vigenère cipher's strength is that it is resistant to frequency analysis since it rotates through many shifts, which means that the same plaintext letter won't always be encrypted to the same ciphertext letter. Say "e," for instance, is the letter that appears most frequently in English words.

Frequency analysis may lead a codebreaker to believe that "e" is the most frequent letter in an encoded message. The assumptions behind frequency analysis are broken, however, because a Vigenère cypher can encode the same letter in a variety of ways, depending on the keyword. As a result, for 300 years they were believed to be indestructible by many.

A Vigenère cypher is challenging to break using brute force since every one of the 26 characters could be used to encode any letter in a message. A given message could be encoded in 26^k different ways, where k is the length of the keyword, because the message's encoding depends on the keyword that is used. For instance, if all we know about the message's encoding is that it uses a word with seven letters, there are 26^7 ~ 8 billion different ways it may be done.

The recurring nature of the Vigenère cipher's key is its main flaw. The ciphertext can be viewed as a series of interconnected Caesar cyphers, each of which is straightforward to decipher if a cryptanalyst accurately predicts the length of the key. For instance, the plaintext THE appears twice in the message of the cryptogram shown above, and in both instances, it completely corresponds with the first two letters of the keyword. As a result, it generates the identical ciphertext BUK.

The gap between such repeats gives a signal as to the length of the keyword. Repetition in the ciphertext denotes repetition in the plaintext. In reality, a Vigenère cypher will result in a lot of these repeated instances in any message. Even though not all instances of repetition will result from the same plaintext being encrypted, many will, which is the basis for decrypting the cypher. The Kasiski examination is the name of this analytical technique.

1.6.1.6   One-Time Pad

A random key that has the same length as the message is employed in this approach. The encryption and decryption of a single message are performed using the key, which is subsequently discarded. Each new message needs its own key that is the same length as the new message. It is impossible to defeat this plan.

Random results that have no statistical connection to the plaintext are generated by it. Simply put, the code cannot be broken since the ciphertext includes absolutely no information about the plaintext. There exists a key that creates a plaintext for any plaintext that is the same length as the ciphertext. Consequently, if you conducted an exhaustive search using all potential keys, you would end up with a large number of plaintexts that are readable but you would have no way of knowing which was the intended plaintext. As a result, the code cannot be cracked. The key's unpredictability is solely responsible for the one-time pad's security.

Although the one-time pad promises absolute security, **there are two major issues** that arise in use:

- The issue of **producing several random keys** in a realistic manner. Any system that receives a lot of traffic could frequently need millions of random characters. It is a huge challenge to provide truly random characters in this volume.
- Key protection and distribution are another issue. Both the sender and the receiver must have keys that are the same length for a message to be transmitted.

The one-time pad is the only cryptosystem that demonstrates absolute secrecy, therefore because of these challenges, it is utilized whenever very high security is necessary.

Analysis of One-Time Pad Cipher   The only cypher that is absolutely safe is the One Time Pad. This means that even if a malicious person manages to obtain a ciphertext generated using the One Time Pad, they will be unable to deduce the accompanying plaintext or key. There is no information in the ciphertext (such as the frequency of letters) that the malicious user can use to determine the plaintext/key because the **key is random and the same length as the plaintext**. Furthermore, even if a brute force attack could be used, in which the malicious user attempts to decrypt the ciphertext using every key available, he or she would have no means of knowing which plaintext is the original plaintext. This is because a brute force attack will generate numerous possible plaintexts that are comprehensible to a hostile user.

1.6.2   Transposition Algorithms

By applying some sort of permutation to the plaintext characters, a very different kind of mapping is produced. A transposition cipher is the name for this method. The rail fence method is the most straightforward encryption of this type.

1.6.2.1   Rail Fence Cipher

A traditional form of transposition cypher is the rail fence cypher, often known as the zigzag cypher. It gets its name from the way encryption is done, which is like building a fence out of horizontal rails. In order to encrypt data, plaintext letters are written diagonally over a number of rows, and the cypher is then read off row by row. As an illustration, the phrase "meet me after the party" can be expressed as follows (in two rows):

```
m e m a t r h p r y
e t e f e t e o a t
```

Row after row, ciphertext is read from the example above: MEMATRHPRYETEFETEAT.

Because there is no key involved, it is quite simple to examine this method. The security of a transposition cypher can be greatly increased by conducting multiple stages of transposition. A more complicated permutation that is difficult to rebuild is the end outcome.

1.7   Symmetric Key Algorithms

Data can be encrypted and decrypted using the same key in symmetric encryption, depicted in fig. 1.27. The key is same for both the sender and the recipient, who keep it private and do not divulge it to anyone.

This is distinct from asymmetric encryption, which employs two keys—a public key (that everyone can access) to encrypt data and a private key to decode data—to encrypt and decrypt data, respectively. Let us quickly examine how encryption generally functions in case it is useful:

- When sending a message, the sender encrypts it using an encryption key, which is often a combination of letters and numbers.
- It is impossible for anyone to decipher the encrypted communication, known as ciphertext, which seems to be jumbled letters.
- To turn the ciphertext back into readable text, the recipient employs a decryption key.

The data can only be viewed and accessed by these two people (the sender and recipient). For this reason, it is sometimes referred to as symmetric cryptography, symmetric key encryption, private key cryptography, and secret key cryptography.

The encryption procedure is made easier by using a single key for both encryption and decryption. After all, you are using a single key to convert legible plaintext data into unintelligible nonsense (ciphertext), and vice versa.

Symmetric encryption offers data protection and secrecy without the added complication of many keys, which is one of its benefits. For some applications, symmetric key encryption can be used alone. When not publicly transmitting data between parties, for instance, it's helpful for encrypting databases and files. However, adopting symmetric key encryption has additional benefits and drawbacks, such as key management and distribution concerns, just like any other technical procedure.

Although symmetric key encryption as it is used to encode digital data using computers is relatively recent (it has been around since the middle of the twentieth century), the idea behind it is not. It is believed that the process of symmetric cryptography was developed thousands of years ago.

One can encrypt a communication with symmetric key encryption so that only you and the intended receiver can decipher it. Although it is one sort of data encryption, it is not the only one. Asymmetric encryption is a separate sort of encryption with a similar name but a different purpose. The ability to authenticate and exchange symmetric keys over public channels is made feasible by asymmetric encryption, which we just explained (such as the internet).

However, we no longer exchange paper messages in the modern era. Information exchanges in the modern day take place via virtual channels such as computers, websites, and the internet in general. While the internet certainly makes life immensely convenient, there are risks involved with using it for ridesharing or banking.

The Function of Symmetric Key Encryption in the Security of Websites A component of the public key infrastructure (PKI) ecosystem, symmetric key encryption transforms plain text (readable) data into unintelligible ciphertext in order to enable safe communication across the unsecured internet. You are currently connecting to TheSSLStore.com to read this article utilizing PKI-based technologies

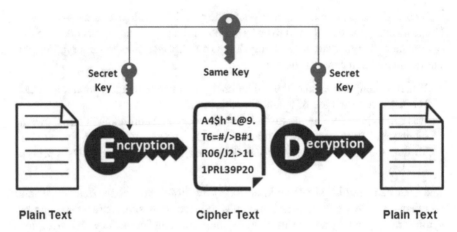

Fig. 1.27 Symmetric Key Algorithm

and procedures. Check out the lock in the URL bar of your browser. It indicates that you are sending data over a secure, encrypted connection and that our website has a website security certificate (SSL/TLS certificate) installed.

Using the secure HTTPS protocol to access our website rather than the insecure HTTP one is made possible to this. This implies that your browser (the "client") has already authenticated the server hosting our website, bargained with the server about the encryption techniques to be used, and generated symmetric session keys.

In order to exchange symmetric session keys and authenticate the website server, HTTPS uses asymmetric encryption. This is a step of the TLS handshake, which has three different iterations (TLS 1.0, TLS 1.2, and TLS 1.3):

- Authenticating our website's server,
- Negotiating with the server on the encryption algorithms to use, and
- Generating symmetric session keys.

Most of the data encryption that occurs throughout your session after that uses symmetric encryption.

1.8   Asymmetric Key Algorithms

Asymmetric cryptography, sometimes known as public-key cryptography, is the study of cryptographic systems that employ pairs of linked keys. A public key and its accompanying private key make up each key pair. The asymmetric key algorithm pictorial representation is given in fig. 1.28.

Cryptographic algorithms that are based on one-way functions are used to create key pairs. The private key must be kept hidden for public-key cryptography to be secure; nevertheless, security is not compromised if the public key is freely distributed. Anyone with access to a public key can encrypt a message in a public-key encryption system, creating a ciphertext. However, only those who have access to the associated private key can decrypt the ciphertext to reveal the original message.

For instance, a journalist can make the public key of a pair of encryption keys available online so that sources can send them ciphertext messages that are private. The ciphertexts must be decrypted by the journalist in order to access the sources' messages; they cannot be decrypted by an eavesdropper reading email that is being forwarded to the journalist. Public-key encryption, however, does not mask meta-data, such as the computer a source sent a message from, the time it was sent, or its length. By itself, public-key encryption also does not reveal to the recipient who sent a message; rather, it only encrypts the message's content into a ciphertext that can only be deciphered with the private key.

A sender can sign a message using a private key and a message in a digital signature system. Anyone with the appropriate public key can check if the message and signature match, but a forger without access to the private key is unable to create any message/signature pairs that will pass public key verification.

A software publisher, for instance, may make a pair of signature keys and incorporate the public key into programmes that are installed on PCs. Any machine receiving an update can certify it is authentic by confirming the signature using the public key, and the publisher can then disseminate an update to the programme that was signed using the private key. Even though a forger can provide malicious updates to computers, they cannot persuade the computers that any malicious updates are real if the software publisher maintains the private key hidden.

Modern cryptosystems, comprising programmes and protocols that provide assurance of the confidentiality, authenticity, and non-reputability of electronic communications and data storage, use public key algorithms as essential security primitives. They support several Internet standards, including PGP, S/MIME, SSH, and Transport Layer Security (TLS). Digital signatures are provided by some public key methods, such as the Diffie-Hellman key exchange, while key distribution and secrecy are provided by others (e.g., RSA).

The following are the top two applications of public key cryptography:

- Public key encryption encrypts a communication using the public key of the intended recipient. Messages cannot be decoded by anybody without the corresponding private key, who is therefore assumed to be the owner of that key and consequently the person linked with the public key, for correctly chosen and utilised algorithms. This can be used to protect a message's privacy.
- Digital signatures, which enable anybody with access to the sender's public key to validate a message after it has been signed with the sender's private key. By demonstrating that the sender has access to the private key, this verification strongly suggests that the sender is the person identified by the public key. Since verification will be unsuccessful for any other message one could concoct without utilising the private key, it also demonstrates that the signature was created specifically for that message.

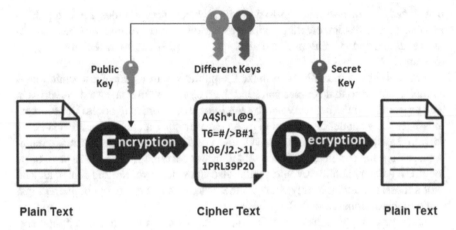

Fig. 1.28 Asymmetric Key Algorithm

1.9   Common Attacks in Cryptography

An attack entails performing a process on the information that modifies it in some way. For instance,

- Altering the data in an unlawful way.
- Initiating unlawful or unwanted information transmission.
- Altering authentication information, such as the information's timestamp or originator name.
- Unauthorised data deletion
- Denying reputable users access to information (denial of service).

> **Assumptions of Attacks   Environment around Cryptosystem:** It is essential to understand the environment of the cryptosystem while thinking about potential assaults against it. The assumptions and background information of the adversary determine his capabilities. The security environment and an attacker's capabilities are predicated on the following three premises in cryptography.
>
> - **Specifications of the Encryption Method:** The following two cryptography algorithms serve as the foundation for the building of a cryptosystem:
> - Public Algorithms – In this case, all of the algorithm's specifics are in the public domain and are known to everyone.
> - Private algorithms Only system designers and users have access to the algorithm's specifics.
> - Security is provided in the case of proprietary algorithms via obscurity. Given that they are created internally and may not have had their weaknesses thoroughly examined, private algorithms may not be the strongest algorithms. Second, they only permit closed group conversation. They are therefore inappropriate for modern communication, which involves a huge number of

known and unknown entities. Additionally, the Kerckhoff principle states that it is preferable for the algorithm to be made public and that the key is what gives encryption its power. As a result, the first presumption regarding the security environment is that the attacker is aware of the encryption scheme.

- **Availability of Plaintext and Ciphertext:** Both plaintext and ciphertext are available. Not as evident as other presumptions. However, there might be circumstances in which an attacker has access to both the ciphertext and the matching plaintext. Some of these scenarios include. In order to get the ciphertext, the attacker persuades the sender to convert plaintext of his choosing. Inadvertently, the recipient might reveal the plaintext to the attacker. The equivalent ciphertext obtained from an open channel is available to the attacker. The encryption key in a public-key cryptosystem is in the public domain and is known to any possible attacker. He can produce pairs of corresponding plaintexts and ciphertexts with this key.

- An attacker's primary goal is to disassemble a cryptosystem and separate the plaintext from the ciphertext. The attacker simply must learn the secret decryption key to get the plaintext because the algorithm is already known to the general public. Based on the methodology used, attacks on cryptosystems are categorized as follows −

  - **Ciphertext Only Attacks (COA)** − In this method, the attacker has access to a set of ciphertext(s). He does not have access to corresponding plaintext. COA is said to be successful when the corresponding plaintext can be determined from a given set of ciphertext. Occasionally, the encryption key can be determined from this attack. Modern cryptosystems are guarded against ciphertext-only attacks.

  - **Known Plaintext Attack (KPA)** − In this method, the attacker knows the plaintext for some parts of the ciphertext. The task is to decrypt the rest of the ciphertext using this information. This may be done by determining the key or via some other method. The best example of this attack is linear cryptanalysis against block ciphers.

  - **Chosen Plaintext Attack (CPA)** − In this method, the attacker has the text of his choice encrypted. So, the ciphertext-plaintext pair of his choice are available. This simplifies his task of determining the encryption key. An example of this attack is differential cryptanalysis applied against block ciphers as well as hash functions. A popular public key cryptosystem, RSA is also vulnerable to chosen-plaintext attacks.

  - **Dictionary Attack** − This attack has many variants, all of which involve compiling a 'dictionary'. In simplest method of this attack, attacker builds a dictionary of ciphertexts and corresponding plaintexts that he has learnt over a period. In future, when an attacker gets the ciphertext, he refers the dictionary to find the corresponding plaintext.

  - **Brute Force Attack (BFA)** − In this method, the asttacker tries to determine the key by attempting all possible keys. If the key is 8 bits long, then the number of possible keys is 2^8 = s256. The attacker knows the ciphertext and the algorithm, now he attempts all the 256 keys one by one for decryption. The time to complete the attack would be very high if the key is long.

- **Birthday Attack** – This attack is a variant of brute-force technique. It is used against the cryptographic hash function. When students in a class are asked about their birthdays, the answer is one of the possible 365 dates. Let us assume the first student's birthdate is third Aug. Then to find the next student whose birthdate is third Aug; we need to enquire $1.25*\square\sqrt{365} \approx 25$ students. Similarly, if the hash function produces 64-bit hash values, the possible hash values are 1.8×10^{19}. By repeatedly evaluating the function for different inputs, the same output is expected to be obtained after about 5.1×10^9 random inputs. If the attacker is able to find two different inputs that give the same hash value, it is a collision and that hash function is said to be broken.
- **Man in Middle Attack (MIM)** – The targets of this attack are mostly public key cryptosystems where key exchange is involved before communication takes place.

  - Host A wants to communicate to host B, hence requests public key of B.
  - An attacker intercepts this request and sends his public key instead.
  - Thus, whatever host A sends to host B, the attacker is able to read.
  - In order to maintain communication, the attacker re-encrypts the data after reading with his public key and sends to B.
  - The attacker sends his public key as A's public key so that B takes it as if it is taking it from A.

- **Side Channel Attack (SCA)** – This type of attack is not against any cryptosystem or algorithm. Instead, it is launched to exploit the weakness in physical implementation of the cryptosystem.
- **Timing Attacks** – They exploit the fact that different computations take different times to compute on processor. By measuring such timings, it is be possible to know about a particular computation the processor is carrying out. For example, if the encryption takes a longer time, it indicates that the secret key is long.
- **Power Analysis Attacks** – These attacks are like timing attacks except that the amount of power consumption is used to obtain information about the nature of the underlying computations.
- **Fault analysis Attacks** – In these attacks, errors are induced in the cryptosystem and the attacker studies the resulting output for useful information.

1.10   The Basic Principles of Modern Cryptography

This book places a strong emphasis on the scientific nature of contemporary cryptography. The key concepts and paradigms that set modern cryptography apart from the classical cryptography we examined in the previous section are outlined in this section. There are three key ideas:

1. **Principle 1:** The construction of an exact and rigorous definition of security is the first step in solving any cryptographic challenge.
2. **Principle 2:** An unproven assumption must be clearly expressed when a cryptographic construction's security depends on it. Additionally, the assumption ought to be as small as possible.
3. **Principle 3:** A rigorous proof of security for cryptographic constructions should be provided in relation to a definition developed in accordance with Principle 1 and in relation to an assumption indicated in Principle 2. (If an assumption is needed at all).

1.10.1   Principle 1 – Formulation of Exact Definitions

The insight that formal definitions of security are necessary precondition for the creation, use, or study of any cryptographic primitive or protocol has been one of the major intellectual achievements of modern cryptography. Let us go over each of these one at a time:

- **Importance for design:** Let us assume that we want to build a secure encryption system. How can we possibly know whether (or when) we have achieved it if we do not have a clear knowledge of what it is we are trying to accomplish? A definition in mind makes it possible to assess the calibre of what we create and directs us toward creating the appropriate item. In instance, it is far preferable to identify what is required before starting the design phase than to define what has been accomplished after the design is complete. The latter strategy runs the danger of having the design phase finish before the goal has been reached (rather than when it has), or it may lead to a construction that accomplishes more than is required and is therefore less efficient than a superior option.
- **Relevance to usage:** Let us say that we wish to implement a cryptographic method within a bigger system. How do we choose the right encryption method? How can we determine whether an encryption method is adequate for our application if one is provided? We can respond to these queries if we have a detailed definition of the security attained by a certain scheme. To be more specific, we can specify the level of security we need for our system, then check to see if a certain encryption scheme meets that need. As an alternative, we might define the definition that the encryption scheme must meet and then search for an encryption scheme that meets this definition. Noting that it might not be a good idea to select the "most secure" technique, we can employ a more effective one if a weaker definition of security works for our application.
- **Study importance:** How can we compare two different encryption schemes? Efficiency is the only metric that can be used for comparison in the absence of a definition for security, however efficiency is a flawed metric because a highly efficient scheme that is also entirely unsecure is useless. A further point of comparison is provided by the precise specification of the security level that a method

achieves. When two schemes are equally effective but the first one meets a stricter definition of security than the second, it is recommended to use the first one. 4 Alternately, there may be a trade-off between security and effectiveness (see the preceding two points), but at least with exact definitions we can comprehend what this trade-off means.

1.10.2   Principle 2 – Reliance on Precise Assumptions

Most contemporary cryptographic structures cannot be categorically demonstrated to be secure. This is because they depend on computational complexity theory concerns that currently seem to be a long way from being resolved.

This regrettable situation has the effect of making assumptions a common part of security. Modern cryptography's second rule states that presumptions must be clearly stated. This is due to the following key factors:

- **Validation of the assumption:** By definition, assumptions are conjectures that have not been demonstrated to be true. It is important to research the assumption in order to support this conjecture. The fundamental idea is that the more often an assumption is examined without being contradicted, the more certain we are that it is correct. Studying an assumption can also demonstrate that it is indicated by another widely held assumption, which is positive proof of its validity. The assumption cannot be examined and (perhaps) disproved if it is not clearly expressed and presented. Therefore, having a clear statement of what is assumed is a prerequisite to increasing our trust in it.
- **Comparison of the schemes:** In cryptography, it is common to be presented with two schemes that, although each may be shown to satisfy a certain definition, do so under a different premise. Which plan should be chosen, if both are equally effective? The first scheme is to be preferred if the first assumption is stronger than the second assumption on which the second scheme is predicated (i.e., the second assumption implies the first assumption). This is because it may turn out that the first assumption is true while the second assumption is false. The general rule is to favour the scheme that is based on the more thoroughly researched assumption where the assumptions employed by the two schemes are incomparable (for the reasons outlined in the preceding paragraphs).
- **Facilitating a proof of security:** As mentioned and will go into more detail in principle 3, contemporary cryptographic structures are offered with proofs of security. A mathematical demonstration that "the construction is safe if the assumption is true" can only be given if there is a clear description of the assumption if the scheme's security cannot be established unconditionally and must rely on some assumption.

One finding is that one might always presume that a building is secure on its own. This assumption is accurate if security is clearly stated (and proving security for the construction is simple)! Of fact, for a variety of reasons, this is not generally recognised practise in the field of cryptography. First, as was stated before, it is preferable to use an assumption that has been proven correct over time rather than one that was created solely to demonstrate the security of a certain structure. Second, since straightforward assumptions are simpler to analyse and challenge, there is a general preference for them. So, for instance, it is easier to study and work with the assumption that a mathematical issue is difficult to answer than the assumption that an encryption system fulfils a complicated (and possibly arbitrary) security criterion. We are more certain that a basic assumption is true when it has been thoroughly examined and has not yet been refuted. Another benefit of using "lower-level" assumptions rather than just assuming that a method is secure is that most constructions can use the same low-level assumptions. A different instantiation of the assumption can take its place within the higher-level structures if a particular instantiation of the assumption turns out to be untrue.

1.10.3   Principle 3 – Rigorous Proofs of Security

The previous two ideas are naturally related to this one. Modern cryptography emphasises the significance of thorough security justifications for proposed systems. Such a proof of security is feasible because specific definitions and presumptions are employed. But why is a proof required? The primary issue is that a construction's or protocol's security cannot be verified in the same way that software is usually verified. For instance, just because encryption and decryption "work" and the ciphertext appears jumbled does not guarantee that a knowledgeable adversary cannot defeat the technique. We must rely on our intuition that this is the case as we lack a proof that no adversary of the required power can defeat the system. Of know, intuition is generally a pretty difficult thing. Experience has proven that using intuition when it comes to computer security and cryptography is disastrous. Numerous instances of dubious ideas that were abandoned exist (sometimes right away, sometimes years after being presented or even put into use).

The potential harm that could be caused by using an unsafe system is another factor in why proofs of security are crucial. Even though software errors can occasionally be highly expensive, a bank could suffer a great deal of harm if its authentication or encryption systems were compromised. Finally, it should be noted that even though software often has defects, most users do not intentionally aim to make their software malfunction. In contrast, attackers assault security measures with the explicit goal of breaching them using incredibly elaborate and intricate methods (using aspects of the construction). Therefore, even if they are always desired in computer science, proofs of correctness are vitally necessary in the fields of cryptography and computer security. We emphasise that the observations are not simply hypothetical; rather, they are the result of years of empirical research and experience, which have shown us that intuition in this area should not be relied.

Bibliography

1. Stallings, William. *Cryptography and network security, 4/E.* Pearson Education India, 2006.
2. Karate, Atul. *Cryptography and network security.* Tata McGraw-Hill Education, 2013.
3. Frozen, Behrouz A., and Debdeep Mukhopadhyay. *Cryptography and network security.* Vol. 12. New York, NY, USA: McGraw Hill Education (India) Private Limited, 2015.
4. Easttom, C. (2015). Modern cryptography. *Applied mathematics for encryption and information security. McGraw-Hill Publishing.*
5. Katz, J., & Lindell, Y. (2020). *Introduction to modern cryptography.* CRC press.
6. Bellare, M., & Rogaway, P. (2005). Introduction to modern cryptography. Ucsd Cse, *207*, 207.
7. Zheng, Z. (2022). Modern Cryptography Volume 1: A Classical Introduction to Informational and Mathematical Principle.
8. Shemanske, T. R. (2017). *Modern Cryptography and Elliptic Curves* (Vol. 83). American Mathematical Soc..
9. Bhat, Bawna, Abdul Wahid Ali, and Apurva Gupta. "DES and AES performance evaluation." *International Conference on Computing, Communication & Automation.* IEEE, 2015.
10. Rihan, Shaza D., Ahmed Khalid, and Saife Eldin F. Osman. "A performance comparison of encryption algorithms AES and DES." *International Journal of Engineering Research & Technology (IJERT)* 4.12 (2015): 151-154.
11. Mahajan, Prerna, and Abhishek Sachdeva. "A study of encryption algorithms AES, DES and RSA for security." *Global Journal of Computer Science and Technology* (2013).
12. Mao, Wenbo. *Modern cryptography: theory and practice.* Pearson Education India, 2003.
13. B Rajkumar "Vulnerability Analysis and Defense Against Attacks: Implications of Trust – Based Cross – Layer Security Protocol for Mobile Adhoc Networks "presented at the International" Conference on IT FWP 09, Andhra Pradesh, India. in 2009.
14. B Rajkumar, G Arunakranthi, "Implementation and Mitigation for Cyber Attacks with proposed OCR Process Model" in Int.J. of Natural Volatiles & Essential Oils, 2021; vol.8(5): 2149-2160.

Chapter 2
Security Standards for Classical and Modern Cryptography

2.1 Overview

This chapter gives the knowledge about different encryption standards and how they are used for example **Data Encryption Standard (DES),** why there is a need to overcome the problems of DES and need of Triple Data Encryption Standard (TDES) and operational modes of TDES as well as it shows how the **Stream Cipher** works. These two are symmetric block cyphers, however **Advanced Encryption Standard (AES)** technology is comparatively more advanced than DES. As a result, several of its flaws are fixed. AES and DES now differ significantly from one another. Before the main algorithm begins, the plaintext block in DES is split into two halves. However, in the case of AES, the complete block is processed in order to acquire the ciphertext. Due to its reduced key size, DES is considerably less secure. To address this particular problem, Triple DES was developed, however its general operation proved to be somewhat slow. As a result, the AES was later presented by the NITS (National Institute of Standard Technology). It shows some cryptography terms like Pseudorandom Sequence and how they used, advancement of Stream Cipher which is LFRS based Stream Cipher, also discussed in this chapter.

2.2 Data Encryption Standard (DES)

Numerous standards are connected to cryptography. Standards for widely used applications draw a lot of cryptanalyses, while standard algorithms and procedures give a subject for study. Data Encryption Standard (DES), Advanced Encryption Standard (AES), RSA, the first public key technique, and OpenPGP are a few examples of well-known encryption standards. **This section will talk about DES.**

A symmetric-key method called the **Data Encryption Standard** is used to encrypt digital data. Although its 56-bit key length renders it too short for use in modern applications, it has had a significant impact on the development of cryptography.

The algorithm was created in the early 1970s at IBM and was based on an earlier invention by **Horst Feistel**. It was sent to the National Bureau of Standards (NBS) in response to the organization's request for a candidate for the security of sensitive, unclassified electronic government data. The algorithm underwent extensive scholarly inspection over time, which contributed to the development of block cyphers and cryptanalysis, which is now widely used.

Due to the comparatively small 56-bit key size, DES is unsafe. Distributed.net and the Electronic Frontier Foundation worked together in January 1999 to publicly decrypt a DES key in 22 h and 15 m (see chronology). Additionally, some analytical findings show cypher theoretical flaws that are impossible to exploit in practise. Although there are theoretical vulnerabilities, the algorithm in the form of Triple DES is thought to be practically secure. The Advanced Encryption Standard has replaced this encryption (AES). The National Institute of Standards and Technology has revoked DES as a standard. In certain papers, the DES standard is distinguished from its algorithm, which is known as the DEA (Data Encryption Algorithm).

2.2.1 Feistel Structure

The Feistel cypher serves as a design template or framework for several **symmetric block cyphers**, including DES. Invertible, non-invertible, and self-invertible components are all possible for this design approach. *The Feistel block cypher further makes use of the same encryption and decryption techniques*.

The 1945 Shannon structure, confusion, and diffusion implementation processes, served as the foundation for the Feistel structure. Using a substitution method, confusion creates a convoluted link between the encryption key and the ciphertext. On the other hand, diffusion uses a permutation algorithm to establish a complicated link between plain text and encrypted text.

A structure that alternately uses substitution and permutation was proposed by the Feistel cypher. Cyphertext is substituted for ordinary text in substitution. Instead of having one element replaced by another as is the case with substitution, permutation simply rearranges the plain text components.

Feistel Encryption
There are several stages of processing plain text involved in the Feistel cypher encryption process. The substitution step and the permutation step are both included in each round. The Feistel Encryption is depicted in Fig. 2.1 (left). See how this design model's encryption structure is described in the example below.

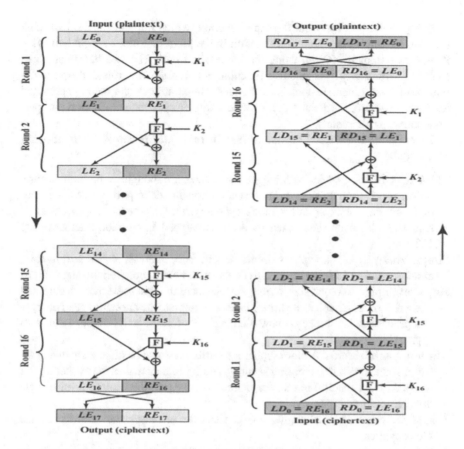

Fig. 2.1 Feistel Encryption (left) and Decryption (right) process

Step 1: In the first step, the plain text is separated into fixed-sized blocks, with only one block being processed at a time. A block of plain text and the key K make up the input for the encryption process.

Step 2: Split the plain text block in half. The plain text block's left and right halves will be designated as **LE₀ and RE₀**, respectively. To create the ciphertext block, both halves of the plain text block (LE₀ and RE₀) will undergo multiple rounds of plain text processing.

Every round, the plain text block's right half **RE$_i$** and the key **K$_i$** are both subject to the encryption process. The left half of **LE$_j$** is then XORed with the function results.

In cryptography, the logical operator known as **XOR** compares two input bits and yields one output bit.

For the subsequent round **RE$_{i+1}$**, the output of the XOR function serves as the new right half. For the following round, the old right half **RE$_i$** becomes the new left half **LE$_{i+1}$**.

Every round will carry out the same function, which implements a substitution function by employing the round function in the plain text block's right half. This function's output is XORed using the block's left half. The two halves are then switched, which uses a permutation function. For the following round, the permutation results are given. In fact, in a manner comparable to the below-mentioned Shannon structure, the Feistel cypher model implements the substitution and permutation steps alternately.

Features of the Feistel cipher design to take into account when utilising block cyphers:

Block size: Block cyphers with bigger block sizes are thought to be more secure. Larger block sizes do slow down the encryption and decryption process's execution, though. Block sizes for block cyphers are typically 64 bits, while more recent blocks, such those used by AES (Advanced Encryption Standard), are 128 bits.

Simple analysis: Block cyphers should be simple to analyse, as this will make it easier to spot and fix any cryptanalytic flaws and build more reliable algorithms.

Key size: Similar to block size, higher key sizes are thought to be more secure, but at the risk of lengthening the time it takes to complete the encryption and decryption process. A 128-bit key is now used in place of the older 64-bit key in modern cyphers.

The number of rounds: A block cipher's security may also be affected by the number of rounds. While increasing security, adding rounds makes the cypher harder to crack. As a result, the number of rounds relies on the desired level of data protection for an organisation.

Round function: A challenging round function increases the security of the block cypher.

Subkey creation function: Professional cryptanalysts find it more challenging to crack the cyphers the more complicated the subkey generating function is.

A software programme that can help achieve faster execution speeds for block cyphers is useful for quick software encryption and decryption.

Feistel Decryption

The Feistel cipher model uses the same encryption and decryption technique, which might surprise some people. The Feistel Decryption process is shown in Fig. 2.1(right). During the decryption procedure, it's important to keep in mind the following rules:

- The encrypted text block is divided into **two parts**, the **left (LD_0)** and the **right (RD_0)**, as seen in the picture.
- When using the key K_{16} and the right half of the cypher block, the round function operates similarly to the encryption algorithm.
- The left half of the encrypted text block is combined with the function's output in an **XOR operation**.
- The output of the XOR operation becomes the new **right half (RD_1)**, and RD_0 switches with LD_0 for the subsequent round.

- Every round does, in fact, employ the **same function**, and after the predetermined number of rounds has been completed, the **plain text block** is obtained.

A well-known cryptography design concept that businesses can utilise to help secure their sensitive data is the Feistel cypher. Strong encryption cyphers should prohibit hackers from deciphering plain text even if they are aware of the cypher algorithm without the key or key sets.

To help stop threat actors from stealing or disclosing their sensitive information, firms should implement a multi-layered cybersecurity plan in addition to this cypher model. An efficient method is tokenization, which substitutes tokens—unique, randomly generated numbers—for the original data. Through a safe cloud platform, tokenized data may be handled and saved. In the event of a breach, the only thing the hackers will have been tokens devoid of any useful data.

2.2.2 How Does DES Work?

DES uses the same key to encrypt and decrypt a message, so both the sender and the receiver must know and use the same private key. DES was once the go-to, symmetric key algorithm for the encryption of electronic data, but it has been superseded by the more secure Advanced Encryption Standard (AES) algorithm. The Feistel function of DES is depicted in Fig. 2.2.

Figure 2.3 depicts the general Feistel structure of the DES algorithm, which consists of 16 identical processing rounds.

Additionally, there is an inverse initial and final permutation known as IP and FP (IP "undoes" the action of FP, and vice versa). IP and FP were added to make it easier to load and unload blocks onto 8-bit based hardware from the middle of the 1970s even though they had no cryptographic importance.

The block is split into two 32-bit halves and processed alternately before the main rounds; this crisscrossing is referred classified as the Feistel scheme. *The*

Fig. 2.2 Feistel Function of DES

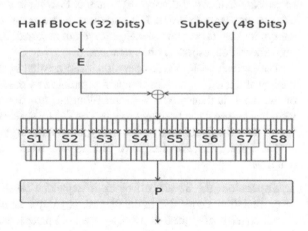

Fig. 2.3 Feistel Structure
of DES

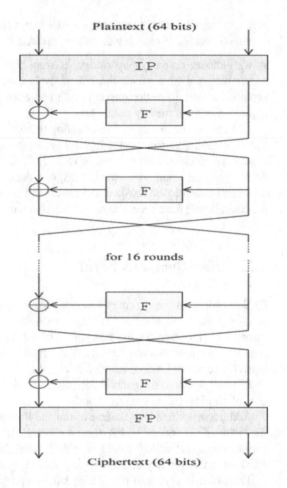

Feistel structure makes sure that the operations of encryption and decryption are
relatively identical; the only difference is that while decrypting, the subkeys are
used in the opposite order. The algorithm is the same throughout. Since separate
encryption and decryption techniques are not required, this considerably simplifies
implementation, especially in hardware.

The exclusive-OR (XOR) operation is represented by the symbol ⊕. A portion of
the key and a half of a block are both scrambled by the **F-function**. The other half
of the block is then mixed with the F-output, function's and then the halves are
switched before the subsequent round. The Feistel structure's feature that swaps the
halves after the final round makes encryption and decryption identical processes.

The Feistel function has **four phases** and works on a **half-block (32 bits)**
at a time.

1. **Expansion:** the 32-bit half-block is expanded to 48 bits using the expansion
   permutation, denoted **E** in the diagram, by duplicating half of the bits. The output consists of eight 6-bit (8 × 6 = 48 bits) pieces, each containing a copy of 4

corresponding input bits, plus a copy of the immediately adjacent bit from each of the input pieces to either side.

2. **Key mixing:** the result is combined with a subkey using an XOR operation. Sixteen 48-bit subkeys—one for each round—are derived from the main key using the key schedule (described below).

3. **Substitution:** after mixing in the subkey, the block is divided into eight 6-bit pieces before processing by the S-boxes, or substitution boxes. Each of the eight S-boxes replaces its six input bits with four output bits according to a non-linear transformation, provided in the form of a lookup table. The S-boxes provide the core of the security of DES—without them, the cipher would be linear, and trivially breakable.

4. **Permutation:** finally, the 32 outputs from the S-boxes are rearranged according to a fixed permutation, the P-box. This is designed so that, after permutation, the bits from the output of each S-box in this round are spread across four different S-boxes in the next round.

Confusion and diffusion, terms coined by Claude Shannon in the 1940s as a requirement for a secure yet practicable encryption, are produced, respectively, by the alternating of substitution from the **S-boxes** and **permutation of bits** from the **P-box and E-expansion.**

Key Schedule of DES

The key schedule for encryption—the algorithm that creates the subkeys, is shown in Fig. 2.4. The initial 56 bits of the key are chosen using Permuted Choice 1 (PC-1)

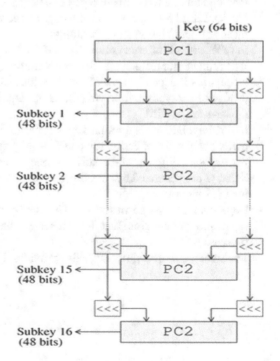

Fig. 2.4 Key Schedule of DES

from the initial 64 bits; the final eight bits are either ignored or utilised as parity check bits. After splitting the 56 bits into two 28-bit portions, each half is then handled separately. Permuted Choice 2 (PC-2) selects 48 subkey bits—24 from the left half and 24 from the right—after rotating both halves left by one or two bits (depending on the round's specification) in each subsequent round. Every subkey uses a distinct set of bits as a result of the rotations; each bit is utilised in around 14 out of the 16 subkeys.

Similar to encryption, the subkeys for decryption are ordered in the opposite direction from those for encryption. The procedure is the same as for encryption except from that alteration. Each rotating box receives the same set of 28 bits. The ≪ represents rounds.

The mathematical computation of DES is difficulty, but Simplified DES (SDES) was created solely for educational reasons to teach pupils about cutting-edge cryptanalytic methods.

SDES is identical to DES in terms of structure and features, but it has been simplified to make encryption and decryption considerably simpler to carry out manually with a pencil and paper. Some believe that knowing SDES can help one better understand DES and other block cyphers as well as various cryptanalytic techniques that can be used against them.

Some key features affecting how DES works include the following:

- **Block cipher.** The Data Encryption Standard is a block cipher, meaning a cryptographic key and algorithm are applied to a block of data simultaneously rather than one bit at a time. To encrypt a plaintext message, DES groups it into 64-bit blocks. Each block is enciphered using the secret key into a 64-bit ciphertext by means of permutation and substitution.
- **Several rounds of encryption.** The DES process involves encrypting 16 times. It can run in four different modes, encrypting blocks individually or making each cipher block dependent on all the previous blocks. Decryption is simply the inverse of encryption, following the same steps but reversing the order in which the keys are applied.
- **64-bit key.** DES uses a 64-bit key, but because eight of those bits are used for parity checks, the effective key length is only 56 bits. The encryption algorithm generates 16 different 48-bit subkeys, one for each of the 16 encryption rounds. Subkeys are generated by selecting and permuting parts of the key as defined by the DES algorithm.
- **Replacement and permutation.** The algorithm defines sequences of replacement and permutation that the ciphertext undergoes during the encryption process.
- **Backward compatibility.** DES also provides this capability in some instances.

2.2.2.1   Why Is DES Unsafe?

For any cipher, the most basic method of attack is brute-force, which involves trying each key until you find the right one. The length of the key determines the number of possible keys—and hence the feasibility—of this type of attack.

The effective DES key length of 56 bits would require a maximum of 2^{56}, or about 72 quadrillion, attempts to find the correct key. This is not enough to protect data with DES against brute-force attempts with modern computers.

Few messages encrypted using DES before it was replaced by AES were likely subjected to this kind of code-breaking effort. Nevertheless, many security experts felt the 56-bit key length was inadequate even before DES was adopted as a standard. There have always been suspicions that interference from the National Security Agency weakened the original algorithm.

DES remained a trusted and widely used encryption algorithm through the mid-1990s. However, in 1998, a computer built by the Electronic Frontier Foundation (EFF) decrypted a DES-encoded message in 56 h. By harnessing the power of thousands of networked computers, the following year, EFF cut the decryption time to 22 h.

Currently, a DES cracking service operated at the crack.sh website promises to crack DES keys, for a fee, in about 26 h as of this writing. Crack.sh also offers free access to a rainbow table for known plaintexts of 1122334455667788 that can return a DES key in 25 s or less.

Today, reliance on DES for data confidentiality is a serious security design error in any computer system and should be avoided. There are much more secure algorithms available, such as AES. Much like a cheap suitcase lock, DES will keep the contents safe from honest people, but it won't stop a determined thief.

2.2.2.2   DES Analysis

The DES satisfies both the desired properties of block cipher. These two properties make cipher very strong.

- **Avalanche effect**—A small change in plaintext results in the very great change in the ciphertext.
- **Completeness**—Each bit of ciphertext depends on many bits of plaintext.

The DES cryptosystem has received more information on its cryptanalysis than any other block cypher, although the most useful attack to date is still a brute-force strategy. Numerous minor cryptanalytic properties are known, and three theoretical attacks are conceivable. These attacks, while theoretically less complex than a brute-force attack, require an irrational amount of known or selected plaintexts to execute and are therefore unimportant in real-world applications.

The most fundamental attack strategy for any encryption is brute force, which involves testing each key individually. The number of potential keys and, thus, the viability of this strategy, depend on the length of the key. DES's key size was questioned early on, even before it was accepted as a standard, and the demand for a new algorithm was driven more by the algorithm's short key size than by theoretical cryptanalysis. The key size was decreased from 128 bits to 56 bits in order to fit on a single chip as a consequence of discussions involving outside advisors.

2.2.3 Triple DES

The Triple Data Encryption Algorithm (TDEA or Triple DEA), sometimes known as Triple DES (3DES or TDES), is a symmetric-key block cypher that uses the DES cypher algorithm three times to encrypt each data block.

The 56-bit key of the Data Encryption Standard (DES) is no longer regarded as sufficient considering contemporary cryptanalytic methods and supercomputing capacity. A significant security flaw in the DES and 3DES encryption algorithms was revealed by CVE-2016-2183, which was published in 2016. NIST deprecated DES and 3DES for new applications in 2017, and for all applications by the end of 2023 due to this CVE and the insufficient key size of DES and 3DES. The more reliable and secure AES has taken its place.

While the acronyms TDES (Triple DES) and TDEA (Triple Data Encryption Algorithm) are used by the government and industry, RFC 1851 originally referred to the algorithm as 3DES. Since then, most suppliers, users, and cryptographers have adopted this nomenclature.

In general, Triple DES with three separate keys (keying option 1) has a key length of 168 bits (three 56-bit DES keys), but the actual amount of protection it offers is only 112 bits because of the meet-in-the-middle attack. The effective key size is reduced to 112 bits by keying option 2. (Because the third key is the same as the first). However, this choice only has 80 bits of security according to NIST because it can be vulnerable to some chosen-plaintext or known-plaintext attacks. As a result, Triple DES was deprecated by NIST in 2017. This can be viewed as insecure.

If 3DES is used to encrypt large amounts of data with the same key, block collision attacks may be possible due to the tiny block size of 64 bits. The Sweet32 attack demonstrates how TLS and OpenVPN can be used to exploit this. Researchers were fortunate to get a collision just after about 220 blocks, which took only 25 min to complete a practical Sweet32 attack on 3DES-based cypher suites in TLS.

2.2.4 Simplified Data Encryption Standard (S-DES)

This algorithm **given mathematical understanding of DES**. Simplified DES is an educational encryption algorithm rather than a secure one. With far less parameters, it is similar in structure and properties to DES.

An **8-bit** block of plaintext (for example, **10111101**) and a **10-bit key** are the inputs for the S-DES encryption technique, which yields an **8-bit** block of ciphertext as the output.

The **10-bit key** that was used to encrypt the initial 8-bit block of plaintext is entered into the S-DES decryption method together with an 8-bit block of ciphertext. **Five functions** make up the encryption algorithm:

1. An **initial permutation (IP)**
2. A complicated function called **fK**, which depends on a key input and combines permutation and substitution operations
3. A straightforward permutation function called SW that switches the two halves of the data
4. fK again, and
5. Finally, a permutation function that is the inverse of the initial permutation.

In addition to the data being encrypted, an 8-bit key is also passed as input to the function fK. One 8-bit subkey, one used for each occurrence of fK, might have been utilised to create a 16-bit key for the method. It was also possible to use a single 8-bit key, repeating it twice throughout the process.

A workaround is to construct two 8-bit subkeys from a 10-bit key. In this scenario, a permutation is initially applied to the key (P10). A shift operation is then carried out. After the shift operation, a permutation function is applied to the output, which results in an 8-bit output (P8) for the **first subkey (K1)**.

The **second subkey (K2)** is created using the output of the shift operation as well as another shift and another instance of P8 (K2).

The encryption algorithm can be succinctly described as a composition of functions as follows:

$$\text{IP}^{-1} \circ f_{K_2} \circ \text{SW} \circ f_{K_1} \circ \text{IP}$$

which can also be written as:

$$\text{ciphertext} = \text{IP}^{-1}\left(f_{K_2}\left(\text{SW}\left(f_{K_1}\left(\text{IP}\left(\text{plaintext}\right)\right)\right)\right)\right)$$

where

$$K_1 = \text{P8}\left(\text{Shift}\left(\text{P10}\left(\text{key}\right)\right)\right)$$

$$K_2 = \text{P8}\left(\text{Shift}\left(\text{Shift}\left(\text{P10}\left(\text{key}\right)\right)\right)\right)$$

$$\text{plaintext} = \text{IP}^{-1}\left(f_{K_1}\left(\text{SW}\left(f_{K_2}\left(\text{IP}\left(\text{ciphertext}\right)\right)\right)\right)\right)$$

Let's look more closely at the components of S-DES.

2.2.4.1 S-DES Key Generation

A 10-bit key that is shared between the sender and receiver is the foundation of S-DES.

- Two 8-bit subkeys are generated from this key for usage at various points in the encryption and decryption method. First, permute the key in the manner described below.
- Let us use the designations (k_1, k_2, k_3, k_4, k_5, k_6, k_7, k_8, k_9, k_{10}) for the 10-bit key.
- So, the definition of the permutation P10 is:

$$P10(k_1,k_2,k_3,k_4,k_5,k_6,k_7,k_8,k_9,k_{10}) = (k_3,k_5,k_2,k_7,k_4,k_{10},k_1,k_9,k_8,k_6)$$

P10 can be concisely defined as follows:

P10									
3	5	2	7	4	10	1	9	8	6

- Reading this table from left to right reveals the identification of the input bit that created the output bit in each position.
- Thus, bit 3 from the input serves as the first output bit, bit 5 from the input serves as the second output bit, and so on.
- The key (1010000010), for instance, can be permuted to (1000001100). Next, individually rotate the first five bits and the second five bits using a circular left shift (LS-1). The outcome in this scenario is (00001 11000).
- Apply P8, which selects and reorders 8 of the 10 bits in accordance with the following principle:

P8							
6	3	7	4	8	5	10	9

- This yields subkey 1 (K1). For instance, this produces (10100100) after which you return to the pair of 5-bit strings generated by the two LS-1 functions and give each string a circular left shift of 2-bit positions.
- The value (00001 11000) in our case becomes (00100 00011). In order to create K2, P8 is then applied once more. The outcome in this scenario is (01000011).

2.2.4.2 S-DES Encryption

The consecutive application of five functions is required for encryption, as was previously explained. We look at each one of these.

Initial and Final Permutations

- The input to the algorithm is an 8-bit block of plaintext, which we first permute using the IP function as follows:

IP							
2	6	3	1	4	8	5	7

- This retains all 8 bits of the plaintext but mixes them up. At the end of the algorithm, the inverse permutation is used as:

IP^{-1}							
4	1	3	5	7	2	8	6

By way of example, it is simple to demonstrate that the second permutation is, in fact, the opposite of the first.

The Function fK

The function f_K, which combines permutation and substitution functions, is the most intricate part of S-DES.

The following is an expression for the functions.

- Let F be a mapping (not necessarily one to one) from 4-bit strings to 4-bit strings, and let L and R be the leftmost 4 bits and rightmost 4 bits of the 8 bit input to fK.

$$f_K(L,R) = \left(L \oplus F(R,SK), R \right)$$

Where SK is a subkey and $\oplus$ is the bit-by-bit exclusive-OR function.

- Let's say, for instance, that the output of the IP stage is (10111101) and that F(1101, SK) = (1110) for a particular key SK. Because (1011)! (1110) =, f_K(10111101) = (01011101). (0101).
- We will now discuss mapping F. It's a 4-bit number as the input $(n_1 n_2 n_3 n_4)$.
- An expansion/permutation procedure is the initial step:

E/P							
4	1	2	3	2	3	4	1

- For what follows, it is clearer to depict the result in this fashion

$$
\begin{array}{cc|cc}
n_4 & n_1 & n_2 & n_3 \\
n_2 & n_3 & n_4 & n_1
\end{array}
$$

- The 8-bit subkey K1 = (k11, k12, k13, k14, k15, k16, k17, k18) is added to this value using exclusive OR:

$$
\begin{array}{cc|cc}
n_4 \oplus k_{11} & n_1 \oplus k_{12} & n_2 \oplus k_{13} & n_3 \oplus k_{14} \\
n_2 \oplus k_{15} & n_3 \oplus k_{16} & n_4 \oplus k_{17} & n_1 \oplus k_{18}
\end{array}
$$

- Let us rename these 8 bits:

$$
\begin{array}{cc|cc}
p_{0,0} & p_{0,1} & p_{0,2} & p_{0,3} \\
p_{1,0} & p_{1,1} & p_{1,2} & p_{1,3}
\end{array}
$$

The **S-box S0** receives the first 4 bits (first row of the previous matrix) to generate a 2-bit output, and the **S-box S1** receives the remaining 4 bits (second row) to generate a second 2-bit output.

The following defines these two boxes:

$$
S0 = \begin{array}{c} \\ 0 \\ 1 \\ 2 \\ 3 \end{array}
\begin{array}{cccc}
0 & 1 & 2 & 3 \\
\begin{bmatrix} 1 & 0 & 3 & 2 \\ 3 & 2 & 1 & 0 \\ 0 & 2 & 1 & 3 \\ 3 & 1 & 3 & 2 \end{bmatrix}
\end{array}
\qquad
S1 = \begin{array}{c} \\ 0 \\ 1 \\ 2 \\ 3 \end{array}
\begin{array}{cccc}
0 & 1 & 2 & 3 \\
\begin{bmatrix} 0 & 1 & 2 & 3 \\ 2 & 0 & 1 & 3 \\ 3 & 0 & 1 & 0 \\ 2 & 1 & 0 & 3 \end{bmatrix}
\end{array}
$$

The following is how the S-boxes work.

- A row of the S-box is specified by the first and fourth input bits, which are both considered as 2-bit numbers, and a column of the S-box is specified by the second and third input bits.
- The 2-bit output is the entry in that row and column in base 2.
- For instance, if (p0,0p0,3) = (00) and (p0,1p0,2) = (10), then row 0, column 2 of S0, which is 3, or (11) in binary, produces the output.
- Like this, S1's row and column are indexed using (p1,0p1,3) and (p1,1p1,2) to provide an extra 2 bits.
- The four bits produced by S0 and S1 are then subjected to the following additional permutation:

P4			
2	4	3	1

The output of P4 is the output of the function F.

2.2.5 *The Switch Function*

Only the leftmost 4 bits of the input are changed by the function f_K. The second instance of f_K uses a different set of 4 bits thanks to the switch function (SW), which switches the left and right 4 bits. The E/P, S0, S1, and P4 operations are identical in the second case. K2 is the crucial input.

2.3 Modes of Operation

Encryption algorithms are divided into two categories based on the input type, as a **block cipher and stream cipher.** Block cipher is an encryption algorithm that takes a fixed size of input say b bits and produces a ciphertext of b bits again. If the input is larger than b bits it can be divided further.

Block Cipher: A block cypher uses a block of plaintext bits to create an equivalent-sized block of ciphertext bits. In the specified system, the block size is fixed. The encryption scheme's strength is not directly impacted by the block size selection. The length of the key has an impact on the cipher's strength.

Block Size: Although any block size is appropriate, the following factors should be taken into consideration when choosing a block size.

Say a block size is m bits; stay away from very small block sizes. The number of plaintext bit combinations that can be made is then 2 m. The attacker can conduct a form of "dictionary attack" by compiling a dictionary of plaintext/ciphertext combinations supplied with that encryption key if they identify the plain text blocks that correspond to certain previously sent ciphertext blocks. Attacks are more difficult when blocks are bigger because a bigger dictionary is required.

Avoid having a very big block size, as this makes the cypher run inefficiently. Such plaintexts will require padding prior to encryption.

Eight-bit multiples A multiple of 8 is a favoured block size since it is simple to create and most computer processors handle data in multiples of 8 bits.

Padding in Block Cipher: Most plaintext lengths are not multiples of the block size. For instance, a 150-bit plaintext contains three blocks totalling 22 bits, two of which are balanced 64-bit blocks. To make the final block of bits equal to the scheme's block size, it is necessary to pad it out with extra information. To give a complete block in our case, an additional 42 superfluous bits must be added to the remaining 22 bits. Padding is the practise of adding bits to the final block.

The system is rendered ineffective by excessive padding. Additionally, if padding is always done with the same bits, it may occasionally make the system vulnerable.

Block Cipher Schemes

There are several different block cyphers in use today. Many of them are well-known to the public. Below is a list of the most well-known and prominent block cyphers.

The well-liked block cypher of the 1990s was called Digital Encryption Standard (DES). Its tiny key size is mostly to blame for the block cipher's current reputation as being "broken."

Triple DES is a variation of the DES algorithm that uses multiple applications. Although still regarded, it is ineffective when compared to the newer, faster block cyphers that are currently available.

The block cypher known as Advanced Encryption Standard (AES), which won the AES design competition, is based on the encryption algorithm Rijndael.

With a block size of 64 and a key size of 128 bits, IDEA is a block cypher that is adequately secure. IDEA encryption is used by a number of programmes, notably early iterations of the Pretty Good Privacy (PGP) protocol. Due of patent concerns, the IDEA concept has a limited adoption.

Block cypher Two-fish employs a key with a variable length and a block size of 128 bits. It was a finalist for the AES. It has a block size of 64 bits and is based on the older block cypher Blowfish.

Serpent, a block cypher that placed in the top three of the AES competition, has a block size of 128 bits and key lengths of 128, 192, or 256 bits.

For different applications and uses, there are several modes of operations for a block cipher.

2.3.1   Electronic Code Book Mode

Electronic code book is the easiest block cipher mode of functioning. It is easier because of direct encryption of each block of input plaintext and output is in form of blocks of encrypted ciphertext. Generally, if a message is larger than b bits in size, it can be broken down into a bunch of blocks and the procedure is repeated.

This mode is the easiest approach to process a list of message blocks that are listed in order. The user takes the first block of plaintext and encrypts it with the key to create the first block of ciphertext. The user then takes the second block of plaintext and repeats the procedure with the same key, and so on.

The ECB mode is deterministic, meaning that the output ciphertext blocks will be the same if plaintext blocks P1, P2..., Pm are encrypted twice using the same key. Technically speaking, we are able to produce a codebook of ciphertexts for every possible block of plaintext for a given key. Then, all that would need to be done to encrypt data is to look up the necessary plaintext and choose the associated ciphertext.

As a result, the action is comparable to assigning code words in a codebook, and as a result, it is given the moniker Electronic Codebook mode of operation (ECB). The schematic diagram of ECB depicted in Fig. 2.5.

Analysis of ECB

In truth, any application data typically contains ambiguous information that can be inferred. One can anticipate, for instance, the pay range. If the plaintext message is predictable, an attacker could use a ciphertext from ECB to try and guess the plaintext.

For instance, if a ciphertext from the ECB mode is known to encrypt a salary figure, an attacker will be able to recover the value after a limited number of trials.

The ECB mode should not be used in the majority of applications since we generally don't want to use a deterministic cypher.

Advantages of Using ECB:
- Parallel encryption of blocks of bits is possible, thus it is a faster way of encryption.
- Simple way of the block cipher.

Disadvantages of Using ECB:
- Prone to cryptanalysis since there is a direct relationship between plaintext and ciphertext.

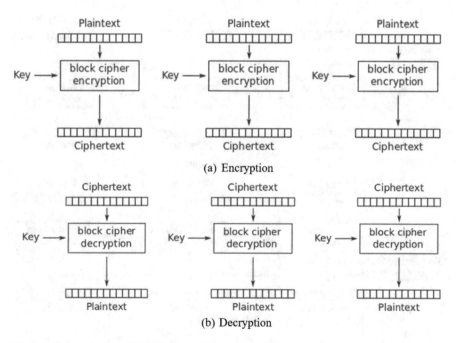

(a) Encryption

(b) Decryption

Fig. 2.5 Electronic Code Book Mode. (**a**) Encryption; (**b**) decryption

2.3.2 Cipher Block Chaining Mode

Cipher block chaining or CBC is an advancement made on ECB since ECB compromises some security requirements.

In CBC, the previous cipher block is given as input to the next encryption algorithm after XOR with the original plaintext block.

In a nutshell here, a cipher block is produced by encrypting an XOR output of the previous cipher block and present plaintext block.

The system is non-deterministic due to the CBC mode of operation's message reliance for ciphertext generation. The pictorial illustration CBC mode is presented in Fig. 2.6.

Following are the steps of CBC mode:

- Activate the top register and load the n-bit Initialization Vector (IV).
- The data value in the top register should be XORed with the n-bit plaintext block.
- Use the block cipher's underlying key K to encrypt the output of the XOR operation.
- Fill the top register with ciphertext blocks and keep going until all plaintext blocks have been processed.
- IV data and the first decrypted ciphertext block are XORed to perform decryption. In order to replace IV in the register that holds the first ciphertext block, the first ciphertext block is also put into the IV.

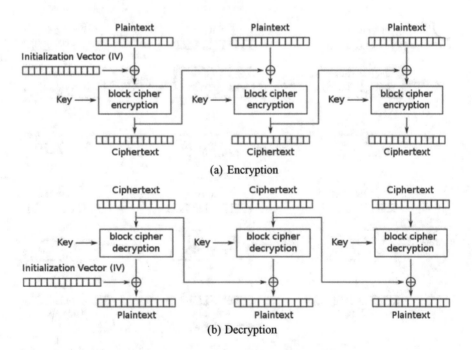

(a) Encryption

(b) Decryption

Fig. 2.6 Cipher block chaining mode. (a) Encryption; (b) decryption

Advantages of CBC:
- CBC works well for input greater than *b* bits.
- CBC is a good authentication mechanism.
- Better resistive nature towards cryptanalysis than ECB.

Disadvantages of CBC:
- Parallel encryption is not possible since every encryption requires a previous cipher.

Analysis of CBC

In CBC mode, the key is used to encrypt the result after adding the most recent plaintext block to the most recent ciphertext block. The act of decrypting the current ciphertext and then adding the preceding ciphertext block to the result is called decryption, which is the opposite of encryption.

Changing IV results in a different ciphertext for an identical message, which gives CBC an advantage over ECB. On the negative side, the chaining effect during decryption causes the transmission error to spread to a few further blocks.

It is important to note that CBC mode serves as the foundation for a well-known method of data origin authentication. It benefits applications that need both symmetric encryption and data origin authentication, as a result.

2.3.3 Cipher Feedback Mode

In this mode the cipher is given as feedback to the next block of encryption with some new specifications:

- First, an initial vector IV is used for first encryption and output bits are divided as a set of *s* and *b-s* bits.
- The left-hand side *s* bits are selected along with plaintext bits to which an XOR operation is applied.
- The result is given as input to a shift register having b-s bits to left hand sides (lhs), s bits to right hand side (rhs) and the process continues.

In this method, each block of ciphertext is "fed back" into the encryption process to encrypt the following block of plaintext. The Fig. 2.7 shows how the CFB mode operates.

For example, in the present system, a message block has a size 's' bit where $1 < s < n$. The initial random n-bit input block for the CFB mode must be an initialization vector (IV). No need to keep the IV a secret.

Operation Steps Are
- Fill the top register with the IV load.
- Data value in the top register should be encrypted using the underlying block cypher and key K.

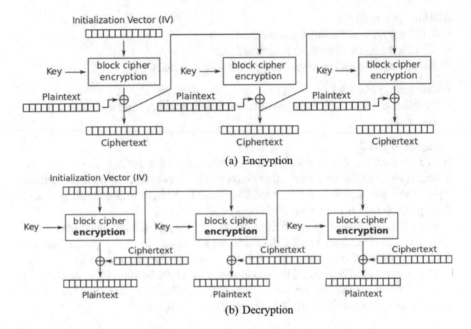

Fig. 2.7 Cipher feedback mode. (**a**) Encryption; (**b**) decryption

- To create a ciphertext block, XOR only the 's' number of most important bits (left bits) from the result of the encryption procedure with the 's' bit plaintext message block.
- Shift any existing data to the left in order to feed the ciphertext block into the top register. Repeat this step until all plaintext blocks have been processed.
- In essence, the current plaintext block is XORed to the preceding ciphertext block after it has been encrypted with the key.
- For decryption, the same procedures are used. The pre-decided IV is initially loaded when decryption begins.

Advantages of CFB:
- Since, there is some data loss due to the use of shift register, thus it is difficult for applying cryptanalysis.

Analysis of CFB
The ciphertext corresponding to a given plaintext block depends on both that plaintext block and the key as well as the preceding ciphertext block in CFB mode, which is very different from ECB mode. The ciphertext block is therefore message-dependent.

A highly peculiar aspect of CFB. In this mode, the user simply uses the block cipher's encryption algorithm to decrypt the ciphertext. Never is the underlying block cipher's decryption algorithm employed.

Evidently, CFB mode transforms a block cypher into a certain class of stream cypher. The key-stream that is stored in the bottom register is created using the encryption technique as a key-stream generator. The plaintext and key stream are then XORed together, much like in a stream cypher.

CFB mode preserves the benefits of a block cypher while also offering some of the benefits of a stream cypher by transforming a block cypher into a stream cypher. The switching of blocks, on the other hand, causes the transmission fault to spread.

2.3.4 Output Feedback Mode

The output feedback mode follows nearly the **same process as the Cipher Feedback mode** *except that it sends the encrypted output as feedback instead of the actual* cipher which is XOR output.

- In this output feedback mode, all bits of the block are sent instead of sending selected *s* bits. The Output Feedback mode of block cipher holds great resistance towards bit transmission errors.
- It also decreases the dependency or relationship of the cipher on the plaintext.
- It entails giving the underlying block cypher back successive output blocks from that cypher.
- These feedback blocks offer a string of bits to feed the key-stream generator used in CFB mode's encryption method.
- The plaintext chunks and the key stream created are XORed.

The initial random n-bit input block for the OFB mode must be an IV. The IV need not be kept a secret. The illustration of output feedback mode is given in Fig. 2.8.

Advantages of OFB:
- In the case of CFB, a single bit error in a block is propagated to all subsequent blocks. This problem is solved by OFB as it is free from bit errors in the plaintext block.

2.3.5 Counter Mode

The Counter Mode or CTR is a simple counter-based block cipher implementation. Every time a counter-initiated value is encrypted and given as input to XOR with plaintext which results in ciphertext block.

The CTR mode is independent of feedback use and thus can be implemented in parallel. It may be thought of as a counter-based variation of CFB mode without the feedback.

In this mode, each party must have access to a trustworthy counter that generates a fresh shared value after each exchange of a ciphertext block. The difficulty is that both parties must maintain the counter's synchronisation.

This shared counter need not necessarily include a secret value.

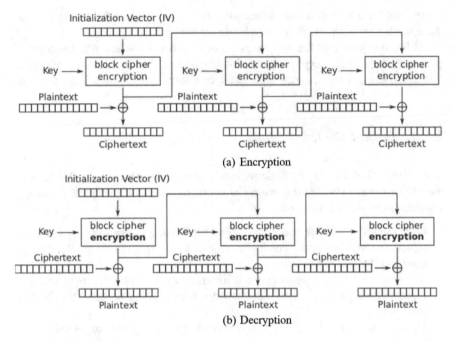

Fig. 2.8 Output feedback mode. (**a**) Encryption; (**b**) decryption

The Actions Taken Are
- Both the sender and the receiver should load the same initial counter value into the top register. In CFB (and CBC) mode, it performs the same function as the IV.
- Put the result in the bottom register after encrypting the counter's contents with the key.
- Add the bottom register's contents to the first plaintext block P1 and XOR it. C1 is the outcome of this. Update the counter and send C1 to the recipient. In CFB mode, the counter update takes the role of the ciphertext feedback.
- This process should be repeated until the final plaintext block has been encrypted.
- The opposite method is used for decryption. The output of the encrypted contents of the counter value is XORed with the ciphertext block. Each ciphertext block counter is updated after decoding, just like it was with encryption.

Its simple implementation is shown in Fig. 2.9.

Analysis of Counter Mode
A ciphertext block is independent of earlier plaintext blocks because it lacks message dependency. CTR mode, like CFB mode, does not require the block cypher to be decrypted. This is so that the CTR mode can really generate a key-stream that is encrypted with the XOR function by employing the block cypher.

In other words, CTR mode also converts a block cypher to a stream cypher. The fact that CTR mode requires a synchronous counter at both the transmitter and the receiver is a severe drawback.

The recovery of plaintext is erroneous when synchronisation is lost. But practically all of CFB mode's benefits are also present in CTR mode. Additionally, it completely avoids transmission error propagation.

Advantages of Counter:
- Since there is a different counter value for each block, the direct plaintext and ciphertext relationship is avoided. This means that the same plain text can map to different ciphertext.
- Parallel execution of encryption is possible as outputs from previous stages are not chained as in the case of CBC.

There have been many additional suggestions for block cypher operating modes. Some are in use, completely acknowledged, and detailed in detail (even standardised).

Some others have been deemed unsafe and ought to never be utilised.

Others, such key feedback mode, and Davies-Meyer hashing, don't fall under the confidentiality, authenticity, or authenticated encryption categories. Block cyphers' proposed modes are kept on file by NIST at Modes Development.

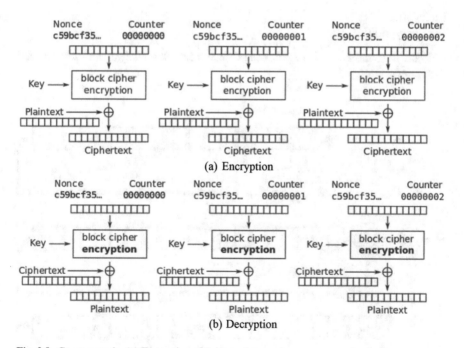

Fig. 2.9 Counter mode. (**a**) Encryption; (**b**) decryption

2.4   Stream Cipher

A stream cipher, one byte is encrypted at a time while in block cipher ~128 bits are encrypted at a time.

Initially, a key(k) will be supplied as input to pseudorandom bit generator and then it produces a random 8-bit output which is treated as keystream. Stream cipher schematic is depicted in Fig. 2.10.

The resulted keystream will be of size 1 byte, i.e., 8 bits.

1. Stream Cipher follows the sequence of pseudorandom number stream.
2. One of the benefits of following stream cipher is to make cryptanalysis more difficult, so the number of bits chosen in the Keystream must be long in order to make cryptanalysis more difficult.
3. By making the key longer it is also safe against brute force attacks.
4. The longer the key the stronger security is achieved, preventing any attack.
5. Keystream can be designed more efficiently by including a greater number of 1s and 0s, for making cryptanalysis more difficult.
6. Considerable benefit of a stream cipher is, it requires few lines of code compared to block cipher.

Encryption
For Encryption,

- Plain Text and Keystream produces Cipher Text (Same keystream will be used for decryption.).

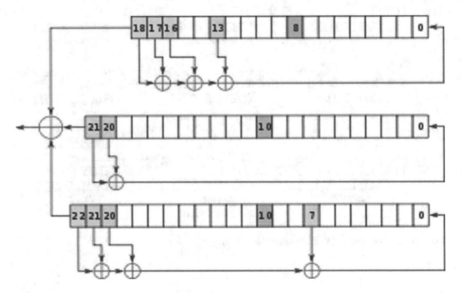

Fig. 2.10 Stream cipher

- The Plaintext will undergo XOR operation with keystream bit-by-bit and produces the Cipher Text.

Example:
Plain Text: 10011001
Keystream: 11000011

Cipher Text: 01011010

Decryption
For Decryption,

- Cipher Text and Keystream gives the original Plain Text (Same keystream will be used for encryption.).
- The Ciphertext will undergo XOR operation with keystream bit-by-bit and produces the actual Plain Text.

Example:
Cipher Text: 01011010
Keystream: 11000011

Plain Text: 10011001

Decryption is just the reverse process of Encryption i.e., performing XOR with Cipher Text.

How Does Stream Cipher Works?
A stream cipher is an encryption algorithm that uses a symmetric key to encrypt and decrypt a given amount of data. A symmetric cipher key, as opposed to an asymmetric cipher key, is an encryption tool that is used in both encryption and decryption.

Asymmetric keys will sometimes use one key to encrypt a message and another to decrypt the respective ciphertext. What makes stream ciphers particularly unique is that they encrypt data one bit, or byte, at a time. This makes for a fast and relatively simple encryption process.

Basic Components of Stream Cipher
Basic encryption requires three main components:

  (i)   a message, document or piece of data
 (ii)   a key
(iii)   an encryption algorithm

The key typically used with a stream cipher is known as a one-time pad. Mathematically, a one-time pad is unbreakable because it's always at least the exact same size as the message it is encrypting.

2.5   Advanced Encryption Standard (AES)

The Advanced Encryption Standard (AES) was developed by the National Institute of Standards and Technology (NIST) of the United States in 2001 as a specification for the encryption of electronic data.

Three members of the group, each with a block size of 128 bits but three distinct key lengths—128, 192, and 256 bits—were chosen by NIST for use with AES. The U.S. government has adopted AES.

Data Encryption Standard is no longer applicable (DES). The AES algorithm uses symmetric keys, which means that the same key is used to both encrypt and decode data.

AES is effective in both software and hardware and is based on a design idea called a **substitution-permutation network**.

AES does not employ a Feistel network, in contrast to its predecessor DES. AES is a variation with a fixed block size of 128 bits and a key size of 128, 192, or 256 bits. In contrast, it is described with block and key sizes that may be any multiple of 32 bits, with a minimum of 128 and a maximum of 256 bits.

A specific finite field (discussed in Chap. 3) is used for the majority of AES calculations. AES operates on a 4×4 column-major order array of 16 bytes termed the state.

$$\begin{bmatrix} b_0 & b_4 & b_8 & b_{12} \\ b_1 & b_5 & b_9 & b_{13} \\ b_2 & b_6 & b_{10} & b_{14} \\ b_3 & b_7 & b_{11} & b_{15} \end{bmatrix}$$

The number of transformation rounds required to transform the input, known as the plaintext, into the desired output, known as the ciphertext, is determined by the key size used for an AES cypher.

There are as follows how many rounds:

- *10 rounds for keys with 128 bits.*
- *12 rounds for keys with 192 bits.*
- *14 rounds for keys with 256 bits.*

There are numerous processing steps in each cycle, one of which is dependent on the encryption key itself. Using the same encryption key, a series of reverse rounds are used to convert the ciphertext back into the original plaintext.

2.5.1 High-Level Description of the AES Encryption

The high-level description of AES encryption is depicted in Fig. 2.11, which mainly includes following things:

- **Key Expansion**—round keys are derived from the cipher key using the AES key schedule. AES requires a separate 128-bit round key block for each round plus one more.
- **Initial round key addition:**
  - Add Round Key—each byte of the state is combined with a byte of the round key using bitwise XOR.
- **9, 11 or 13 rounds:**
  - **Sub-Bytes**—a non-linear substitution step where each byte is replaced with another according to a lookup table.
  - **Shift-Rows**—a transposition step where the last three rows of the state are shifted cyclically a certain number of steps.
  - **Mix-Columns**—a linear mixing operation which operates on the columns of the state, combining the four bytes in each column.
  - Add Round Key
- **Final round (making 10, 12 or 14 rounds in total):**
  - Sub-Bytes
  - Shift-Rows
  - Add Round Key

2.5.2 Sub-Bytes

In the Sub-Bytes stage, an 8-bit substitution box is used to replace each byte in the state array with a Sub-Byte. Keep in mind that the state array is just plaintext/input before round 0.

The non-linearity in the cypher is provided by this process. The multiplicative inverse over GF, which is well known to have good non-linearity qualities, is how the S-box was created.

The S-box is built by fusing the inverse function with an invertible affine transformation, preventing assaults based on elementary algebraic features. The S-box was chosen in order to avoid both any fixed points that are opposite to one another and any derangements.

The Inv-Sub-Bytes step (the inverse of Sub-Bytes), which entails first taking the inverse of the affine transformation and then calculating the multiplicative inverse, is utilised to execute the decryption. The depiction of Sub-Byte is given in Fig. 2.12.

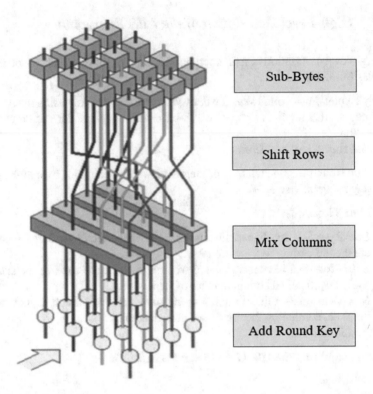

Fig. 2.11 High-level description of AES

2.5.3   Shift Rows

The Shift-Rows step cycles through the state's rows, shifting each row's bytes by a specific offset. The first row is left unaltered for AES. The second row's bytes are shifted one to the left. The third and fourth rows are also displaced by two and three offsets, respectively.

Bytes from each column of the input state are then used to create each column of the output state of the Shift-Rows step. This step is crucial because if the columns were encrypted separately, AES would break down into four separate block cyphers. Shift-Rows depicted in Fig. 2.13.

2.5.4   Mix-Columns

The four bytes of each state column are mixed using an invertible linear transformation in the Mix-Columns step, depicted in Fig. 2.14. Each input byte has an impact on all four output bytes when using the Mix-Columns function, which accepts four bytes as input and outputs four bytes. Diffusion in the cypher is provided by

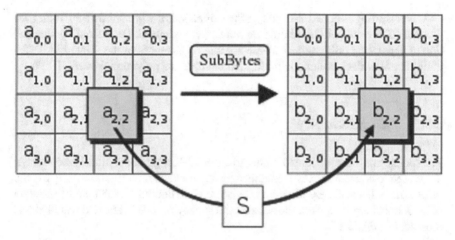

Fig. 2.12 Sub-bytes

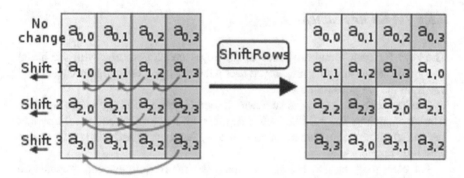

Fig. 2.13 Shift-rows

Mix-Columns in conjunction with Shift-Rows. Each column is converted throughout this procedure using a fixed matrix.

For Example:

$$\begin{bmatrix} b_{0,j} \\ b_{1,j} \\ b_{2,j} \\ b_{3,j} \end{bmatrix} = \begin{bmatrix} 2 & 3 & 1 & 1 \\ 1 & 2 & 3 & 1 \\ 1 & 1 & 2 & 3 \\ 3 & 1 & 1 & 2 \end{bmatrix} \begin{bmatrix} a_{0,j} \\ a_{1,j} \\ a_{2,j} \\ a_{3,j} \end{bmatrix} \quad 0 \le j \le 3$$

The entries are multiplied and added together in matrix multiplication. Bytes used as entries are considered as x^7-order polynomial coefficients. Just use XOR to add. Incompressible polynomial $x^8 + x^4 + x^3 + x + 1$ is modulo irreducible multiplication.

When shifting is done bit-by-bit, if the shifted value is greater than FF16, a conditional XOR with 1B (16) should be run (overflow must be corrected by subtraction of generating polynomial). These are unique instances of the standard GF (2^8) multiplication. Each column is multiplied modulo as a polynomial over GF (2^8).

2.5.5 Add Round Key

The subkey and state are joined in the Add-Round-Key phase. Rijndael's key schedule is used to create a subkey from the main key for each round; each subkey has the same size as the state. By utilising bitwise XOR to combine each byte of the state with its matching byte from the subkey, the subkey is added. The add round key is presented in Fig. 2.15.

2.5.6 AES Key Schedule

The keys for each round are listed in the key schedule. Starting with the initial encryption key as the whitening key, it uses a recursive process to derive each round key from the previous round key.

The key schedule generates keys with a round number of N_{r+1}, where N_r is the number of rounds. The AES key schedule offers effective distribution of the cypher key variations, the right amount of non-linearity for security, and good performance with little memory use.

For each AES variant, the key schedule is slightly different and operates on 4-byte blocks (words). The initial cypher key is the input to the key schedule.

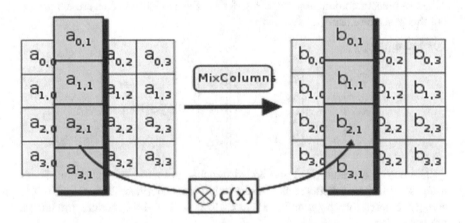

Fig. 2.14 Mix-columns

The initial key can be 128, 192, or 256 bits long depending on the AES type, which corresponds to $N_k = 4, 6,$ or 8 words, respectively. The key schedule's first N_k output words are also directly drawn from the beginning key (the whitening key).

2.5.7 AES Decryption

All the procedures that were used during the encryption process must be undone in order to decrypt an AES-generated ciphertext.

To do this, we both perform the round transformations (Sub-Bytes, Shift-Rows, and Mix-Columns) on the ciphertext in reverse order and invert each round transformation individually. Since Shift-Rows simply requires rotating each row by a set amount, it is relatively easy to invert.

We just reverse the rotation's direction to obtain the inverse operation Inv-Shift-Rows. We only need to develop a second lookup table that uses inverse substitution to obtain Inv-Sub-Bytes because Sub-Bytes is a bijective mapping.

The Inv-Mix-Columns phase involves multiplying each column by the inverse coefficient matrix, as was already explained above.

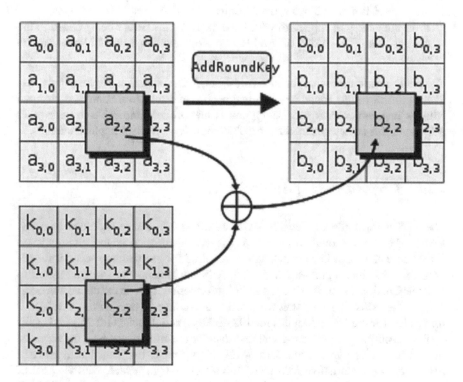

Fig. 2.15 Add round key

The Add-Round-Key step must be reversed as the final step. We may just add the same round key again to reverse the key addition because x $\oplus$ x = 0.

Following are the steps that make up a whole decryption round:

- Add-Round-Key
- Inv-Mix-Columns
- Inv-Shift-Rows
- Inv-Sub-Bytes

Be aware that the Mix-Columns transformation is skipped in the encryption algorithm's last round. Therefore, we must omit the Inv-Mix-Columns from the first inverse round during decryption.

The initial Add-Round-Key with the whitening key can be described so. We would have to write new code for the entire decryption process in order to handle this crude inversion of the encryption process. We could reuse code fragments in software implementations and reduce space in hardware implementations as a result.

AES's fundamental operations have some algebraic aspects that can be leveraged to make decryption more like encryption.

The method that results uses the following two characteristics and is known as an equivalent decryption algorithm:

- Since Inv-Sub-Bytes and Inv-Shift-Rows operate on each byte separately and use the same S-Box for all bytes, the order in which they are run is irrelevant.
- If the round key is applied to with Inv-Mix-Columns before being added to the current state, the order of Add-Round-Key and Inv-Mix-Columns can be changed.

The only variations are that for each Add-Round-Key operation, we first apply Inv-Mix-Columns to this round key and that each round transformation is exchanged with its inverted counterpart. Decryption is now quite comparable to encryption because to this advancement, which enables similarly effective implementations.

2.5.8   Cryptanalysis of AES

The AES algorithm's key lengths—128, 192, and 256—have been designed and tested to be strong enough to safeguard sensitive information up to the secret level. Either the 192 or 256 key lengths will be required for use with top secret information. Prior to being purchased and used, AES implementation in items meant to safeguard national security systems and/or information must be examined and certified by the NSA. The best-known attacks, according to one survey, involved 7 rounds for 128-bit keys, 8 rounds for 192-bit keys, and 9 rounds for 256-bit keys.

For the purpose of protecting sensitive data for the military and banking services, the Advanced Encryption Standard (AES) algorithm is frequently utilised. As a result, study on alternative AES algorithm attacks has increased, with the goal of either testing the algorithm's security or obtaining the secret data, or key. Since its debut in 2001, the AES algorithm has been frequently the target of numerous crypt-analytic assaults.

Most of these attacks, meanwhile, are theoretical and have not been able to entirely defeat the AES algorithm. In terms of time and data complexity, these attacks against the AES algorithm's decreased rounds are put up against the brute force attack. The most successful cryptanalytic technique is the brute force attack, which tries all possible key values.

The following are some of the different cryptanalysis attacks that can be made against AES:

- **Linear-Cryptanalysis-Attack:**

- The foundation of linear cryptanalysis is the identification of affine approxima-tions to a cypher element. It aims to make use of the high probability linear relationship between a function block's inputs and outputs. When using a block cypher, a linear set of key bits is separated from a linear set of plain text patterns and linear sets of ciphertext patterns. Finding a relationship that is proven either significantly more or less than 50% of the time is the primary goal of linear cryptanalysis.

- **Differential-Cryptanalysis-Attack:**
- Differential cryptanalysis takes use of connections between variations in a func-tion block's input and output. Determined are plaintext patterns with fixed differ-ences in an encryption algorithm's technique. Finding "characteristics" is differential cryptanalysis's major goal. Characteristics are particular variations in a collection of plaintext patterns that, for a given key, have a propensity to pro-duce particular variations in the ciphertext pairs. Utilizing pairs of plaintext pair-ings and giving probability to a number of potential subkeys are both components of a differential attack. The probabilities will rely on the cryptanalyst's under-standing of the features of the method. There are enough trails run for the correct key to be determined. In differential cryptanalysis, the attacker's analysis of modifications to a few chosen plaintexts and the variations in the outputs that arise from encrypting each one is crucial in order to uncover some of the key.

- **Boomerang-Attack:** The boomerang attack developed by Wagner may be thought of as a modernization of the traditional differential cryptanalysis that utilises quadruples of data rather than pairs with a fixed difference. Correlating quadruples of ciphertexts and middle states are used to precisely pick and acquire quadruples of plaintexts. Wagner demonstrated the application of this technique against various obscure block cyphers.

- **Square-Attack, Truncated-Differentials, and Interpolation-Attacks:**

- In differential cryptanalysis, when partially decided differentials are handled, truncated differentials are a generalisation.

- These partial differentials offer the ability to group difference pairs into pools. The statistics that this feature can return can greatly reduce the difficulty of launching a successful attack.

- The Square attack is a broadening of a strategy that was first put forth to attack the Square Block Cipher. A "multiset" of plaintexts deliberately chosen to have particular characteristics is used for this attack.

- The cypher is modelled using a big order polynomial to protect against interpolation attacks. As a result, the polynomial's key-dependent coefficients are found. When a low degree, compact expression that defines the cypher is appropriate, the method is very effective.

2.6 Pseudo Random Number Generator (PRNG)

Pseudo Random Number Generator (PRNG) refers to an algorithm that uses mathematical formulas to **produce sequences of random numbers**. PRNGs generate a sequence of numbers approximating the properties of random numbers.

A PRNG starts from an arbitrary starting state using a seed state. Many numbers are generated in a short time and can also be reproduced later, if the starting point in the sequence is known. Hence, the numbers are deterministic and efficient.

Why Do We Need PRNG?
With the advent of computers, programmers recognized the need for a means of introducing randomness into a computer program. However, surprising as it may seem, it is difficult to get a computer to do something by chance as computer follows the given instructions blindly and is therefore completely predictable.

It is not possible to generate truly random numbers from deterministic thing like computers so PRNG is a technique developed to generate random numbers using a computer.

How PRNG Works?
Linear Congruential Generator is most common and oldest algorithm for generating pseudo-randomized numbers. The generator is defined by the recurrence relation:

$$X_{n+1} = \left(a^* X_n + c\right) \bmod m,$$

Where:

X is the sequence of pseudo-random values
m, $0 < m$—modulus
a, $0 < a < m$—multiplier
c, $0 \leq c < m$—increment
x_0, $0 \leq x_0 < m$—the seed or start value

We generate the next random integer using the previous random integer, the integer constants, and the integer modulus. To get started, the algorithm requires an initial seed, which must be provided by some means. The appearance of randomness is provided by performing modulo arithmetic.

Characteristics of PRNG
- **Efficient:** PRNG can produce many numbers in a short time and is advantageous for applications that need many numbers.
- **Deterministic:** A given sequence of numbers can be reproduced at a later date if the starting point in the sequence is known. Determinism is handy if you need to replay the same sequence of numbers again at a later stage.
- **Periodic:** PRNGs are periodic, which means that the sequence will eventually repeat itself. While periodicity is hardly ever a desirable characteristic, modern PRNGs have a period that is so long that it can be ignored for most practical purposes.

Applications of PRNG
- PRNGs are suitable for applications where many random numbers are required and where it is useful that the same sequence can be replayed easily. Popular examples of such applications are simulation and modelling applications.
- PRNGs are not suitable for applications where it is important that the numbers are really unpredictable, such as data encryption and gambling.

2.7   LFRS Based Stream Cipher

Binary stream ciphers are often constructed using linear-feedback shift registers (LFSRs) because they can be easily implemented in hardware and can be readily analysed mathematically.

The use of LFSRs on their own, however, is insufficient to provide good security.

Various schemes have been proposed to increase the security of LFSRs, few are discussed below.

- **Non-linear combining functions**
- One approach is to use n LFSRs in parallel, their outputs combined using an n-input binary Boolean function (F). Because LFSRs are inherently linear, one technique for removing the linearity is to feed the outputs of several parallel LFSRs into a non-linear Boolean function to form a combination generator. Various properties of such a combining function are critical for ensuring the security of the resultant scheme, for example, in order to avoid correlation attacks.
- **Clock-controlled generators**
- Normally LFSRs are stepped regularly. One approach to introducing non-linearity is to have the LFSR clocked irregularly, controlled by the output of a second LFSR. Such generators include the stop-and-go generator, the alternating step generator and the shrinking generator.
- An alternating step generator comprises three LFSRs, which we will call LFSR0, LFSR1 and LFSR2 for convenience. The output of one of the registers decides which of the other two is to be used; for instance, if LFSR2 outputs a 0, LFSR0

is clocked, and if it outputs a 1, LFSR1 is clocked instead. The output is the exclusive OR of the last bit produced by LFSR0 and LFSR1. The initial state of the three LFSRs is the key.

- The stop-and-go generator consists of two LFSRs. One LFSR is clocked if the output of a second is a 1, otherwise it repeats its previous output. This output is then (in some versions) combined with the output of a third LFSR clocked at a regular rate.

- The shrinking generator takes a different approach. Two LFSRs are used, both clocked regularly. If the output of the first LFSR is 1, the output of the second LFSR becomes the output of the generator. If the first LFSR outputs 0, however, the output of the second is discarded, and no bit is output by the generator. This mechanism suffers from timing attacks on the second generator, since the speed of the output is variable in a manner that depends on the second generator's state. This can be alleviated by buffering the output.

- **Filter generator**

- Another approach to improving the security of an LFSR is to pass the entire state of a single LFSR into a non-linear filtering function.

Bibliography

1. Stallings, William. *Cryptography and network security, 4/E*. Pearson Education India, 2006.
2. Karate, Atul. *Cryptography and network security*. Tata McGraw-Hill Education, 2013.
3. Frozen, Behrouz A., and Debdeep Mukhopadhyay. *Cryptography and network security*. Vol. 12. New York, NY, USA: McGraw Hill Education (India) Private Limited, 2015.
4. Easttom, C. (2015). Modern cryptography. *Applied mathematics for encryption and information security. McGraw-Hill Publishing*.
5. Katz, J., & Lindell, Y. (2020). *Introduction to modern cryptography*. CRC Press.
6. Bellare, M., & Rogaway, P. (2005). Introduction to modern cryptography. *Ucsd Cse, 207*, 207.
7. Zheng, Z. (2022). Modern Cryptography Volume 1: A Classical Introduction to Informational and Mathematical Principle.
8. Shemanske, T. R. (2017). *Modern Cryptography and Elliptic Curves* (Vol. 83). American Mathematical Soc.
9. Bhat, Bawna, Abdul Wahid Ali, and Apurva Gupta. "DES and AES performance evaluation." *International Conference on Computing, Communication & Automation*. IEEE, 2015.
10. Rihan, Shaza D., Ahmed Khalid, and Saife Eldin F. Osman. "A performance comparison of encryption algorithms AES and DES." *International Journal of Engineering Research & Technology (IJERT)* 4.12 (2015): 151–154.
11. Mahajan, Prerna, and Abhishek Sachdeva. "A study of encryption algorithms AES, DES and RSA for security." *Global Journal of Computer Science and Technology* (2013).
12. Mao, Wenbo. *Modern cryptography: theory and practice*. Pearson Education India, 2003.
13. B Rajkumar "Vulnerability Analysis and Defense Against Attacks: Implications of Trust – Based Cross – Layer Security Protocol for Mobile Adhoc Networks" presented at the International" Conference on IT FWP 09, Andhra Pradesh, India. in 2009.
14. B Rajkumar, G Arunakranthi, "Implementation and Mitigation for Cyber Attacks with proposed OCR Process Model" in Int. J. of Natural Volatiles & Essential Oils, 2021; vol. 8(5): 2149–2160.

15. Daemen, J., & Rijmen, V. (1999). AES proposal: Rijndael.
16. Zodpe, H., & Shaikh, A. (2021). A Survey on Various Cryptanalytic Attacks on the AES Algorithm. *International Journal of Next-Generation Computing*, 115–123.
17. Sharma, N. (2017). A Review of Information Security using Cryptography Technique. *International Journal of Advanced Research in Computer Science*, 8(4).
18. Gupta, A., & Walia, N. K. (2014). Cryptography Algorithms: a review.
19. Amalraj, A. J., & Jose, J. J. R. (2016). A survey paper on cryptography techniques. *International Journal of Computer Science and mobile computing*, 5(8), 55–59.
20. Pachghare, V. K. (2019). *Cryptography and information security*. PHI Learning Pvt. Ltd.

Chapter 3
Mathematical Foundation for Classical and Modern Cryptography

3.1 Overview

The foundation of cryptography is mathematics. Cryptography is nothing more than mathematical operations. Any of the current encryption protocols or standards, such RSA, would serve as an illustration. This is referred to as a public-key encryption technique.

Each participant has a unique private key that they use to decrypt incoming traffic. A public key is generated when the connection is established. These keys are actually very huge integers that are generated using various mathematical processes and then used to check the validity of communications.

Feistel cyphers, often known as block cyphers, include some of the older and less reliable techniques, such as DES. These encrypt and decrypt data using a series of passes through a collection of blocks. These blocks each have a unique mathematical transform to apply to the message that is provided into them.

A self-contained introduction to modern cryptography is provided by an Introduction to Mathematical Foundations of Cryptography, with a focus on the mathematics underlying the theory of public key cryptosystems and digital signature techniques. Hence, this chapter cover mathematical foundation for cryptography:

- Modular arithmetic,
- Groups,
- Finite fields,
- Elliptic curves, and
- Elliptic curve cryptography.

R. Banoth, R. Regar, *Classical and Modern Cryptography for Beginners*, https://doi.org/10.1007/978-3-031-32959-3_3

3.2   Modular Arithmetic

In mathematics, modular arithmetic is a method of integer arithmetic in which numbers "wrap around" after they reach a predetermined value known as the modulus. Carl Friedrich Gauss invented the current method of modular arithmetic.

Another notation of modular arithmetic is—the branch of arithmetic mathematics associated with the "mod" functionality is known as modular arithmetic. Modular arithmetic basically has to do with computing an expression's "**mod**." Expressions may contain numerals as well as **addition, subtraction, multiplication, division,** and other computational symbols.

3.2.1   Quotient Remainder Theorem

The quotient-remainder theorem asserts that there are two distinct integers q and r such that for any pair of integers a and b (b is positive):

$$a = b \times q + r$$

where $0 < = r < b$.

Example
Case 1:
If $a = 22, b = 4$
then $q = 5, r = 2$
$22 = 4 \times 5 + 2$

Case 2:
If $a = -19, b = 5$
then $q = -4, r = 1$
$-19 = 5 \times - 4 + 1$

It is used to demonstrate the concepts of modular addition, modular multiplication, and a great deal more.

3.2.2   Modular Addition

$$(a + b) \bmod m = ((a \bmod m) + (b \bmod m)) \bmod m$$

Example
case 1:

$$(15+17)\%7$$
$$=((15\%7)+(17\%7))\%7$$
$$=(1+3)\%7$$
$$=4\%7$$
$$=4$$

Modular subtraction is also same as addition. Although, modular subtraction is not needed in many cases but can compute following modular addition unlike the addition operator.

3.2.3 Modular Multiplication

$$(a\times b)\bmod m = ((a\bmod m)\times(b\bmod m))\bmod m$$

Example
case 1:

$$(12\times13)\%5$$
$$=((12\%5)\times(13\%5))\%5$$
$$=(2\times3)\%5$$
$$=6\%5$$
$$=1$$

3.2.4 Modular Division

Modular addition, subtraction, and multiplication are completely distinct from modular division. It also does not always exist.

$$(a/b)\bmod m \text{ is not equal to} ((a\bmod m)/(b\bmod m))\bmod m.$$

This is calculated using the following formula:

$$(a/b)\bmod m = (a\times(\text{inverse of } b \text{ if exists}))\bmod m$$

3.2.5 Modular Inverse

The modular inverse of a mod m exists only if a and m are relatively prime i.e., greatest common divisor—gcd (a, m) = 1. Hence, for finding the inverse of an under modulo m, if (a × b) mod m = 1 then b is the modular inverse of a.

Example
case 1:
a = 5,
m = 7 (5 × 3) % 7 = 1
hence, 3 is modulo inverse of 5 under 7.

3.2.6 Modular Exponentiation

Finding a^b mod m is the modular exponentiation.
      There are two approaches for this—recursive and iterative.

Example
case 1:
a = 5,
b = 2,
m = 7
(5^2) % 7 = 25 % 7 = 4

3.2.7 Congruence

Given an integer n > 1, called a modulus, two integers a and b are said to be congruent modulo n, if n is a divisor of their difference (that is, if there is an integer k such that a − b = kn).

- Congruence modulo n is a congruence relation, meaning that it is an equivalence relation that is compatible with the operations of addition, subtraction, and multiplication.
- Congruence modulo n is denoted: a ≡ (b mod n).
- The parentheses mean that (mod n) applies to the entire equation, not just to the right-hand side.

Following are properties of congruence:
      The congruence relation satisfies all the conditions of an equivalence relation:

- **Reflexivity:** a ≡ a (mod n)
- **Symmetry:** a ≡ b (mod n) if b ≡ a (mod n) for all a, b, and n.
- **Transitivity:** If a ≡ b (mod n) and b ≡ c (mod n), then a ≡ c (mod n)

If $a_1 \equiv b_1$ (mod n) and $a_2 \equiv b_2$ (mod n), or if $a \equiv b$ (mod n), then:

- **$a + k \equiv b + k$ (mod n)** for any integer k (compatibility with translation)
- **$k\,a \equiv k\,b$ (mod n)** for any integer k (compatibility with scaling)
- **$k\,a \equiv k\,b$** (mod kn) for any integer k
- **$a_1 + a_2 \equiv b_1 + b_2$ (mod n)** (compatibility with addition)
- **$a_1 - a_2 \equiv b_1 - b_2$ (mod n)** (compatibility with subtraction)
- **$a_1\,a_2 \equiv b_1\,b_2$ (mod n)** (compatibility with multiplication)
- **$a^k \equiv b^k$ (mod n)** for any non-negative integer k (compatibility with exponentiation)
- **$p(a) \equiv p(b)$ (mod n)**, for any polynomial $p(x)$ with integer coefficients (compatibility with polynomial evaluation)

If $a \equiv b$ (mod n), then it is generally false that $k^a \equiv k^b$ (mod n). However, the following is true:

- If $c \equiv d$ (mod $\varphi(n)$), where φ is Euler's totient function, then $a^c \equiv a^d$ (mod n)— provided that a is coprime with n.

For cancellation of common terms, we have the following rules:

- If **$a + k \equiv b + k$ (mod n)**, where k is any integer, then $a \equiv b$ (mod n)
- If **$k\,a \equiv k\,b$ (mod n)** and k is coprime with n, then $a \equiv b$ (mod n)
- If **$k\,a \equiv k\,b$ (mod kn)** and $k \neq 0$, then $a \equiv b$ (mod n)

The modular multiplicative inverse is defined by the following rules:

- **Existence:** there exists an integer denoted a^{-1} such that $aa^{-1} \equiv 1$ (mod n) if and only if a is coprime with n. This integer a^{-1} is called a modular multiplicative inverse of a modulo n.
- If $a \equiv b$ (mod n) and a^{-1} exists, then $a^{-1} \equiv b^{-1}$ (mod n) (compatibility with multiplicative inverse, and, if $a = b$, uniqueness modulo n)
- If $a\,x \equiv b$ (mod n) and a is coprime to n, then the solution to this linear congruence is given by $x \equiv a^{-1}b$ (mod n)

If p is a prime number, then a is coprime with p for every a such that $0 < a < p$; thus, a multiplicative inverse exists for all a that is not congruent to zero modulo p.

Some of the more *advanced properties of congruence relations are the following*:

- **Fermat's little theorem:** If p is prime and does not divide a, then $a^{p-1} \equiv 1$ (mod p).
- **Euler's theorem:** If a and n are coprime, then $a^{\varphi(n)} \equiv 1$ (mod n), where φ is Euler's totient function
- A simple consequence of Fermat's little theorem is that if p is prime, then $a^{-1} \equiv a^{p-2}$ (mod p) is the multiplicative inverse of $0 < a < p$. More generally, from Euler's theorem, if a and n are coprime, then $a^{-1} \equiv a^{\varphi(n)-1}$ (mod n).
- Another simple consequence is that if $a \equiv b$ (mod $\varphi(n)$), where φ is Euler's totient function, then $k^a \equiv k^b$ (mod n) provided k is coprime with n.

- **Wilson's theorem:** p is prime if and only if $(p - 1)! \equiv -1$ (mod p).
- **Chinese remainder theorem:** For any a, b and coprime m, n, there exists a unique x (mod mn) such that $x \equiv a$ (mod m) and $x \equiv b$ (mod n). In fact, $x \equiv b\, m_n^{-1}\, m + a\, n_m^{-1}\, n$ (mod mn) where m_n^{-1} is the inverse of m modulo n and n_m^{-1} is the inverse of n modulo m.
- **Lagrange's theorem:** The congruence $f(x) \equiv 0$ (mod p), where p is prime, and $f(x) = a_0\, x^n + \ldots + a_n$ is a polynomial with integer coefficients such that $a_0 \neq 0$ (mod p), has at most n roots.
- **Primitive root modulo n:** A number g is a primitive root modulo n if, for every integer a coprime to n, there is an integer k such that $g^k \equiv a$ (mod n). A primitive root modulo n exists if and only if n is equal to 2, 4, p^k or $2p^k$, where p is an odd prime number and k is a positive integer. If a primitive root modulo n exists, then there are exactly $\varphi(\varphi(n))$ such primitive roots, where φ is the Euler's totient function.
- **Quadratic residue:** An integer a is a quadratic residue modulo n, if there exists an integer x such that $x^2 \equiv a$ (mod n). Euler's criterion asserts that, if p is an odd prime, and a is not a multiple of p, then a is a quadratic residue modulo p if and only if $a^{(p-1)/2} \equiv 1$.

Congruence Classes
- Like any congruence relation, congruence modulo n is an equivalence relation, and the equivalence class of the integer a, denoted by an, is the set $\{\ldots, a - 2n, a - n, a, a + n, a + 2n, \ldots\}$.
- This set, consisting of all the integers congruent to a modulo n, is called the congruence class, residue class, or simply residue of the integer a modulo n.
- When the modulus n is known from the context, that residue may also be denoted [a].

Residue System
Although we often represent each residue class by the smallest nonnegative integer that belongs to that class, each residue class modulo n may be represented by any one of its members. Modulo n, any two members of dissimilar residue classes are incongruent. Every integer furthermore belongs to a single residue class modulo n.

3.2.8   Application of Modular Arithmetic

Theoretical mathematics uses modular arithmetic extensively in group theory, ring theory, knot theory, and abstract algebra. It is one of the foundations of number theory, touching on nearly every part of its study.

Computer algebra, cryptography, computer science, chemistry, and the visual and performing arts are all areas of applied mathematics that employ it.

A very practical application is to **calculate checksums** within serial number identifiers. For example, **International Standard Book Number (ISBN)** uses modulo 11 (for 10 digit ISBN) or modulo 10 (for 13 digit ISBN) arithmetic for error detection.

Likewise, **International Bank Account Numbers (IBANs)**, for example, make use of modulo 97 arithmetic to spot user input errors in bank account numbers. In chemistry, the last digit of the CAS registry number (a unique identifying number for each chemical compound) is a check digit, which is calculated by taking the last digit of the first two parts of the CAS registry number times 1, the previous digit times 2, the previous digit times 3 etc., adding all these up and computing the sum modulo 10.

Modular arithmetic is used in several *symmetric key algorithms*, including Advanced Encryption Standard (AES), International Data Encryption Algorithm (IDEA), and RC4. It also directly *supports public key systems*, such as RSA and Diffie-Hellman, and provides finite fields that support elliptic curves. Exponentiation is done modularly in RSA and Diffie-Hellman.

Modular arithmetic is frequently used in *computer algebra to restrict the size of integer coefficients* in intermediate calculations and data.

Modular arithmetic is employed in *polynomial factorization*, a problem for which all currently used effective techniques.

The most effective applications of the Gröbner basis, exact linear algebra, and polynomial GCD over integers and rational numbers all make use of it.

In computer science, *bitwise operations and other operations using fixed-width, cyclic data structures frequently make use of modular arithmetic*.

An application of modular arithmetic that is frequently used in this setting is the *modulo operation*, which is available in a wide variety of *programming languages and calculators*. XOR is a logical operation that sums two bits modulo 2.

In music, arithmetic modulo 12 is used in the consideration of the system of 12-tone equal temperament, where octave and enharmonic equivalency occurs (that is, pitches in a 1:2 or 2:1 ratio are equivalent, and C-sharp is considered the same as D-flat).

The method of *casting out nines offers* a quick check of decimal arithmetic computations performed by hand. It is based on modular arithmetic modulo 9, and specifically on the crucial property that $10 \equiv 1 \pmod 9$.

Arithmetic modulo 7 is used in algorithms that determine the day of the week for a given date. In particular, *Zeller's congruence and the Doomsday algorithm make heavy use of modulo-7 arithmetic.*

Modular arithmetic is useful in fields like law (e.g., apportionment), *economics* (e.g., game theory), and other social sciences, where the examination of proportional division and distribution of resources is crucial.

3.2.9   Computational Complexity

- Knowing how challenging a system of congruences is to solve is crucial since modular arithmetic has so many uses. For more information, the linear congruence theorem. A linear system of congruences can be solved in polynomial time using a variant of Gaussian elimination.
- There are further algorithms, like the Montgomery reduction, that make it possible to efficiently perform common arithmetic operations on huge numbers, such multiplication and exponentiation modulo n.
- Finding discrete logarithms and quadratic congruences, two procedures that seem to be as difficult as integer factorization, serve as the basis for many encryption and cryptography systems.

3.3   Groups

In mathematics, *a group is a set and an operation that joins any two elements of the set to create a third element of the set in a fashion that is associative, has an identity element and an inverse for each element.*

Numerous additional mathematical structures as well as number systems adhere to these three axioms.

For instance, a group is formed by the addition operation and the integers. The idea of a group and the axioms that describe it were developed in order to handle the fundamental structural characteristics of a variety of very distinct mathematical entities, such as numbers, geometric shapes, and polynomial roots, in a coherent manner.

Some authors view the idea of groups as the main organizing principle of modern mathematics due to its pervasiveness in many fields both inside and outside of mathematics.

Definition

A group G, sometimes denoted by $\{G,.\}$, is a set of elements with a binary operation denoted by . that associates to each ordered pair (a, b) of elements in G an element (a . b) in G, such that the following axioms are obeyed:

- **Closure:** If a and b belong to G, then a . b is also in G.
- **Associative:** a . (b . c) = (a . b) . c for all a, b, c in G.
- **Identity element:** There is an element e in G such that a . e = e . a = a for all a in G.
- **Inverse element:** For each a in G, there is an element a^{-1} in G such that a . a^{-1} = a^{-1} . a = e.

A group is referred to be a finite group if it contains a finite number of elements, and its order is determined by the number of elements. The group is an infinite group if such is the case.

The set of integers is one of the better-known groups.

$$\mathbb{Z} = \{\ldots, -4, -3, -2, -1, 0, 1, 2, 3, 4, \ldots\}$$

There various types of groups and compositions of groups are:

1. *Abelian Groups*
2. *Cyclic Groups*
3. *Rings*
4. *Fields*

3.3.1   Abelian Groups

A group is said to be abelian if it satisfies the following additional condition:
Commutative: a . b = b . a for all a, b in G.
The set of integers (positive, negative, and 0) under addition is an abelian group. The set of nonzero real numbers under multiplication is an abelian group.

3.3.2   Cyclic Groups

A group G is cyclic if every element of G is a power a^k (k is an integer) of a fixed element a $\in$ G. The element a is said to generate the group G or to be a generator of G. A cyclic group is always abelian and may be finite or infinite.

3.3.3   Rings

A ring is a set R equipped with two *binary operations + (addition) and · (multiplication)* satisfying the following three sets of axioms, called the ring axioms

1. *R is an abelian group under addition, meaning that*:

   - $(a + b) + c = a + (b + c)$ for all a, b, c in R (that is, + is associative).
   - $a + b = b + a$ for all a, b in R (that is, + is commutative).
   - There is an element 0 in R such that $a + 0 = a$ for all a in R.
   - For each a in R there exists −a in R such that $a + (-a) = 0$.

2. R is a *monoid under multiplication*, meaning that:

   - $(a \cdot b) \cdot c = a \cdot (b \cdot c)$ for all a, b, c in R.
   - There is an element 1 in R such that $a \cdot 1 = a$ and $1 \cdot a = a$ for all a in R.

3. *Multiplication is distributive with respect to addition*, meaning that:

- $a \cdot (b + c) = (a \cdot b) + (a \cdot c)$ for all a, b, c in R (left distributivity).
- $(b + c) \cdot a = (b \cdot a) + (c \cdot a)$ for all a, b, c in R (right distributivity).

The term "**ring**" in the context of this section is defined as a structure with a multiplicative identity, whereas the term "**ring**" is used to refer to a structure with the same axiomatic definition but without the requirement for a multiplicative identity.

Ring multiplication does not have to be commutative; ab need not always equal ba.

Ring addition is commutative. Commutative rings, such as the ring of integers, are rings that also meet commutativity for multiplication.

To simplify vocabulary, books on commutative algebra or algebraic geometry frequently follow the assumption that ring refers to a commutative ring.

Multiplicative inverses are not necessary in rings. A field is a nonzero commutative ring where each nonzero member has a multiplicative inverse.

The underlying set of a ring that only has the addition operation available is known as the additive group. Although the additive group must be abelian to satisfy the definition, this can be deduced from the other ring axioms.

3.3.4   Fields

A field is a set, along with two operations defined on that set: an addition operation written as a + b, and a multiplication operation written as a · b, both of which behave similarly as they behave for rational numbers and real numbers, including the existence of an additive inverse −a for all elements a, and of a multiplicative inverse b^{-1} for every nonzero element b. This allows one also to consider the so-called inverse operations of subtraction, a − b, and division, a/b, by defining: $a - b := a + (-b), a / b := a \cdot b^{-1}$. Formally, *a field is a set F together with two binary operations on F called addition and multiplication.*

These operations are required to satisfy the following properties, referred to as field axioms (in these axioms, a, b, and c are arbitrary elements of the field F):

- **Associativity of addition and multiplication:** $a + (b + c) = (a + b) + c$, and $a \cdot (b \cdot c) = (a \cdot b) \cdot c$.
- **Commutativity of addition and multiplication:** $a + b = b + a$, and $a \cdot b = b \cdot a$.
- **Additive and multiplicative identity:** there exist two different elements 0 and 1 in F such that $a + 0 = a$ and $a \cdot 1 = a$.
- **Additive inverses:** for every a in F, there exists an element in F, denoted −a, called the additive inverse of a, such that $a + (-a) = 0$.
- **Multiplicative inverses:** for every $a \neq 0$ in F, there exists an element in F, denoted by a^{-1} or 1/a, called the multiplicative inverse of a, such that $a \cdot a^{-1} = 1$.
- **Distributivity of multiplication over addition:** $a \cdot (b + c) = (a \cdot b) + (a \cdot c)$.

Fields can also be defined in a variety of ways that are all comparable. The four binary operations (addition, subtraction, multiplication, and division) and their necessary attributes can also be used to create a field. Division by zero is not included.

Fields can be defined by two binary operations, two unary operations (yielding the additive and multiplicative inverses, respectively), and two nullary operations in order to avoid existential quantifiers. The conditions are then applicable to these procedures. In constructive mathematics and computers, it is crucial to stay away from existential quantifiers.

3.4   Finite Fields

A field with a finite number of elements is known as a finite field or Galois field in mathematics. A finite field is a set on which the *operations of multiplication, addition, subtraction, and division* are defined and comply with some fundamental principles, just like any other field.

The integers mod p when p is a prime number provide the most prevalent examples of finite fields. The quantity of elements in a finite field, which is either a prime integer or a prime power, determines the field's order.

There are **isomorphic fields of order p^k** for each prime number p and each positive integer k. Numerous branches of mathematics and computer science, such as number theory, algebraic geometry, Galois theory, finite geometry, cryptography, and coding theory, all depend on finite fields.

Multiplication, addition, subtraction, and division (aside from division by zero) are defined and satisfy the laws of arithmetic known as the field axioms in a finite field, which is a finite set that is a field.

A finite field's order or size, depending on the situation, refers to how many elements are there. A finite field of order q exists if and only if q is a prime power p^k (where p is a prime number and k is a positive integer).

In a field of order p^k, adding p copies of any element always results in zero; that is, the characteristic of the field is p.

If $q = p^k$, all fields of order q are isomorphic. Moreover, a field cannot contain two different finite subfields with the same order. One may therefore identify all finite fields with the same order, and they are unambiguously denoted $\mathbf{F_q}$ or $\mathbf{GF(q)}$, where the letters **GF** stand for "Galois field". In a finite field of order q, the polynomial $X^q - X$ has all q elements of the finite field as roots. The non-zero elements of a finite field form a multiplicative group. This group is cyclic, so all non-zero elements can be expressed as powers of a single element called a *primitive element of the field*. (In general, there will be several primitive elements for a given field.) The simplest examples of finite fields are the fields of prime order: for each prime number p, the prime field of order p, may be constructed as the integers modulo p, Z/pZ.

Integers in the range of $0\ldots, p - 1$ can be used to represent the elements of the prime field of order p. The residual of dividing the outcome of the corresponding integer operation by p is the sum, difference, and product. The extended Euclidean algorithm can be used to compute an element's multiplicative inverse.

Let F be a finite field. For any element x in F and any integer n, denote by $n \cdot x$ the sum of n copies of x. The least positive n such that $\mathbf{n \cdot 1 = 0}$ is the characteristic p of the field. This allows defining a multiplication of an element k of GF(p) by an element x of F by choosing an integer representative for k. This multiplication makes F into a GF(p)-vector space. It follows that the number of elements of F is p^n for some integer n.

The identity: $(\mathbf{x + y})^p = \mathbf{x}^p + \mathbf{y}^p$ (sometimes called the freshman's dream) is true in a field of characteristic p. This follows from the binomial theorem, as each binomial coefficient of the expansion of $(\mathbf{x + y})^p$, except the first and the last, is a multiple of p.

Fermat's little theorem, if p is a prime number and x is in the field GF(p) then $\mathbf{x}^p = \mathbf{x}$.

This implies the equality:

$$X^p - X = \prod_{a \in GF(p)} (X - a)$$

for polynomials over GF(p). More generally, every element in GF(p^n) satisfies the polynomial equation $\mathbf{x}^{p^n} - \mathbf{x} = \mathbf{0}$.

Any extension of a finite field that is finite is simple and separable.

In other words, if E is a finite field and F is a subfield of E, then E can be created by attaching a single element whose minimal polynomial can be separated from F. Finite fields are perfect, to use a technical term. A division ring is a more general algebraic structure that meets all a field's other axioms but whose multiplication is not required to be commutative (or sometimes skew field).

Any finite division ring is commutative and hence a finite field according to Wedderburn's small theorem. The uniqueness up to isomorphism of splitting fields implies thus that all fields of order q are isomorphic. Also, if a field F has a field of order $\mathbf{q = p}^k$ as a subfield, its elements are the q roots of $\mathbf{X}^q - \mathbf{X}$, and F cannot contain another subfield of order q.

3.4.1   Types of Finite Fields

Non-prime Fields
Given a prime power $\mathbf{q = p}^n$ with p prime and n > 1, the field **GF(q)** may be explicitly constructed in the following way.

- One first chooses an *irreducible polynomial P in GF(p)[X] of degree n* (such an irreducible polynomial always exists).
- Then the *quotient ring of the polynomial ring GF(p)[X]* by the ideal generated by P is a field of order q.

More explicitly, the elements of **GF(q)** are the polynomials over GF(p) whose degree is strictly less than n. The addition and the subtraction are those of polynomials over GF(p). The product of two elements is the remainder of the Euclidean division by P of the product in GF(p)[X]. The multiplicative inverse of a non-zero element may be computed with the extended Euclidean algorithm; see Extended Euclidean algorithm.

Except in the construction of GF(4), there are several possible choices for P, which produce isomorphic results. To simplify the Euclidean division, one commonly chooses for P a polynomial of the form which make the needed Euclidean divisions very efficient. However, for some fields, typically in characteristic 2, *irreducible polynomials of the form $X^n + aX + b$* may not exist. In characteristic 2, if the polynomial $X^n + X + 1$ is reducible, it is recommended to choose $X^n + X^k + 1$ with the lowest possible k that makes the polynomial irreducible. If all these trinomials are reducible, one chooses "**pentanomials**" $X^n + X^a + X^b + X^c + 1$, as polynomials of degree greater than 1, with an even number of terms, are never irreducible in characteristic 2, having 1 as a root.

A possible choice for such a polynomial is given by Conway polynomials. They ensure a certain compatibility between the representation of a field and the representations of its subfields.

In the next sections, we will show how the general construction method outlined above works for small finite fields.

Field with Four Elements

The smallest non-prime field is the field with four elements **0, 1, α and α^2** which is commonly denoted **GF(4)**. The other operation results being easily deduced from the distributive law. See below for the complete operation Table 3.1. This may be deduced as follows from the results of the preceding section. Over GF(2), there is only one *irreducible polynomial of degree 2: $X^2 + X + 1$*. Therefore, for GF(4) the construction of the preceding section must involve this polynomial, and

$$GF\left(4\right) = GF\left(2\right)[X] / \left(X^2 + X + 1\right)$$

Let α denote a root of this polynomial in GF(4).

Table 3.1 Results of the operations in GF(4)

Addition $x+y$					Multiplication $x\cdot y$					Division x/y			
x \ y	0	1	α	$1+\alpha$	x \ y	0	1	α	$1+\alpha$	x \ y	1	α	$1+\alpha$
0	0	1	α	$1+\alpha$	0	0	0	0	0	0	0	0	0
1	1	0	$1+\alpha$	α	1	0	1	α	$1+\alpha$	1	1	$1+\alpha$	α
α	α	$1+\alpha$	0	1	α	0	α	$1+\alpha$	1	α	α	1	$1+\alpha$
$1+\alpha$	$1+\alpha$	α	1	0	$1+\alpha$	0	$1+\alpha$	1	α	$1+\alpha$	$1+\alpha$	α	1

This implies that $\alpha^2 = 1 + \alpha$, and that α **and** $1 + \alpha$ are the elements of GF(4) that **are not in GF(2)**. The tables of the operations in **GF(4)** result from this, and are as follows:

GF(p^2) for an Odd Prime p
For applying the construction of *finite fields in the case of GF(p^2)*, one must find an irreducible polynomial of degree 2.

For $p = 2$, this has been done in the preceding section. If p is an odd prime, there are always irreducible polynomials of the form $X^2 - r$, *with r in GF(p)*.

More precisely, the polynomial $X^2 - r$ is irreducible over GF(p) if and only if r is a quadratic non-residue modulo p (this is almost the definition of a quadratic non-residue).

There are $(p - 1)/2$ quadratic non-residues modulo p.

For example:
2 is a quadratic non-residue for $p = 3, 5, 11, 13, \ldots$,
and
3 is a quadratic non-residue for $p = 5, 7, 17, \ldots$.
If $p \equiv 3 \bmod 4$, that is $p = 3, 7, 11, 19, \ldots$,
one may choose $-1 \equiv p - 1$ as a quadratic non-residue, which allows us to have a
very simple irreducible polynomial $X^2 + 1$.

Having chosen a **quadratic non-residue r**, let α be a symbolic square root of r, that is a symbol which has the property $\alpha^2 = r$, in the same way as the complex number i is a symbolic square root of -1.

Then, the elements of **GF(p^2)** are all the linear expressions $\alpha + b\,\alpha$ with α and b in GF(p).

The operations on GF(p^2) are defined as follows (the operations between elements of GF(p) represented by Latin letters are the operations in GF(p)):

$$-(a + b\alpha) = -a + (-b)\alpha$$

$$(a + b\alpha) + (c + d\alpha) = (a + c) + (b + d)\alpha$$

$$(a + b\alpha)(c + d\alpha) = (ac + rbd) + (ad + bc)\alpha$$

$$(a + b\alpha)^{-1} = a(a^2 - rb^2)^{-1} + (-b)(a^2 - rb^2)^{-1}\alpha$$

3.4.2   Applications

Several popular protocols, including the **Diffie-Hellman protocol**, are based on the complexity of the discrete logarithm problem in finite fields or in elliptic curves.

For instance, the **elliptic curve Diffie-Hellman protocol (ECDHE)** over a sizable finite field was used in 2014 to establish a secure internet connection to Wikipedia. Many codes in coding theory are built as subspaces of vector spaces over finite fields.

Many **errors correction codes**, including the **Reed-Solomon error correcting code and the BCH code, rely on finite fields**.

Since computer data is stored in binary, the finite field usually always has the characteristic of 2. A byte of data, for instance, could be interpreted as a GF element (128). The PDF417 bar code, which is GF, is one example (929). For finite fields of characteristic 2, several CPUs feature specialized instructions that are typically carry-less product variations.

Since many issues over the integers can be solved by reducing them modulo one or more prime numbers, finite fields are commonly employed in number theory.

The quickest techniques for linear algebra and polynomial factorization, for instance, reduce the problem by one or more primes and then reconstruct the solution using the *Chinese remainder theorem, Hensel lifting*.

Like this, a lot of theoretical issues in number theory can be resolved by taking their reductions modulo some or all prime numbers into consideration. Take the Hasse principle, for instance. The need to increase the capabilities of these modular approaches served as the driving force behind many recent discoveries in algebraic geometry.

A complex result involving a variety of mathematical techniques, including finite fields, can be seen in **Wiles' proof of Fermat's Last Theorem**. The Weil conjectures are about how many points there are on algebraic varieties over finite fields, and the theory has various uses, such as character sum and exponential estimates.

The definition of Paley Graphs and the associated construction for *Hadamard Matrices are two well-known applications of finite fields in combinatorics*. Finite fields and finite field models are frequently employed in arithmetic combinatorics, notably in Szemerdi's theorem on arithmetic progressions.

3.5   Elliptic Curves

An elliptic curve in mathematics is a projective, algebraic curve with a specified point O that is smooth. Over a field K, known as the Cartesian product of K and itself, K^2, an elliptic curve is defined that characterizes points.

If the field has properties other than those of 2 and 3, the curve can be characterized as a planar algebraic curve that, with a linear change in the variables, consists of solutions (x, y) for:

$y^2 = x^3 + ax + b$ (represented in Fig. 3.1).

For some a and b coefficients in K. The curve must not have cusps or self-intersections in order to be considered non-singular. It is generally accepted that the

Fig. 3.1 Curve of
$y^2 = x^3 + ax + b$

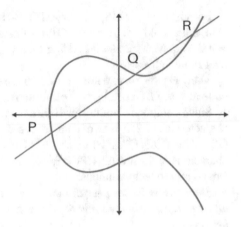

curve resides in the projective plane, with point O acting as the unique infinity point. A curve that is given by an equation of this kind is frequently used to define an elliptic curve.

An elliptic curve is an example of an abelian variety or group, meaning it has an algebraically defined group law that makes it an abelian group, and O acts as the identity element.

A nonsingular plane curve of genus one, an elliptic curve, is the solution set if

$$\mathbf{y}^2 = \mathbf{P(x)},$$

where P is any polynomial of degree three in x with no repeated roots.

This equation again defines a plane curve of genus one if **P** has degree four and is square-free, but it lacks a naturally occurring identity element.

More generally, any algebraic curve of genus one is referred to as an elliptic curve if it has a marked point that serves as the identity, such as the intersection of two quadric surfaces contained in three-dimensional projective space.

It can be demonstrated using the theory of elliptic functions that elliptic curves defined over complex numbers correspond to torus embeddings in the complex projective plane. The correspondence is also a group isomorphism for the torus, which is likewise an abelian group.

An elliptic curve differs from a **projective conic**, which has genus zero; for more information on the definition of an ellipse, see the elliptic integral. However, ellipses in the hyperbolic plane are a natural representation of real elliptic curves with shape invariant **j > =1**.

The Steiner ellipses in the hyperbolic plane are specifically created by the intersections of the Minkowski hyperboloid with quadric surfaces that exhibit a specific constant-angle attribute. Any ellipse in the hyperbolic plane described as a locus relative to two foci is exclusively the elliptic curve sum of two Steiner ellipses, which is obtained by adding the pairs of intersections on each orthogonal trajectory.

Furthermore, the orthogonal trajectories of these ellipses comprise the elliptic curves with **j** < =**1**. Here, the identity on each trajectory curve is the vertex of the hyperboloid. A complex elliptic curve is a sphere topologically, while a complex ellipse is a torus.

3.5.1 *Elliptic Curve over the Real Numbers*

It is feasible to describe several characteristics of elliptic curves over the real numbers using only basic algebra and geometry, despite the formal definition of an elliptic curve requiring some knowledge in algebraic geometry.

After a linear change in the variables, an elliptic curve is a plane curve specified by the equation:

$$y^2 = x^3 + ax + b \quad \text{(a and b are real numbers)}.$$

Weierstrass form, also known as Weierstrass normal form, is the name given to this sort of equation.

The curve must also be non-singular in order to meet the definition of an elliptic curve. This implies that there are no cusps, self-intersections, or isolated points on the graph geometrically speaking.

3.5.2 *Elliptic Curves over the Rational Numbers*

In the field of real numbers, a curve E that is defined over the field of rational numbers is also defined. As a result, E can be used to apply the law of addition (of points with real coordinates) through the tangent and secant approach.

The precise formulae demonstrate that because the line connecting P and Q has rational coefficients, the sum of two points P and Q with rational coordinates also has rational coordinates. In this manner, it is demonstrated that the group of real points of E is a subgroup of the set of rational points of E. It is an abelian group, meaning that

$$P + Q = Q + P, \quad \text{just like this group.}$$

3.5.3 *Elliptic Curves over Finite Fields*

Over finite fields, *elliptic curves yield finite Abelian groups*.

For example, the curve:

$$y^2 = x^3 + 3x + 2,$$

over F_{11} has the corresponding group

$$\{(2,\pm 4),(3,\pm 4),(4,\pm 1),(6,\pm 4),(7,\pm 5),(10,\pm 3),I\}.$$

Since the order of the group is 13 any non-identity element acts as a generator. The exact size of these groups is open to conjecture but **Hasse's theorem** on elliptic curves provides a bound to give some idea,

if **N** is the number of points that satisfy some elliptic curve over F_q then

$$\left|N-(q+1)\right| \le 2\sqrt{q}$$

Schoof's algorithm gives a method of counting points on Elliptic curves in polynomial time making use of Hasse's bound as well as the Chinese remainder theorem and division polynomials. The algorithm can be found in Schoof's Counting Points on Elliptic Curves over Finite Fields. *Elliptic curves over finite fields have applications in a few algorithms including cryptography and integer factorization.*

3.5.4   Algorithms that Use Elliptic Curves

Elliptic curves over finite fields are utilized for integer factorization as well as some cryptography applications. The basic concept behind these applications is to rewrite an existing method that uses certain finite groups in order to employ the groups of rational points on elliptic curves.

Elliptic curve cryptography is another resource for details.

- Elliptic curve cryptography
- Elliptic-curve Diffie–Hellman key exchange
- Super singular isogeny key exchange
- Elliptic curve digital signature algorithm
- EdDSA digital signature algorithm
- Dual EC DRBG random number generator
- Lenstra elliptic-curve factorization
- Elliptic curve primality proving

3.6   Elliptic Curve Cryptography

A method of public-key encryption known as elliptic-curve cryptography (ECC) is based on the algebraic structure of elliptic curves over finite fields.

ECC enables similar security to be achieved with smaller keys as compared to non-EC encryption (based on simple Galois fields). Elliptic curves can be used for several applications, including key agreement, digital signatures, and pseudo-random generators.

By combining the key agreement with a symmetric encryption method, they can be used for encryption indirectly. Elliptic curves are also utilized in several elliptic-curve-based integer factorization techniques that have cryptographic applications, such as the Lenstra elliptic-curve factorization.

Based on the intractability of specific mathematical puzzles, public-key cryptography is used. The security of early public-key systems was predicated on the idea that it is challenging to factor a huge integer made up of two or more large prime factors. The "**elliptic curve discrete logarithm problem**" states that it is impossible to find the discrete logarithm of a random elliptic curve element with respect to a publicly known base point. This is the underlying assumption for later **elliptic curve-based protocols (ECDLP)**.

In order to use elliptic curve cryptography, one must be able to calculate a point multiplication and not be able to do so given the original and product points. The difficulty of the issue is determined by the total number of discrete integer pairs that satisfy the curve equation, which is a measure of the size of the elliptic curve.

An elliptic curve group could offer the same level of security as an RSA-based system with a large modulus and correspondingly larger key, **for example, a 256-bit elliptic curve public key should provide comparable security to a 3072-bit RSA public key.** This is the main benefit promised by elliptic curve cryptography, which is a smaller key size, reducing storage and transmission requirements.

Several discrete logarithm-based procedures have been modified for elliptic curves:

- The Diffie-Hellman system serves as the foundation for the Elliptic-curve Diffie-Hellman (ECDH) key agreement scheme.
- Elliptic Curve Integrated Encryption Scheme (ECIES), also called Elliptic Curve Augmented Encryption Scheme or Elliptic Curve Encryption Scheme.
- The Digital Signature Algorithm serves as the foundation for the Elliptic Curve Digital Signature Algorithm (ECDSA).
- Harrison's p-adic Manhattan metric deformation method.
- Twisted Edwards curves are used in the Edwards-curve Digital Signature Algorithm (EdDSA), which is based on the Schnorr signature.
- Based on the MQV key agreement technique, the ECMQV key agreement system was developed. An authenticated technique for key agreement based on the Diffie-Hellman algorithm is called MQV (Menezes-Qu-Vanstone). MQV offers defense against a live attacker, like other authenticated Diffie-Hellman methods. The protocol can be changed to operate in any finite group, but it is most effective in elliptic curve groups, where it is referred to as elliptic curve MQV (ECMQV).

3.6.1 Elliptic Curve Cryptography Implementation

Following are a few typical implementation factors:

- **Domain Parameters:** To utilize ECC, both parties must concur on the domain parameters, or the variables that define the elliptic curve. The size of the field is usually either prime (and is denoted by p) or a power of two; the latter situation is known as the binary case and requires the selection of an auxiliary curve, which is denoted by f.
- In the prime case, p defines the field, and in the binary case, m and f define it. The constants a and b in its defining equation determine the elliptic curve.
- Finally, the generator (also known as base point) G of the cyclic subgroup is defined. The order of G, which is the lowest positive number n such that nG = O (the point at infinity of the curve and the identity element), is often prime for cryptographic applications.
- The domain parameters must be checked before use unless there is confirmation that they were generated by a party that can be trusted with respect to their use. Because it requires computing the number of points on a curve, which is time-consuming and difficult to execute, the production of domain parameters is typically not done by each participant. As a result, elliptic curve domain parameters for various typical field widths were published by several standard bodies. These types of domain parameters are frequently referred to as "standard curves" or "named curves"; a named curve may be referred to by its name or by the object identifier specified in the standard documents:

  I. Elliptic Curves Recommended for Government Use by NIST.
  II. Recommended Elliptic Curve Domain Parameters (SECG, SEC 2).
  III. ECC Brainpool Standard Curves and Curve Generation (RFC 5639), Archived on April 17, 2018, at the Wayback Machine.

- There are other SECG test vectors available. There is a considerable overlap between the NIST and SECG requirements because NIST has certified numerous SECG curves. Either a name or a value can be used to specify an EC domain parameter. Despite the foregoing, if one wishes to create their own domain parameters, they should first choose the underlying field and then employ one of the following techniques to locate a curve with the proper (i.e., near prime) number of points:

  - Use a universal point-counting technique and a random curve, such as the Schoof or Schoof-Elkies-Atkin algorithms.
  - Choose a random curve from a family that makes it simple to determine the number of points, or
  - Using the complex multiplication technique, choose the number of points and create a curve with that many points.

- There are several sorts of weak curves that should be avoided.

- **Key Sizes:** The size of the underlying field should be around twice the security parameter because all the fastest known methods that enable one to solve the ECDLP require order of under-root n steps.
- For instance, one requires a curve over F_q for 128-bit security. Contrast this with integer factorization cryptography (e.g., RSA), which requires a 3072-bit value of n, where the private key should be just as large, and finite-field cryptography (e.g., DSA), which requires 3072-bit public keys and 256-bit private keys.
- The public key, however, might be smaller to support effective encryption, particularly when processor power is constrained.
- **Projective Co-ordinates:** A close examination of the addition rules shows that in order to add two points, one needs not only several additions and multiplications F_q in but also an inversion operation. The inversion is one to two orders of magnitude slower than multiplication.
- However, points on a curve can be represented in different coordinate systems which do not require an inversion operation to add two points. Several such systems were proposed: in the projective system each point is represented by three coordinates (X, Y, Z) using the following relation:

$$x = (X / Z),$$

$$y = (Y / Z);$$

- in the Jacobian system a point is also represented with three coordinates (X, Y, Z) but a different relation is used:

$$x = (X / Z^2),$$

$$y = (Y / Z^3).$$

- **Fast Reduction:** If the prime p is a pseudo-Mersenne prime, reduction modulo p (which is required for addition and multiplication) can be completed significantly more quickly. There may be a speedup of an order of magnitude above Barrett reduction.

- The speedup in this case is practical rather than theoretical and results from the fact that computers using bitwise operations on binary numbers can efficiently execute the moduli of numbers against numbers close to powers of two. NIST suggests using pseudo-Mersenne p curves over F_q. The NIST curves also have the benefit of using a = −3, which facilitates addition in Jacobian coordinates. Many of the judgments made in NIST FIPS 186-2 regarding efficiency, in the opinion of Bernstein and Lange, are not the best ones. Other curves run just as quickly and are safer.

3.6.2   Elliptic Curve Cryptography Applications

Elliptic curves can be used for several applications, **including encryption, digital signatures, and pseudo-random generation**. They are also utilized in several cryptographic techniques for integer factorization, including the Lenstra elliptic-curve factorization. NIST suggested a total of 15 elliptic curves. FIPS 186-4 recommends the following 10 finite fields in particular:

- Five prime fields F_q for certain primes p of sizes 192, 224, 256, 384, and 521 bits. For each of the prime fields, one elliptic curve is recommended.
- Five binary fields F_q for m equal 163, 233, 283, 409, and 571. For each of the binary fields, one elliptic curve and one Koblitz curve was selected.

Thus, the NIST guideline includes 10 binary curves and a total of 5 prime curves. The curves were supposedly selected for the best implementation efficiency and security. According to The New York Times, the NSA had a hand in making Dual Elliptic Curve Deterministic Random Bit Generation a national standard by including a purposeful flaw in the algorithm and the suggested elliptic curve.

Bitcoin is a cryptocurrency that makes use of elliptic curve cryptography. For cryptographically ensuring that a specific Eth2 validator has verified a specific transaction, Ethereum version 2.0 makes considerable use of elliptic curve couples employing BLS signatures, as stated in the IETF draught BLS specification.

3.6.3   Security

Side-Channel-Attacks
The method for doubling and general addition in the elliptic curves differs greatly depending on the coordinate system employed, unlike most other systems (where it is possible to apply the same process for squaring and multiplication). It is crucial to defend against side-channel attacks (such as timing or simple/differential power analysis assaults) by adopting techniques like fixed pattern window methods, for instance (note that this does not increase computation time). A different option is to use an Edwards curve, a unique family of elliptic curves where doubling and adding can be accomplished using the same operation. Fault attacks are a worry for ECC systems as well, especially when they use smart cards.

Backdoors
One or more elliptic curve-based pseudo random generators may have had a kleptographic backdoor added, according to concerns raised by cryptographic specialists. Internal memos that Edward Snowden, a former NSA contractor, disclosed indicate that the NSA added a backdoor to the Dual EC DRBG standard. According to one examination of the potential backdoor, an adversary with the secret key to the technique might get encryption keys from 32 bytes of PRNG output. The Safe-Curves project was started in order to catalogue curves that are simple to implement securely

and are created in a method that is completely open to public verification to reduce the likelihood of a backdoor.

Quantum Computing Attack

On a fictitious quantum computer, Shor's technique can be used to crack elliptic curve cryptography by computing discrete logarithms. The most recent quantum resource estimates are 2330 qubits and 126 billion Toffoli gates for breaking a curve with a 256-bit modulus (128-bit security level). Nine hundred six qubits are required for the binary elliptic curve (to break 128 bits of security). ECC is a more straight-forward target for quantum computers than RSA, according to Shor's technique, which requires 4098 qubits and 5.2 trillion Toffoli gates for a 2048-bit RSA key. The construction of such computers is predicted to be at least a decade away, and all of these numbers much exceed any quantum computer that has yet been developed.

By employing isogenies to carry out Diffie-Hellman key exchanges, the super-singular Isogeny Diffie-Hellman Key Exchange claimed to provide a post-quantum secure version of elliptic curve cryptography. This key exchange involves computational and transmission overhead resembling many currently in use public key systems and makes extensive use of the same field arithmetic as elliptic curve encryption. However, this protocol's security was compromised by recent classic assaults. The NSA declared in August 2015 that it would switch to a new cypher suite that is immune to quantum assaults "in the not-too-distant future." Unfortunately, the expansion of elliptic curve use has collided with the fact that quantum computing research is still moving forward, prompting a re-evaluation of our cryptographic approach.

Bibliography

1. Stallings, William. *Cryptography and network security, 4/E*. Pearson Education India, 2006.
2. Karate, Atul. *Cryptography and network security*. Tata McGraw-Hill Education, 2013.
3. Frozen, Behrouz A., and Debdeep Mukhopadhyay. *Cryptography and network security*. Vol. 12. New York, NY, USA: McGraw Hill Education (India) Private Limited, 2015.
4. Easttom, C. (2015). Modern cryptography. *Applied mathematics for encryption and information security. McGraw-Hill Publishing*.
5. Katz, J., & Lindell, Y. (2020). *Introduction to modern cryptography*. CRC press.
6. Bellare, M., & Rogaway, P. (2005). Introduction to modern cryptography. *Ucsd Cse, 207*, 207.
7. Zheng, Z. (2022). Modern Cryptography Volume 1: A Classical Introduction to Informational and Mathematical Principle.
8. Shemanske, T. R. (2017). *Modern Cryptography and Elliptic Curves* (Vol. 83). American Mathematical Soc.
9. Bhat, Bawna, Abdul Wahid Ali, and Apurva Gupta. "DES and AES performance evaluation." *International Conference on Computing, Communication & Automation*. IEEE, 2015.
10. Rihan, Shaza D., Ahmed Khalid, and Saife Eldin F. Osman. "A performance comparison of encryption algorithms AES and DES." *International Journal of Engineering Research & Technology (IJERT)* 4.12 (2015): 151–154.
11. Mahajan, Prerna, and Abhishek Sachdeva. "A study of encryption algorithms AES, DES and RSA for security." *Global Journal of Computer Science and Technology* (2013).

12. Mao, Wenbo. *Modern cryptography: theory and practice*. Pearson Education India, 2003.
13. B Rajkumar "Vulnerability Analysis and Defense Against Attacks: Implications of Trust – Based Cross – Layer Security Protocol for Mobile Adhoc Networks "presented at the International" Conference on IT FWP 09, Andhra Pradesh, India. in 2009.
14. B Rajkumar, G Arunakranthi, "Implementation and Mitigation for Cyber Attacks with proposed OCR Process Model" in Int. J. of Natural Volatiles & Essential Oils, 2021; vol. 8(5): 2149–2160.
15. Daemen, J., & Rijmen, V. (1999). AES proposal: Rijndael.
16. Zodpe, H., & Shaikh, A. (2021). A Survey on Various Cryptanalytic Attacks on the AES Algorithm. *International Journal of Next-Generation Computing*, 115–123.
17. Sharma, N. (2017). A Review of Information Security using Cryptography Technique. *International Journal of Advanced Research in Computer Science*, 8(4).
18. Gupta, A., & Walia, N. K. (2014). Cryptography Algorithms: a review.
19. Amalraj, A. J., & Jose, J. J. R. (2016). A survey paper on cryptography techniques. *International Journal of Computer Science and mobile computing*, 5(8), 55–59.
20. Pachghare, V. K. (2019). *Cryptography and information security*. PHI Learning Pvt. Ltd.
21. Koblitz, N., Menezes, A., & Vanstone, S. (2000). The state of elliptic curve cryptography. *Designs, codes and cryptography*, 19(2), 173–193.
22. Hankerson, D., Menezes, A. J., & Vanstone, S. (2006). *Guide to elliptic curve cryptography*. Springer Science & Business Media.
23. Kapoor, V., Abraham, V. S., & Singh, R. (2008). Elliptic curve cryptography. *Ubiquity*, 2008(May), 1–8.
24. Amara, M., & Siad, A. (2011, May). Elliptic curve cryptography and its applications. In *International workshop on systems, signal processing and their applications, WOSSPA* (pp. 247–250). IEEE.
25. Cilardo, A., Coppolino, L., Mazzocca, N., & Romano, L. (2006). Elliptic curve cryptography engineering. *Proceedings of the IEEE*, 94(2), 395–406.

Chapter 4
Asymmetric Key Cryptography

4.1 Overview

Asymmetric cryptography, often known as public-key cryptography, refers to cryptographic methods that employ pairs of related keys. Every key pair consists of a corresponding private key and a corresponding public key. Cryptographic algorithms are used to create key pairs; these methods are based on one-way functions, a class of mathematical problems. Public-key cryptography's security depends on keeping the private key a secret; security is unaffected by the public key's free distribution.

Anyone with a public key in a public-key encryption system can encrypt a message to create a ciphertext, but only those who also know the associated private key can decrypt the ciphertext to reveal the original message.

This chapter broadly covers following:

1. Introduction to asymmetric-key cryptography
2. Applications
3. Hybrid cryptosystems
4. Public Key Infrastructure
5. Weaknesses of asymmetric-key cryptography
6. Algorithms

   - RSA
   - RC4
   - ElGamal
   - Digital Signature
   - Diffie-Hellman
   - Password authentication key agreements

7. Protocols uses asymmetric-key cryptography algorithms

© The Author(s), under exclusive license to Springer Nature Switzerland AG 2023   109
R. Banoth, R. Regar, *Classical and Modern Cryptography for Beginners*,
https://doi.org/10.1007/978-3-031-32959-3_4

- S/MIME
- PGP
- IPsec
- SSH
- TLS and previous versions

4.2   Introduction to Asymmetric Key Cryptography

The area of cryptographic systems that use pairs of related keys is known as public-key cryptography, also known as asymmetric cryptography. The generic illustration of asymmetric key cryptography depicted in fig. 4.1. A public key and its accompanying private key make up each key pair. Cryptographic algorithms that are based on one-way functions are used to create key pairs. *The private key must be kept hidden for public-key cryptography to be secure; nevertheless, security is not compromised if the public key is freely distributed.*

Anyone with access to a public key can encrypt a message in a public-key encryption system, creating a ciphertext. However, only those who have access to the associated private key can decrypt the ciphertext to reveal the original message.

Asymmetric-key cryptography's fundamental challenge is demonstrating that a public key is genuine and has not been altered or restored by an unintentional third party. Using a public-key infrastructure (PKI), where one or more certificate authorities attest ownership of key pairs, is a good solution to this issue. The "**web of trust**" mechanism is another strategy employed by **PGP** to guarantee the authenticity of key pair.

- For instance, a journalist can make the public key of a pair of encryption keys available online so that sources can submit ciphertext messages to a news organization.

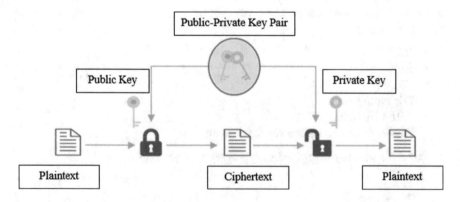

Fig. 4.1 Asymmetric Key Cryptography

- The ciphertexts must be decrypted by the journalist in order to access the sources' messages; they cannot be decrypted by an eavesdropper reading email that is being forwarded to the journalist.
- Public-key encryption, however, does not mask metadata, such as the computer a source sent a message from, the time it was sent, or its length.
- By itself, public-key encryption also does not reveal to the recipient who sent a message; rather, it only encrypts the message's content into a ciphertext that can only be deciphered with the private key.

A sender can sign a message using a private key and a message in a digital signature system. Anyone with the appropriate public key can check if the message and signature match, but a forger without access to the private key is unable to create any message/signature pairs that will pass public key verification.

A **software publisher**, for instance, may make a pair of signature keys and incorporate the public key into programs that are installed on PCs. Any machine receiving an update can certify it is authentic by confirming the signature using the public key, and the publisher can then disseminate an update to the program that was signed using the private key. Even though a forger can provide malicious updates to computers, they cannot persuade the computers that any malicious updates are real if the software publisher maintains the private key hidden.

Modern cryptosystems, comprising programs and protocols that provide assurance of the.

Confidentiality,

Authenticity, and

Non-reputability of electronic communications and data storage, use public key algorithms as essential security primitives.

They support several Internet standards, including PGP, S/MIME, SSH, and Transport Layer Security (TLS).

Digital signatures are provided by some public key methods, such as the **Diffie-Hellman key exchange**, while key distribution and secrecy are provided by others (e.g., RSA). Asymmetric encryption is considerably slower than good symmetric encryption, which is too sluggish for many applications. *Both symmetric and asymmetric encryption are utilized by modern cryptosystems*, which frequently start with asymmetric encryption to safely exchange a secret key before switching to symmetric encryption.

Prior to the middle of the 1970s, all cipher systems utilized symmetric key methods, in which the sender and recipient both share the same cryptographic key with the underlying algorithm and are required to keep it a secret. Every such system required to have the key shared between the communication parties in some secure manner before it could be used, for example, through a secure channel. As the number of players rises, secure channels are not accessible, or keys are frequently changed (as is a sensible cryptographic practice), this requirement is never straightforward and very quickly becoming unmanageable. A unique key is needed for every potential user pair, especially if messages are intended to be secure from other users. In contrast, only the associated private keys must be kept hidden by their owner in a public key system where the public keys can be shared freely and openly.

The following are the *top two applications* of public key cryptography:

- Public key encryption encrypts a communication using the public key of the intended recipient.
- Messages cannot be decoded by anybody without the corresponding private key, who is therefore assumed to be the owner of that key and consequently the person linked with the public key, for correctly chosen and utilized algorithms. This can be used to protect a message's privacy.

Digital signatures, which enable anybody with access to the sender's public key to validate a message after it has been signed with the sender's private key. By demonstrating that the sender has access to the private key, this verification strongly suggests that the sender is the person identified by the public key. Since verification will be unsuccessful for any other message one could concoct without utilizing the private key, it also demonstrates that the signature was created specifically for that message.

Confidence/proof that a specific public key is authentic, i.e., that it is correct and belongs to the person or entity claimed, and has not been altered or substituted by a third party (perhaps intentionally), is a crucial issue.

There are several options, including:

A public key infrastructure (PKI) where one or more certificate authorities (third parties) certify key pair ownership. This is how TLS works. This suggests that everyone involved can trust the PKI system, including the software, hardware, and administration. A "**web of trust**" that uses individual endorsements of connections between users and their public keys to decentralize authentication. Along with looking for information in the domain name system (DNS), PGP employs this technique. This method is also employed by the DKIM system for email digital signatures.

4.3 Applications

Public-key cryptography has several essential applications, including authentication and digital signatures. For instance, you should have some level of confidence that a communication you received from me actually came from me if you were able to decrypt it using my public key after I had encrypted it using my private key. If we decide that it is vital to keep the communication private, I may encrypt it using both your public key and my private key. Only you will be able to decrypt the message and be able to tell that it is mine.

The only prerequisite is that public keys be linked to their owners using a reliable method, such a trusted directory. Key exchange, email security, web security, and other encryption systems that call for key exchange over a public network all use asymmetric encryption. The standards community created a thing called a certificate to fix this issue. The name of the certificate issuer, the name of the subject for whom the certificate is being issued, the subject's public key, and a few time stamps are all included in a certificate. Because the certificate issuer also has a certificate, you can be sure that the public key is valid.

- A public key encryption system's most obvious use is for encrypting communication to provide confidentiality. To do this, a sender uses the recipient's public key to encrypt a message, which can only be decrypted by the recipient's matched private key.
- The use of digital signatures in public key cryptography is another. Schemes for digital signatures can be used to verify the sender.
- Digital signatures are used in non-repudiation systems to ensure that one side cannot effectively contest the authorship of a communication or document.
- Digital currency, password-authenticated key agreements, time-stamping services, and non-repudiation protocols are further applications built on top of this base.

4.4 Hybrid Cryptosystems

Since asymmetric key algorithms are almost always much more computationally intensive than symmetric ones, it is usual to use a public/private asymmetric key-exchange algorithm to encrypt and exchange a symmetric key, which is then used by symmetric-key cryptography to transmit data using the now-shared symmetric key for a symmetric key encryption algorithm.

Because of how PGP, SSH, and the SSL/TLS family of schemes operate, they are referred to as hybrid cryptosystems. The initial asymmetric cryptography-based key exchange to share a server-generated symmetric key from the server to client has the benefit of not requiring a symmetric key to be manually shared in advance, such as on printed paper or discs delivered by a courier, while providing the higher data throughput of symmetric key cryptography over asymmetric key cryptography for the remainder of the shared connection.

4.5 Public Key Infrastructure

The PKI (Public Key Infrastructure) framework, which also contains the associated crypto-mechanisms, permits the encryption of public keys. Any PKI setup's fundamental goal is to manage the keys and certificates that go with it, resulting in a highly secure network environment that can be used by hardware and software. As the means through which cryptography can be established for an endpoint, X.509 certificates and public keys serve as the foundation of PKI. As a result, PKI may

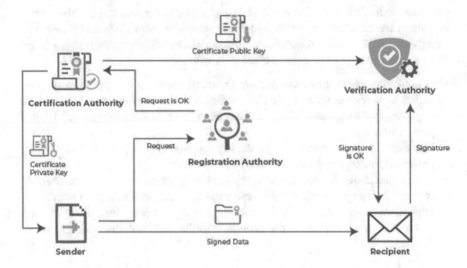

Fig. 4.2 Public Key Infrastructure

refer to any program, policy, process, or procedure that may be used while configuring and managing such certificates and keys.

In a word, PKI is in charge of enhancing the security of online interactions, and it accomplishes this through:

- Determining an endpoint's identification on a network.
- Encrypting the communication channels used by the network to transfer data.

It does this by encrypting data using private keys and decrypting it with public keys, which are made possible by digital certificates (Fig. 4.2).

Mobile devices, IoT-enabled hardware, and payment systems are just a few examples of infrastructures that require PKI for security, without which they would be exposed to cyber risk and would fail to comply with standards imposed on them by regulatory bodies. In today's hyper-connected world, the need for a robust PKI cannot be overstated, especially given the explosion in the number of devices that can leverage the internet to communicate with each other.

Where Is PKI Applied?

PKI is applicable for following:

- Secure Browsing (via SSL/TLS).
- Securing Email (signing and encrypting messages).
- Secure Code-signing.
- Network Security.
- File Security (via Encrypted File Systems).

The Components of an PKI

PKI infrastructures involve the participation of some or all the below entities:

- **Public and Private Keys:** The single most important component(s) of PKI, public and private keys are used to encrypt and decrypt the information transmitted over the web, ensuring that the sending and receiving party are the only ones privy to that information. Public key information is available openly online, but can only be effectively leveraged when the receiving party has an approved private key in order to decrypt a message.
- **Public Key Certificates:** Electronically signed documents that verify ownership of a public key. They are as important as keys, as they act as proof that a key-holder is legitimate. They are issued by Certificate Authorities.
- **Certificate Repository:** An electronic, searchable storage facility for signed certificates with public keys that have been generated. It consists of important certificate information, such as certificate validity details, revocation lists, and root certificates. They are often equipped with LDAP (Lightweight Directory Access Protocol), an online directory service where entries are classified and indexed.
- **Certificate Authority (CA):** A trusted body which enables organizations to get themselves verified as public key holders. It does this by verifying a requesting organization, and generating an electronic document called a digital certificate which also holds the public key. It then signs the certificate with its own private key, which acts as a seal of approval that it is trusted by a Certificate Authority.
- **Registration Authority (RA):** Assists the PKI cycle by verifying that the body requesting a certificate is legitimate. Once the verification is complete, it carries out the request by allowing the request to reach the CA, who uses a certificate server to execute it.
- **Key encryption and storage facilities:** Private keys are valuable documents that can be misused if malicious actors gain access to it. Hence, they are stored in encrypted vaults with secured periodic access.
- **Software to manage and automate PKI operations:** Since certificates act as the face of a PKI system, they must diligently managed, since invalid certificates often result from haphazard management, making them useless measures of security. Certificate Management is a blanket domain involving practices such as issuance, revocations, renewals, and a lot more.

Working of PKI

Public Key Infrastructure uses Public Key Cryptography as the basis for providing encryption, with the underlying principles, procedures, and policies being part of the overlying 'infrastructure' that is compatible with SSL/TLS protocols. Public Key Cryptography uses asymmetric key algorithms to perform its role.

According to this principle, both communicating parties establish a working relationship by verifying each other's identities. Consider the following exchange which enables a server and a web application, for instance, a browser, to communicate with each other:

- When a browser wishes to establish a secure communication channel with a web server, it requests the server to present its public key.
- The server possesses an asymmetric public key, whose copy it presents to the browser.

- The browser generates a 'session key', a symmetric key that is encrypted using the public key that the server provided. This session key is then passed to the server.
- The web server, which has a unique copy of a private key, uses the private key to decrypt the session key. If it can do this, the browser takes it as proof that the server is safe to communicate with, and an encrypted channel is opened.

The entire exchange is facilitated by x.509 certificates (also called digital certificates or PKI certificates), since only those public keys that have been signed by a Certificate Authority and bound to a certificate are considered acceptable for use online.

Role of Certificates in PKI

Certificates are the gatekeepers to ensuring that the underlying PKI works properly. Certificate Authorities (CAs) provide much-needed trust for the entire PKI framework. Several major CAs are trusted across the globe to provide authenticity to certificates, and by extension, signed keys. A typical certificate consists of the following information:

- A Distinguished Name (DN) which is simply a unique name that identifies the user who requested the certificate.
- The date of issuance and the date of expiry, to estimate the certificate's lifetime.
- The public key.
- The purpose of the certificate, which could range from signing code to encrypting communication channels.
- A digital signature, which is the CA's guarantee that the certificate is valid and belongs to the user in question.

A digital certificate, once issued, must be diligently managed to ensure that it remains secure. An expired certificate is of no use to anyone, and neither is a compromised one. Certificate Management is a discipline that overlaps with PKI management, and has its own set of rules and protocols that must be followed.

4.6   Weaknesses of Asymmetric Key Cryptography

Identification of potential flaws is crucial for security-related systems in general. *The main security risk is that the pair's private key is discovered, which can also happen when an asymmetric key technique is chosen incorrectly (there are not many that are generally regarded as good) or when the key length is set too low.* Then, all message security, authentication, and other features will be lost.

Weaknesses related to algorithms, public key infrastructures and alteration of public keys listed below.

4.6.1 Algorithms

Theoretically, any public key scheme could be vulnerable to a "**brute-force key search attack**". But if all possible attackers lack the computing power necessary to succeed, which Claude Shannon called the "work factor," such an attack becomes impracticable.

By just selecting a longer key, the work factor can frequently be enhanced. However, certain techniques may already be far less computationally intensive than others, rendering resistance to a brute-force attack (using longer keys, for example) meaningless.

To help in defeating some public key encryption techniques, some specialized and algorithms have been created; both RSA and ElGamal encryption have known attacks that are far faster than the brute-force method. However, none of these have been sufficiently improved to be useful.

For several formerly promising asymmetric key methods, significant flaws have been discovered. After the creation of a fresh attack, the "knapsack packing" algorithm was discovered to be insecure. Public-key implementations may be subject to side-channel attacks, which use information leakage to their advantage to make it easier to find a secret key, as is the case with all cryptographic operations. These frequently exist without regard to the algorithm in use. Research is being done to find new threats and develop defenses against them.

4.6.2 Alteration of Public Keys

A "man-in-the-middle" attack, in which the communication of public keys is intercepted by a third party (the "man in the middle") and then altered to supply new public keys instead, is another potential security risk associated with the use of asymmetric keys.

To prevent suspicion, encrypted messages and responses must always be intercepted, decrypted, and re-encrypted by the attacker using the appropriate public keys for the various communication segments.

When data is transmitted in a way that makes it possible for someone to intercept it, a communication is said to be insecure (also called "sniffing"). These phrases allude to fully reading the sender's confidential information. When interceptions cannot be stopped or monitored by the sender, a communication is especially hazardous.

Modern security procedures might be complicated to install, making man-in-the-middle attacks challenging. When a sender uses unsecured media, such as open networks, the Internet, or wireless communication, the task is made easier. Instead, then the data itself, an attacker in these circumstances can compromise the communications infrastructure.

An Internet Service Provider (ISP) employee who is hostile in nature might find a man-in-the-middle assault to be rather simple. The only way to intercept the public key would be to look for it as it passes via the ISP's communications equipment; in well-constructed asymmetric key systems, this is not a danger.

One side of the conversation will see the original data in some sophisticated man-in-the-middle attacks, while the other will receive a malicious variant. Man-in-the-middle attacks that are asymmetric can keep consumers from recognizing their connection has been compromised. Because the data seems secure to the other user, this is true even when one user's data is known to have been compromised. This may cause misunderstandings between users, leading to statements like "it must be on your end!" even though neither user is at blame.

Therefore, man-in-the-middle assaults can only be completely avoided when one or both sides physically control the communications infrastructure, such as when using a wired route inside the sender's own building.

In conclusion, when a sender's communications hardware is under the attacker's control, public keys are simpler to change.

4.6.3   Public Key Infrastructure

A public key infrastructure (PKI), a set of roles, policies, and processes required to create, maintain, distribute, utilize, store, and revoke digital certificates and manage public-key encryption, is one strategy for preventing attacks.

However, there might be some issues with this. For instance, before protected communications can start, all parties involved must have confidence in the certificate authority issuing the certificate that it has thoroughly verified the identity of the key-holder, ensured the accuracy of the public key when it issues a certificate, is secure from computer piracy, and has decided with all parties to check all their certificates.

For instance, PKI providers provide web browsers with a broad list of "self-signed identity certificates" that are used to verify the legitimacy of the certificate authority and, in a subsequent step, the certificates of possible communicators. A "man-in-the-middle" attack might then be launched just as easily if the certificate scheme was not being utilized at all by an attacker who managed to trick one of those certificate authorities into issuing a certificate for a false public key. An attacker who infiltrates an authority's servers and takes its cache of certificates and keys (public and private) would, in a rarely addressed alternative scenario, be able to spoof, masquerade, decode, and fabricate transactions without restriction.

This method is frequently employed despite its theoretical limitations and potential issues. TLS and SSL, which are frequently used to offer security for web browser transactions, are two examples (for example, to securely send credit card details to an online store).

When implementing public key systems, security of the certification hierarchy must be considered in addition to a key pair's resistance to attack. By creating a digital certificate, a certificate authority—typically a special program running on a server computer - attests to the identities associated with private keys. The related private keys must be kept safely for the duration of the public key digital certificate's validity period, which is generally several years at a time.

Any subordinate certificate becomes completely insecure if a private key used to create certificates at a higher level in the PKI server hierarchy is compromised or unintentionally made public.

4.7 Asymmetric Key Techniques

There are various techniques or algorithms for asymmetric encryption and decryption. Following are discussed in details in upcoming sections:

1. RSA
2. RC4
3. ElGamal
4. Digital Signature Algorithm
5. Diffie-Hellman

4.7.1 RSA

A popular public-key cryptosystem for secure data transfer is RSA which stands for Rivest-Shamir-Adleman. It is among the oldest. The surnames of Ron Rivest, Adi Shamir, and Leonard Adleman, who first publicly published the algorithm in 1977, are the origin of the abbreviation "RSA."

The encryption key of a public-key cryptosystem is separate from the decryption key, which is kept confidential (private). A user of RSA generates and disseminates a public key using two significant prime integers and an auxiliary value. It is a secret what the prime numbers are. Anyone can encrypt messages using the public key, but only someone who is familiar with the prime numbers can decode them (Fig. 4.3).

The "factoring problem," which is the practical challenge of factoring the product of two huge prime numbers, is the foundation for RSA security. It is debatable if it is equally challenging as the factoring problem. If a large enough key is used, the system cannot be beaten using any disclosed techniques. The RSA algorithm is a slow one. It is not frequently used to directly encrypt user data as a result. Shared keys for symmetric-key cryptography are typically transmitted using RSA, and these keys are then utilized for mass encryption and decryption.

Operation of RSA
Key generation, key distribution, encryption, and decryption are the four phases that make up the RSA algorithm.

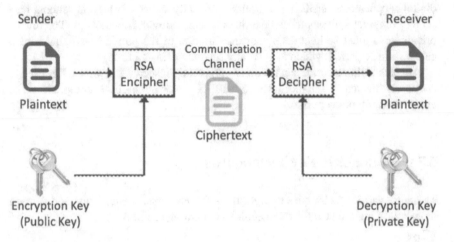

Fig. 4.3 RSA Encryption and Decryption Process

Finding three very large positive integers, **e, d,** and **n,** such that with modular exponentiation for any integers m, is a fundamental tenet of RSA,

$$\left(\mathbf{m^e}\right)^\mathbf{d} \equiv \mathbf{m}\left(\bmod \mathbf{n}\right)$$

and that it might be quite challenging to find d even when one knows e, n, or even m.

Here, the triple bar ($\equiv$) stands for modular congruence. Additionally, it is useful for some operations that this relation also implies that the two exponentiations can be changed in order. Such as:

$$\left(\mathbf{m^d}\right)^\mathbf{e} \equiv \mathbf{m}\left(\bmod \mathbf{n}\right).$$

A public key and a private key are used in RSA. Everyone has access to the public key, which is used to encrypt messages. It is intended that utilizing the private key is the only way to quickly decrypt messages encrypted using the public key.

The integers **n** and **e** stand in for the public key, while the integer **d** stands for the private key (although n is also used during the decryption process, so it might be a part of the private key too). **m** stands for the message.

Key Generation

The keys for the RSA algorithm are generated in the following way:

1. **Choose two large prime numbers p and q.**

   - To make factoring harder, p and q should be chosen at random, be similar in magnitude, but differ in length. Prime integers can be efficiently found using a primality test.
   - p and q should be kept secret.

2. **Compute n = p * q.**

   - n is used as the modulus for both the public and private keys. Its length, usually expressed in bits, is the key length.
   - n is released as part of the public key.

3. **Compute λ(n), where λ is Carmichael's totient function. Since n = p * q,** λ(n) = lcm(λ(p), λ(q)), and since p and q are prime, λ(p) = φ(p) = p − 1, and likewise λ(q) = q − 1. Hence λ(n) = lcm(p − 1, q − 1).

   - The lcm may be calculated through the Euclidean algorithm, since lcm(a, b) = |ab| / gcd (a, b).
   - λ(n) is kept secret.

4. **Choose an integer e such that 1 < e < λ(n) and gcd(e, λ(n)) = 1; that is, e and λ(n) are coprime.**

   - e having a short bit-length and small Hamming weight results in more efficient encryption – the most chosen value for e is $2^{16} + 1 = 65,537$. The smallest (and fastest) possible value for e is 3, but such a small value for e has been shown to be less secure in some settings.
   - e is released as part of the public key.

5. **Determine d as d ≡ e⁻¹ (mod λ(n)); that is, d is the modular multiplicative inverse of e modulo λ(n).**

   - This Solve for d the equation

$$\mathbf{de} \equiv \mathbf{1}\big(\mathrm{mod}\,\lambda\,(\mathbf{n})\big);$$

d can be computed efficiently by using the extended Euclidean algorithm, since, thanks to **e** and **λ(n)** being coprime, said equation is a form of Bézout's identity, where d is one of the coefficients.

   - **d** is kept secret as the private key exponent.

The modulus n and the public (or encryption) exponent e make up the public key. The private (or decryption) exponent d, which needs to be kept a secret, makes up the private key. It is also necessary to keep p, q, and λ(n) a secret because they can be utilized to figure out d. In fact, after d has been calculated, they can all be ignored.

Key Distribution
We assume that there are two parties on communication channel to exchange data or information, Alice, and Bob.

1. Let us say Bob wishes to send Alice some information.
2. If they choose to use RSA, Bob will need access to Alice's public key in order to encrypt the message, and Alice will need to use her private key in order to decrypt it.

3. In order to allow Bob to send his encrypted messages, Alice sends Bob her public key (n, e) over a trustworthy, albeit not always private, channel.
4. The private key (d) of Alice is never shared.

Encryption

After Bob obtains Alice's public key, he can send a message M to Alice.

To do it, he first turns M (strictly speaking, the un-padded plaintext) into an integer m (strictly speaking, the padded plaintext), such that $0 \leq m < n$ by using an agreed-upon reversible protocol known as a padding scheme.

He then computes the ciphertext **C**, using Alice's public key **e**,

$$\mathbf{C} \equiv \mathbf{m}^{\mathbf{e}} \left(\bmod \mathbf{n} \right).$$

This can be done reasonably quickly, even for very large numbers, using modular exponentiation. Bob then transmits **C** to Alice.

Decryption

Alice can recover m from **C** by using her private key exponent d by computing

$$\mathbf{C}^{\mathbf{d}} \equiv \left(\mathbf{m}^{\mathbf{e}} \right)^{\mathbf{d}} \equiv \mathbf{m} \left(\bmod \mathbf{n} \right)$$

Given m, she can recover the original message M by reversing the padding scheme.

Example

- Choose p = 3 and q = 11
- Compute n = p * q = 3 * 11 = 33
- Compute φ(n) = (p - 1) * (q - 1) = 2 * 10 = 20
- Choose e such that $1 < e < \varphi$(n) and e and φ (n) are coprime. Let e = 7
- Compute a value for d such that (d * e) % φ(n) = 1. One solution is d = 3 [(3 * 7) % 20 = 1]
- Public key is (e, n) = > (7, 33)
- Private key is (d, n) = > (3, 33)
- The encryption of m = 2 is c = 2^7% 33 = 29
- The decryption of c = 29 is m = 29^3% 33 = 2

Signing Messages

Consider the scenario where Alice sends Bob an encrypted message using his public key.

- She can identify herself as Alice in the message, but Bob will not be able to confirm that Alice sent it because anyone can send him an encrypted message using his public key.
- RSA can also be used to sign a communication, allowing for origin verification.

Let us say Alice wants to send Bob a message that she has signed.

- She can achieve this by using her personal key.

- When she decrypts a message, she generates a hash value of the message, raises it to the power of d (modulo n), and adds it as a "signature" to the message.
- The same hash algorithm is combined with Alice's public key when Bob uses the signed message. In a similar manner to how he does while encrypting a message, he raises the signature to the power of e (modulo n), compares the resulting hash value to the message's hash value.
- If both parties concur, he will know that Alice's private key was used to send the message and that it has not been tampered with since it was transmitted.

$$h = hash(m),$$

$$\left(h^e\right)^d = h^{ed} = h^{de} = \left(h^d\right)^e \equiv h(\bmod n).$$

As a result, the keys can be switched without compromising generality; specifically, a key pair's private key can be used to:

1. Decrypt a message that was encrypted by the recipient's public key and is only intended for them (asymmetric encrypted transport).
2. Encrypt a message that anyone can decrypt, but only one person can encrypt; this creates a digital signature.

Correctness

The correctness of RSA algorithm can be proved using either Fermat's little theorem or Euler's theorem. In this book the discussion of RSA is limited to Fermat's little theorem.

Proof using Fermat's little theorem

The proof of the correctness of RSA is based on Fermat's little theorem, stating that

$$a^{p-1} \equiv 1(\bmod p)$$

for any integer a and prime p, not dividing a. We want to show that

$$\left(m^e\right)^d \equiv m(\bmod p^* q)$$

for every integer m when **p** and **q** are distinct prime numbers and **e** and **d** are positive integers satisfying

$$e^* d \equiv 1\left(\bmod \lambda\left(p^* q\right)\right).$$

Since

$$\lambda\left(p^* q\right) = lcm(p-1, q-1)$$

is, by construction, divisible by both $p - 1$ and $q - 1$, we can write as:

$$e^* d - 1 = h^* (p - 1) = k^* (q - 1),$$

for some non-negative integers h and k. To check whether two numbers, such as m^{ed} and m, are congruent mod $p * q$, it suffices (and in fact is equivalent) to check that they are congruent mod p and mod q separately.

To show

$$m^{ed} \equiv m \pmod{p},$$

we consider two cases:

1. If $m \equiv 0 \pmod{p}$, m is a multiple of p. Thus, m^{ed} is a multiple of p. So,

$$m^{ed} \equiv 0 \equiv m \pmod{p}.$$

2. If m *not congruent equal to 0 (mod p)*,

$$m^{ed} = m^{ed-1} m = m^{h(p-1)} m = \left(m^{p-1} \right)^h m \equiv 1^h m \equiv m \pmod{p},$$

where Fermat's little theorem used to replace m^{p-1} mod p with 1.

The verification that

$$m^{ed} \equiv m \pmod{q}$$

proceeds in a completely analogous way:

1. If $m \equiv 0 \pmod{q}$,

m^{ed} is a multiple of q. So,

$$m^{ed} \equiv 0 \equiv m \pmod{q}.$$

2. If m **not congruent equal to 0 (mod q)**,

$$m^{ed} = m^{ed-1} m = m^{k(q-1)} m = \left(m^{q-1} \right)^k m \equiv 1^k m \equiv m \pmod{q}.$$

This completes the proof that, for any integer m, and integers e, d such that

$$e^* d \equiv 1 \left(\bmod \lambda \left(p^* q \right) \right),$$

$$\left(m^e \right)^d \equiv m \left(\bmod p^* q \right)$$

Note:

- We cannot trivially break RSA by applying the theorem **(mod p * q)** because **p * q is not prime.**
- In particular, the statement above holds for any e and d that satisfy

$$e^* d \equiv 1 \left(\bmod (p-1) * (q-1) \right),$$

since *(p − 1) * (q − 1)* is divisible by $\lambda(p * q)$, and thus trivially also by **p − 1** and **q − 1**. However, in modern implementations of RSA, it is common to use a reduced private exponent d that only satisfies the weaker, but sufficient condition

$$e^* d \equiv 1 \left(\bmod \lambda \left(p^* q \right) \right).$$

Padding Scheme

Practical RSA implementations often include structured, randomized padding before encrypting the value m to get around these issues. After a message has been padded, it will encrypt to one of the many different potential ciphertexts, ensuring that m does not fall into the range of unsafe plaintexts.

Both message encryption and message signing require secure padding algorithms, such as the Probabilistic Signature Scheme for RSA (RSA-PSS). **Note** that it may be more secure to use different RSA key pairs for encryption and signing.

Attacks against RSA

The following is a list of various attacks that can be made against simple RSA.

- The output of **m^e** (message encryption) is strictly less than the modulus **n** when encrypting with low encryption exponents (for example, e = 3) and small values of the **m**. By dividing the ciphertext's **e**^th root by the integers in this situation, ciphertexts can be easily deciphered.
- The **Chinese remainder theorem** makes it simple to decode the original cleartext message when it is sent encrypted to e or more recipients when the recipients have the same exponent **e** but distinct **p, q,** and consequently different **n**. Johan Hastad found that this approach is still viable if the attacker is aware of a linear relationship between the clear texts, even if they are not equal. Don Coppersmith later made improvements to this attack.
- An attacker can successfully conduct a selected plaintext attack against the cryptosystem by encrypting likely plaintexts under the public key and testing if they are equal to the ciphertext because RSA encryption is a deterministic encryption method (i.e., has no random component). When two encryptions cannot be distinguished from one another by an attacker, even if the adversary is aware of (or has selected) the matching plaintexts, the cryptosystem is said to be semantically secure. Padding is necessary for RSA to be semantically secure.
- RSA has the property that the product of two ciphertexts is equal to the encryption of the product of the respective plaintexts. That is,

$$m_1^e m_2^e \equiv (m_1 m_2)^e \pmod{n}.$$

Because of this multiplicative property, a chosen-ciphertext attack is possible. E.g., an attacker who wants to know the decryption of a ciphertext

$$c \equiv m^e \pmod{n}$$

may ask the holder of the private key d to decrypt an unsuspicious-looking ciphertext

$$c' \equiv c^* r^e \pmod{n}$$

for some value r chosen by the attacker. Because of the multiplicative property, c' is the encryption of m * r (mod n). Hence, if the attacker is successful with the attack, they will learn m * r (mod n), from which they can derive the message m by multiplying m * r with the modular inverse of r modulo n.

- Given the private exponent d, one can efficiently factor the modulus

$$n = p^* q.$$

And given factorization of the modulus n = p * q, one can obtain any private key **(d', n)** generated against a public key **(e', n)**.

4.7.2   RC4

In cryptography, **RC4 (Rivest Cipher 4)** is a stream cipher. While it is remarkable for its simplicity and speed in software, multiple vulnerabilities have been discovered in RC4, rendering it insecure. It is especially vulnerable when the beginning of the output keystream is not discarded, or when nonrandom or related keys are used. Particularly problematic uses of RC4 have led to very insecure protocols such as WEP. There is speculation that some state cryptologic agencies may possess the capability to break RC4 when used in the TLS protocol.

Description of RC4
RC4 generates a pseudorandom stream of bits (a keystream). As with any stream cipher, these can be used for encryption by combining it with the plaintext using bitwise exclusive or; decryption is performed the same way (since exclusive or with given data is an involution). This is like the one-time pad, except that generated pseudorandom bits, rather than a prepared stream, are used.

To generate the keystream, the cipher makes use of a secret internal state which consists of two parts:

- A permutation of all 256 possible bytes (denoted "S" below).
- Two 8-bit index-pointers (denoted "i" and "j").

The permutation is initialized with a variable-length key, typically between 40 and 2048 bits, using the key-scheduling algorithm (KSA). Once this has been completed, the stream of bits is generated using the pseudo-random generation algorithm (PRGA).

Key-Scheduling Algorithm (KSA)

The key-scheduling algorithm is used to initialize the permutation in the array "S". "Key-length" is defined as the number of bytes in the key and can be in the range $1 \leq$ key-length ≤ 256, typically between 5 and 16, corresponding to a key length of 40–128 bits. First, the array "S" is initialized to the identity permutation. S is then processed for 256 iterations in a similar way to the main PRGA, but also mixes in bytes of the key at the same time.

```
for i from 0 to 255
S[i]: = i
endfor
j: = 0
for i from 0 to 255
j: = (j + S[i] + key[i mod key_length]) mod 256
swap values of S[i] and S[j]
endfor
```

Pseudo-Random Generation Algorithm (PRGA)

For as many iterations as are needed, the PRGA modifies the state and outputs a byte of the keystream. In each iteration, the PRGA:

- Increments i;
- Looks up the ith element of S, S[i], and adds that to j;
- Exchanges the values of S[i] and S[j], then uses the sum S[i] + S[j] (modulo 256) as an index to fetch a third element of S (the keystream value K below);
- Then bitwise exclusive ORed (XORed) with the next byte of the message to produce the next byte of either ciphertext or plaintext.

Each element of S is swapped with another element at least once every 256 iterations.

```
i: = 0.
j: = 0.
while Generating_Output:
i: = (i + 1) mod 256.
j: = (j + S[i]) mod 256.
swap values of S[i] and S[j].
K: = S[(S[i] + S[j]) mod 256].
output K.
endwhile.
```

Thus, this produces a stream of K[0], K [1], ... which are XORed with the plaintext to obtain the ciphertext. So ciphertext[l] = plaintext[l] $\oplus$ K[l].

Advantages
- Utilizing RC4 stream cyphers is easy.
- When compared to other ciphers, RC4 has a quick rate of operation.
- RC4 stream cyphers offer robust coding and are simple to use.
- No additional memory is needed for RC4 stream cyphers.
- Large data streams are encrypted using RC4 stream cyphers.

Disadvantages
- Encryption is vulnerable to a bit-flipping attack if RC4 is not used in conjunction with a robust MAC.
- Authentication is not provided by RC4 stream cyphers.
- Before incorporating new systems, more analysis of the RC4 algorithm is necessary.
- Small data streams cannot be encrypted with RC4 stream cyphers.
- RC4 fails to use non-random or linked keys for the method or to discard the output keystream's beginning.

4.7.3   ElGamal

The ElGamal encryption system is a public-key cryptography asymmetric key encryption scheme that is based on the Diffie-Hellman key exchange. Recent iterations of PGP, the free GNU Privacy Guard program, and other cryptosystems all include ElGamal encryption. ElGamal is not to be confused with ElGamal encryption; the Digital Signature Algorithm (DSA) is a variation of the ElGamal signature system.

Any cyclic group G, like a multiplicative group of integers modulo n, can be used to define ElGamal encryption. Its security is based on how challenging a specific discrete logarithm computation problem in G is.

Operation of ElGamal
The **key generator, the encryption algorithm, and the decryption algorithm** are the three parts of the ElGamal encryption system.

Key Generation
The first party, Alice, generates a key pair as follows:

1. Generate an efficient description of a cyclic group G, of order q, with generator g. Let e represent the identity element of G.
2. Choose an integer x randomly from $\{1,......,q-1\}$.
3. Compute $h = g^x$.
4. The public key consists of the values (G, q, g, h). Alice publishes this public key and retains x as her private key, which must be kept secret.

Encryption

A second party, Bob, encrypts a message M to Alice under her public key (G, q, g, h) as follows:

1. Map the message M to an element m of G using a reversible mapping function.
2. Choose an integer y randomly from {1......, q-1}.
3. Compute $s := h^y$. This is called the shared secret.
4. Compute $c_1 := g^y$.
5. Compute $c_2 := m.s$.
6. Bob sends the ciphertext (c_1, c_2) to Alice.

Note that if one knows both the ciphertext (c_1, c_2) and the plaintext m, one can easily find the shared secret s, since $c_2. M^{-1} = s$.

Therefore, a new y and hence a new s is generated for every message to improve security. For this reason, y is also called an ephemeral key.

Decryption

Alice decrypts a ciphertext (c_1, c_2) with her private key x as follows:

1. Compute $s := c_2^x$.

   Since $c_1 = g^y$, $c_1^x = g^{xy} = h^y$, and thus it is the same shared secret that was used by Bob in encryption.

2. Compute s^{-1}, the inverse of s in the group G. This can be computed in one of several ways. If G is a subgroup of a multiplicative group of integers modulo n, where n is prime, the modular multiplicative inverse can be computed using the extended Euclidean algorithm. An alternative is to compute s^{-1} **as** c_1^{q-x}. This is the inverse of s because of Lagrange's theorem, since

$$s.c_1^{q-x} = g^{xy}.g^{(q-x)y} = \left(g^q\right)^y = e^y = e.$$

3. Compute $m := c_2. s^{-1}$. This calculation produces the original message m, because $c_2 = m. s$; hence

$$c_2.s^{-1} = (m.s).s^{-1} = m.$$

4. Map m back to the plaintext message M.

Practical Use of ElGamal Algorithm

The ElGamal cryptosystem, like most public key systems, is typically employed as a component of a hybrid cryptosystem, in which a symmetric cryptosystem is used to encrypt the message itself and ElGamal is then used to encrypt only the symmetric key.

It is quicker to encrypt the message, which can be arbitrary large, with a symmetric cipher and then use ElGamal only to encrypt the symmetric key, which is typically quite small compared to the size of the message, because asymmetric cryptosystems like ElGamal are typically slower than symmetric ones for the same level of security.

Security of ElGamal
The characteristics of the underlying group G and any message padding method applied affect the security of the ElGamal system. The encryption function is one-way if the computational Diffie-Hellman assumption (CDH) is true for the underlying cyclic group G.

- ElGamal provides semantic security if the decisional Diffie-Hellman assumption (DDH) in G is true. By itself, the computational Diffie-Hellman assumption does not imply semantic security.
- ElGamal encryption is always malleable, making it vulnerable to chosen ciphertext attacks. For instance, one can quickly create a valid encryption $(c_1, 2c_2)$ of the message 2 **m** given an encryption (c_1, c_2) of some (potentially unknown) message m.
- The scheme must be further altered, or an appropriate padding scheme must be utilized, to provide chosen-ciphertext security. The DDH assumption may or may not be required depending on the adjustment.
- There have also been other ElGamal-related techniques put out that provide security from certain ciphertext attacks. Assuming DDH holds for G, the Cramer-Shoup cryptosystem is secure against the chosen ciphertext attack. Its demonstration excludes the random oracle concept.
- ElGamal encryption is probabilistic, meaning that a single plaintext can be encrypted to many possible ciphertexts, with the consequence that a general ElGamal encryption produces a 1:2 expansion in size from plaintext to ciphertext.
- Encryption under ElGamal requires two exponentiations; however, these exponentiations are independent of the message and can be computed ahead of time if needed. Decryption requires one exponentiation and one computation of a group inverse, which can, however, be easily combined into just one exponentiation.

4.7.4 Digital Signature Algorithm

The Digital Signature Algorithm (DSA), a public-key cryptosystem is based on the discrete logarithm problem and the mathematical idea of modular exponentiation.

Operation
Key generation, which forms the key pair, key distribution, signing, and signature verification are the four steps that make up the DSA algorithm.

- **Key Generation**

- **Two phases make up key generation**. The system's users may choose from a set of algorithm parameters in the first phase, while a single key pair is computed for just one user in the second phase.

1. Parameter Generation

- Initially a user needs to choose a cryptographic **hash function (H)** along with output length in bits |H|. Modulus length N is used in when output length |H| is greater.
- Then choose a key length L where it should be multiple of 64 and lie in between 512 and 1024 as per Original DSS length. However, lengths 2048 or 3072 are recommended by NIST for lifetime key security.
- The values of L and N need to be chosen in between (1024, 60), (2048, 224), (2048, 256), or (3072, 256) according to FIPS 186–4. Also, a user should choose modulus length N in such a way that modulus length N should be less than key length (N < L) and less than and equal to output length (N < =|H|).
- Later a user can choose a prime number q of N bit and another prime number as p of L bit in such a way that p-1 is multiple of q. And then choose h as an integer from the list (2.........p-2).
- Once you get p and q values, find out

$$g = h^{(p-1)} / q^* \bmod(p).$$

If you get **g = 1**, please try another value for h and compute again for g except 1.

p, q, and g are the algorithm parameters that are shared amongst different users of the systems.

2. Per user keys

To compute the key parameters for a single user, first choose an integer x (private key) from the list (1.......q-1), then compute the public key, y = g^(x)*mod(p).

- **Signature Generation**

  - It passes the original message (M) through the hash function (H#) to get our hash digest(h).
  - It passes the digest as input to a signing function, whose purpose is to give two variables as output, s, and r.
  - Apart from the digest, you also use a random integer k such that 0 < k < q.
  - To calculate the value of r, you use the formula

$$r = \left(g^* k \bmod p\right) \bmod q.$$

  - To calculate the value of s, you use the formula

$$s = \left[K - 1\left(h + x.R\right) \bmod q\right].$$

  - It then packages the signature as **{r, s}**.
  - The entire bundle of the message and signature **{M, r, s}** are sent to the receiver.

- **Key distribution**

- While distributing keys, a signer should keep the private key (x) secret and publish the public key (y) and send the public key (y) to the receiver without any secret mechanism.

- **Signing**

- Signing of message m should be done as follows:
  - first choose an integer k from (1……q-1)
  - compute

$$r = g \wedge (k) * \mod(p) * \mod(q).$$

If you get r = 0, please try another random value of k and compute again for r except 0.

- Calculate,

$$s = \left(k \wedge (-1) * \left(H(m) + x^*r\right)\right) * \mod(q).$$

If you get s = 0, please try another random value of k and compute again for s except 0.

- The signature is defined by two key elements **(r, s).** Also, key elements k and r are used to create a new message. Nevertheless, computing r with modular exponential process is a very expensive process and computed before the message is known. Computation is done with the help of the Euclidean algorithm and Fermat's little theorem.

- **Signature Verification**
  - We use the same hash function (H#) to generate the digest h.
  - We then pass this digest off to the verification function, which needs other variables as parameters too.
  - Compute the value of w such that:

$$s^*w \bmod q = 1$$

- Calculate the value of u1 from the formula,

$$u1 = h^*w \bmod q$$

- Calculate the value of u2 from the formula,

$$u2 = r^*w \bmod q$$

- The final verification component v is calculated as

$$v = \left[\left(\left(gu1 . yu2 \right) \bmod p \right) \bmod q \right].$$

- It compares the value of v to the value of r received in the bundle.
- If it matches, the signature verification is complete.

Sensitivity

The random signature value k's entropy, secrecy, and uniqueness are crucial for DSA. It is so crucial that breaking any one of those three rules can give an attacker access to the full private key. It is sufficient to betray the private key x to use the same value twice (even when k is kept secret), to use a predictable value, or to leak even a little portion of k in each of numerous signatures.

Elliptic Curve Digital Signature Algorithm (ECDSA) and DSA are also impacted by this problem; in December 2010, a group going by the name fail0verflow revealed the recovery of the ECDSA private key that Sony had been using to sign software for the PlayStation 3 gaming console.

Due to Sony's failure to produce a fresh random number for each signature, the attack was made viable. According to RFC 6979, this problem can be avoided by deterministically deriving k from the private key and the message hash.

As a result, each H(m) has a unique value for k, making it unpredictable for attackers who do not possess the private key x.

Additionally, malicious DSA and ECDSA implementations can be developed where k is selected to covertly reveal information via signatures. For instance, a flawless offline device that only released signatures with a clean appearance may leak an offline private key.

DSA Applications

Digital signatures can contribute to the evidence of the origin, identity, and status of an electronic document while also acknowledging the signer's knowledge and consent. Here are a few typical justifications for include a digital signature in communications:

Authentication

Even though communications frequently contain information about the party sending them, this information may not be reliable. The source communications' identities can be verified using digital signatures. When a user is assigned ownership of a digital signature secret key, a valid signature demonstrates that user transmitted the message.

In a financial setting, the significance of having strong confidence in sender legitimacy is very clear. Imagine, for instance, that a bank branch office sends instructions to the main office demanding a modification to an account's balance. Acting on such a request could be a fatal error if the central office is not sure that the message was delivered by an authorized source.

Integrity

The sender and the recipient of a communication may frequently need to have faith that the message was not changed during transmission. Although encryption obscures a message's contents, it might still be feasible to alter an encrypted message without being able to decipher it. This is prevented by some encryption techniques (known as nonmalleable), but not by all.

When a communication is digitally signed, any alterations made after the signature render the message invalid. Furthermore, most cryptographic hash functions still view this as computationally impossible, therefore there is no effective way to change a message and its signature to create a new message with a legitimate signature (see collision resistance).

Non-repudiation

An essential feature of digital signatures is non-repudiation, more especially non-repudiation of origin. By virtue of this feature, a signatory cannot later retract their signature on a document. Like that, a fraudulent party cannot impersonate a legitimate signature if they just have access to the public key.

It should be noted that these properties - authentication, non-repudiation, etc. - depend on the secret key not having been revoked before being used. Leaked secret keys would continue to implicate the key-purported pair's owner without the ability to publicly revoke a key-pair.

Revocation status must be verified "online," for example, by checking a list of revoked certificates or using the Online Certificate Status Protocol. This is somewhat comparable to a merchant who receives credit cards first contacting the credit card company online to determine whether a specific card has been reported lost or stolen. Of course, when key pairs are taken, the theft is frequently only found after the secret key has been used, such as when it has been used to sign a fake certificate for espionage.

4.7.5   Diffie-Hellman Key Exchange Protocol

The Diffie-Hellman (DH) key exchange technique was one of the first public-key protocols, developed by Ralph Merkle and named for Whitfield Diffie and Martin Hellman. It allows for the secure exchange of cryptographic keys via a public channel. One of the earliest applications of public key exchange in the context of cryptography is DH. This is the oldest piece of public knowledge that proposed the concept of a private key and a corresponding public key. It was published in 1976 by Diffie and Hellman.

In the past, exchanging keys between two parties required that they do it first through a safe physical channel, like paper key lists delivered by a reliable messenger. Using an unsecure channel, two parties with no prior knowledge of one another can establish a shared secret key together using the Diffie-Hellman key exchange mechanism. Using a symmetric-key cypher, this key can then be used to encrypt subsequent messages.

Different Internet services are secured using Diffie-Hellman. The parameters being used for many DH Internet apps at the time, according to research published in October 2015, may not have been robust enough to thwart attacks by highly well-funded adversaries, such as the security agencies of some governments.

Despite being a non-authenticated key-agreement protocol in and of itself, Diffie-Hellman key agreement serves as the foundation for several authenticated protocols and is used to ensure forward secrecy in Transport Layer Security's ephemeral modes (referred to as EDH or DHE depending on the cipher suite).

Description
A shared secret is created between two parties via the Diffie-Hellman key exchange, which can then be utilized for confidential data exchange over a public network. An analogy uses colors rather than very large numbers to demonstrate the idea of public key exchange:

- The method starts with Alice and Bob openly deciding on a random starting color that is not required to be kept a secret. The color used in this illustration is yellow.
- In addition, each person chooses a private hidden color, in this example red and cyan. The key step in the procedure is when Alice and Bob blend their own secret colors with the color, they both share to produce combinations of orange-tan and light blue, respectively, and then publicly trade the two combined colors.
- Finally, they each combine their personal color with the hue they received from their spouse. The end-result is a final color combination (in this case, yellow-brown) that is the same as their partner's final color combination.
- A third person who overheard the conversation would only be aware of the common color, yellow, and the first two mixed colors, orange-tan and light blue, but it would be extremely difficult for them to determine the last secret color (yellow-brown).
- This determination is computationally costly, to return to a real-world exchange utilizing huge numbers instead of colors. Even with the most advanced super-computers, it is not possible to compute in a reasonable amount of time.

The illustration of Diffie-Hellman depicted in fig. 4.4.

Cryptographic Explanation
The multiplicative group of integers modulo p, where p is prime, and g is a primitive root modulo p are used in the protocol's initial and most basic implementation. In order to guarantee that the resulting shared secret can take on any value between 1 and p-1, these two values were selected in this manner.

The protocol is illustrated here, with non-secret values shown in blue and secret values shown in red.

1. Alice and Bob publicly agree to use a modulus $p = 23$ and base $g = 5$ (which is a primitive root modulo 23).
2. Alice chooses a secret integer $a = 4$, then sends Bob $A = g^a \bmod p$

- $A = 5^4 \bmod 23 = 4$ (in this example both A and a have the same value 4, but this is usually not the case)

3. Bob chooses a secret integer $b = 3$, then sends Alice $B = g^b \bmod p$

   • $B = 5^3 \bmod 23 = 10$

4. Alice computes $s = B^a \bmod p$

   • $s = 10^4 \bmod 23 = 18$

5. Bob computes $s = A^b \bmod p$

   • $s = 4^3 \bmod 23 = 18$

6. Alice and Bob now share a secret (the number 18).

   • Both Alice and Bob have arrived at the same values because under mod p,

$$A^b \bmod p = g^{ab} \bmod p = g^{ba} \bmod p = B^a \bmod p$$

More specifically,

$$\left(g^a \bmod p\right)^b \bmod p = \left(g^b \bmod p\right)^a \bmod p$$

• Only a and b are kept secret. All the other values – **p, g, g^a mod p**, and **g^b mod p** – are sent in the clear.

The strength of the scheme comes from the fact that

$$g^{ab} \bmod p = g^{ba} \bmod p$$

take extremely long times to compute by any known algorithm just from the knowledge of **p, g, g^a mod p**, and **g^b mod p**.

• Once Alice and Bob compute the shared secret they can use it as an encryption key, known only to them, for sending messages across the same open communications channel.

• Of course, much larger values of a, b, and p would be needed to make this example secure, since there are only 23 possible results of n mod 23.

• However, if p is a prime of at least 600 digits, then even the fastest modern computers using the fastest known algorithm cannot find a given only **g, p** and **g^a mod p**.

• Such a problem is called the discrete logarithm problem. The computation of **g^a mod p** is known as modular exponentiation and can be done efficiently even for large numbers.

Note that g need not be large at all, and in practice is usually a small integer (like 2, 3, ...).

Fig. 4.4 Diffie-Hellman

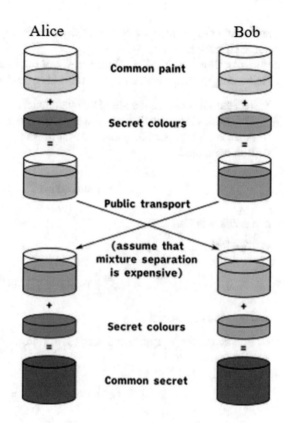

Ephemeral and Static Keys

The employed keys may be either ephemeral or static (long-term), or they may even be mixed - this is known as semi-static DH. These variations have various features, which lead to various use scenarios. Here is a brief list of things to know:

- **Ephemeral, ephemeral:** typically employed for critical agreement. Offers forward secrecy but no authenticity.
- **Static, static:** Would produce a long-lasting shared secret. Provides implicit authenticity rather than outward secrecy. For instance, replay-attack protection would not be available because the keys are static.
- **Ephemeral, static:** It could offer implicit one-sided authenticity if utilized in critical agreement (the ephemeral side could verify the authenticity of the static side). There is no provision for forward secrecy.

Ephemeral and static keys can be used in a single key agreement to increase security.

Operation with More than Two Parties

Negotiating a key that is shared by more than just two people is possible with a Diffie-Hellman key agreement. The agreement protocol can be iterated upon and any number of people may participate by exchanging intermediate data (which does not itself need to be kept secret).

As an illustration, Alice, Bob, and Carol could engage in the following Diffie-Hellman agreement, with all operations being modulo p:

- The parties agree on the algorithm parameters **p** and **g**.
- The parties generate their private keys, named **a**, **b**, and **c**.
- Alice computes **g^a mod p** and sends it to Bob.
- Bob computes

$$\left(g^a \right)^b \bmod p = g^{ab} \bmod p$$

and sends it to Carol.

- Carol computes

$$\left(g^{ab} \right)^c \bmod p = g^{abc} \bmod p$$

and uses it as her secret.

- Bob computes **g^b mod p** and sends it to Carol.
- Carol computes

$$\left(g^b \right)^c \bmod p = g^{bc} \bmod p$$

and sends it to Alice.

- Alice computes

$$\left(g^{bc} \right)^a \bmod p = g^{bca} \bmod p = g^{abc} \bmod p$$

and uses it as her secret.

- Carol computes **g^c mod p** and sends it to Alice.
- Alice computes

$$\left(g^c \right)^a \bmod p = g^{ca} \bmod p$$

and sends it to Bob.

- Bob computes

$$\left(g^{ca} \right)^b \bmod p = g^{cab} \bmod p = g^{abc} \bmod p$$

and uses it as his secret.

An eavesdropper has been able to see g^a mod **p, g^b mod p, g^c mod p, g^{ab} mod p, g^{ac} mod p, and g^{bc} mod p,** but cannot use any combination of these to efficiently reproduce g^{abc} **mod p**.

Two fundamental guidelines must be followed in order to expand this method to larger groups:

- The secret is created by increasing the current value to each participant's private exponent once, in any sequence (the first such exponentiation produces the participant's own public key), starting with an "empty" key consisting just of the letter g.
- Any intermediate value, where N is the total number of group members, may have up to N-1 exponents applied to it; however, the final value, which has all N exponents applied, is the shared secret and should never be made public. Therefore, each user must apply their own private key last to acquire their own copy of the secret (otherwise there would be no way for the last contributor to communicate the final key to its recipient, as that last contributor would have turned the key into the very secret the group wished to protect).

These guidelines leave open several alternatives for selecting the sequence in which contributors to keys are added. The easiest and most straightforward approach is to put the N participants in a circle and rotate the N keys around the circle until every key has been contributed to by all N participants (starting with its owner), and each participant has contributed to N keys (ending with their own). However, this necessitates N modular exponentiations from each participant.

Security

The protocol is considered secure against eavesdroppers if G and g are chosen properly. In particular, the order of the group G must be large, particularly if the same group is used for large amounts of traffic. The eavesdropper must solve the Diffie–Hellman problem to obtain g^{ab}.

This is currently considered difficult for groups whose order is large enough. An efficient algorithm to solve the discrete logarithm problem would make it easy to compute a or b and solve the Diffie–Hellman problem, making this and many other public key cryptosystems insecure. Fields of small characteristic may be less secure.

The order of G should have a large prime factor to prevent use of the Pohlig–Hellman algorithm to obtain a or b.

For this reason, a Sophie Germain prime q is sometimes used to calculate

$$p = 2q + 1,$$

called a safe prime, since the order of G is then only divisible by 2 and q. g is then sometimes chosen to generate the order q subgroup of G, rather than G, so that the Legendre symbol of g^a never reveals the low order bit of a. A protocol using such a choice is for example IKEv2.

g is often a small integer such as 2. Because of the random self-reducibility of the discrete logarithm problem a small g is equally secure as any other generator of the same group.

If Alice and Bob use random number generators whose outputs are not completely random and can be predicted to some extent, then it is much easier to eavesdrop.

In the original description, the Diffie–Hellman exchange by itself does not provide authentication of the communicating parties and is thus vulnerable to a man-in-the-middle attack. Mallory (an active attacker executing the man-in-the-middle attack) may establish two distinct key exchanges, one with Alice and the other with Bob, effectively masquerading as Alice to Bob, and vice versa, allowing her to decrypt, then re-encrypt, the messages passed between them. Note that Mallory must continue to be in the middle, actively decrypting and re-encrypting messages every time Alice and Bob communicate. If she is ever absent, her previous presence is then revealed to Alice and Bob.

They will know that all their private conversations had been intercepted and decoded by someone in the channel. In most cases it will not help them get Mallory's private key, even if she used the same key for both exchanges.

A method to authenticate the communicating parties to each other is generally needed to prevent this type of attack. Variants of Diffie–Hellman, such as STS protocol, may be used instead to avoid these types of attacks.

Other Uses

The Diffie-Hellman can be used in several forms, some are listed below.

Encryptionss On the Diffie-Hellman key exchange, public key encryption techniques have been presented. ElGamal encryption is the first of these systems. The Integrated Encryption Scheme is one of the most recent variations.

Forward Secrecy Forward-secret protocols create fresh key pairs for every session and discard them at the conclusion of the session. Due to its quick key generation, the Diffie-Hellman key exchange is a popular choice for such protocols.

Password-Authenticated Key Agreement A password-authenticated key agreement (PK) version of Diffie-Hellman can be used by Alice and Bob when they share a password to fend off man-in-the-middle attacks. Comparing the hash of s concatenated with the password that was calculated independently on both ends of the channel is one straightforward method.

Because only one password can be tested by an attacker at a time with the other side using these schemes, the system offers strong security even with relatively weak passwords. ITU-T Recommendation X.1035, which is used by the G.hn home networking standard, describes this strategy. The Secure Remote Password protocol is one illustration of such a protocol.

Public Key Diffie-Hellman can also be used as a component of a public key infrastructure. In this case, Bob can encrypt a message so that only Alice will be able to decrypt it without any prior communication between them, provided Bob has reliable access to Alice's public key.

RSA is the most common public key algorithm, and Diffie-Hellman is not utilized in this way. This is primarily due to historical and financial factors; specifically, RSA Security founded Verisign, a certificate authority for key signing.

As shown above, Diffie-Hellman cannot be used to sign certificates directly. The ElGamal and DSA signature algorithms, as well as MQV, STS, and the IKE component of the IPsec protocol suite for securing Internet Protocol communications, are mathematically connected to it, though.

4.7.6   Password-Authenticated Key Agreement

A password-authenticated key agreement technique in cryptography is an interactive way for two or more parties to create cryptographic keys based on the password knowledge of one or more parties. One crucial characteristic is that a man-in-the-middle or eavesdropper cannot gather enough data to brute-force guess a password without interacting with the parties after each (few) guesses. This implies that weak passwords can still provide strong security.

Types of Password-Authenticated Key Agreement
Techniques including

- Balanced password-authenticated key exchange,
- Enhanced password-authenticated key exchange,
- Password-authenticated key retrieval,
- Multi-server methods, and
- Multi-party methods

are all included in password-authenticated key agreement.

The strictest password-only security models do not require the method's user to keep track of any private or public information aside from the password.

Password-authenticated key exchange (PAKE) is a technique in which two or more parties create a cryptographic key by exchanging messages based solely on the knowledge of a shared password, so that an unauthorized party (one who controls the communication channel but does not have the password) is prevented from doing so and is as restrained as possible from brute-forcing the password. (In the best situation, each run exchange produces exactly one guess.) PAKE comes in two flavors: enhanced and balanced ways.

Balanced PAKE   Balanced PAKE presupposes that both parties in a client-client or client-server scenario negotiate and authenticate a shared key using the same secret password. Encrypted Key Exchange (EKE), PAK and PPK, SPEKE (Simple Password Exponential Key Exchange), the Elliptic Curve based Secure Remote

Password protocol, Dragonfly, Advanced Modular Handshake for Key Agreement and Optional Authentication, etc. are a few examples of these.

Augmented PAKE There is a version of PAKE called "augmented PAKE" that can be used in client/server contexts when the server does not keep password-equivalent information. As a result, unless they first use a brute force password search, an attacker who obtained the server data is still unable to pose as the client. Some enhanced PAKE systems mix the user's secret password with the server's secret salt value using an oblivious pseudorandom function such that neither the user nor the server ever learns the user's password (or password-equivalent value) or the final key. AMP, Augmented-EKE, B-SPEKE, PAK-X, SRP, Advanced modular handshake for key agreement and optional authentication, etc. are a few examples.

Key Retrieval In a password-based negotiation with a server that is aware of password-related information, as in the Ford and Kaliski techniques, a client acquires a static key. This procedure is known as password-authenticated key retrieval. In the strictest configuration, one party retrieves a static key using N (two or more) servers and only a password. The process is finished in a way that keeps the password (and key) secure even in the event that N - 1 of the servers are totally compromised.

4.8   Examples of Protocols Using Asymmetric Key Algorithms Include

4.8.1   S/Mime

The Secure/Multipurpose Internet Mail Extensions, or *S/MIME standard, is used to encrypt and sign MIME data with a public key.* S/MIME is described in several documents, most notably RFC 3369, 3370, 3850, and 3851, and is on an IETF standards track. It was initially created by RSA Data Security, and the original definition combined the de facto industry standard secure communication format (PKCS) with the IETF MIME protocol.

Since then, the IETF has taken over change management of S/MIME, and the specification is now overlaid on Cryptographic Message Syntax (CMS), an IETF specification that is nearly identical to PKCS. Most current email programs include S/MIME capability and can communicate with one another. Because MIME is based on CMS, it can also store a sophisticated digital signature.

Functions
The following cryptographic security features are offered by S/MIME for use in electronic messaging applications:

1. Authentication

2. Message integrity
3. Non-repudiation of origin (using digital signatures)
4. Privacy
5. Data security (using encryption)

When data must be enveloped (encrypted), S/MIME specifies the MIME type application (S/MIME-type "enveloped-data") where the entire (prepared) MIME entity to be enveloped is encrypted and packed into an object which is then put into an application MIME entity.

S/MIME Certificates

Before S/MIME can be used in any of the apps, a unique key/certificate must be acquired and installed, either from a private or public certificate authority (CA). Using distinct private keys (and related certificates) for encryption and signing is considered to be the best practice because it allows escrow of the encryption key without compromising the non-repudiation property of the signature key.

Having the destination party's certificate on hand is necessary for encryption (which is typically automatic upon receiving a message from the party with a valid signing certificate). The S/MIME clients will demand the user to install their own certificate before they allow encrypting to others, even though it is technically possible to transmit a message encrypted (using the destination party certificate) without having one's own certificate to digitally sign. This is required so that the message can be encrypted for the receiver and the sender, and so that the sender can retain a copy of the message (in the sent folder) that is readable by the recipient.

A typical basic ("class 1") personal certificate only establishes the sender's "identity" insofar as it states that the sender is the owner of the "From:" email address insofar as the sender can receive email sent to that address, and thus merely establishes that an email received actually originated from the stated "From:" address. The name of the person or the name of the company is not verified. Senders need to obtain a certificate ("class 2") from a CA who performs a more thorough identity verification process, which involves asking questions about the potential certificate holder, if they want to allow email recipients to verify the sender's identity in the sense that a received certificate name contains the sender's name or an organization's name. See the digital signature for additional information on authenticity.

The certificate and all of its contents may be posted publicly for reference and verification, depending on the CA's policies. The name and email address are now publicly visible and potentially searchable. Other CAs do not disclose any personal information; they merely publish serial numbers and revocation status. To maintain the integrity of the public key infrastructure, the latter is at the very least required.

S/MIME Working Group

In 2020, the S/MIME Certificate Working Group of the CA/Browser Forum was chartered to create a baseline requirement applicable to CAs that issue S/MIME certificates used to sign, verify, encrypt, and decrypt email.

That effort is intended to create standards including:

- Certificate profiles for S/MIME certificates and CAs that issue them
- Verification of control over email addresses
- Identity validation
- Key management, certificate lifecycle, CA operational practices, etc.

Obstacles for S/MIME Deployment in Practice
- S/MIME is occasionally viewed as being unsuitable for usage with webmail clients. Although a browser's support can be exploited, some security procedures call for the private key to be maintained accessible to the user but inaccessible from the webmail server, which complicates webmail's main benefit of offering universal accessibility. This problem is not entirely unique to S/MIME; other secure webmail signature techniques may also require the browser to run code; the exceptions are PGP Desktop and some iterations of GnuPG, which take the data out of the webmail, sign it using a clipboard, and then return the signed data to the webmail page. This is a more secure solution when viewed from the perspective of security.
- S/MIME was designed with end-to-end security in mind. It is illogical to have safe end-to-end interactions while a third-party scans emails for malware. Malware will also be encrypted via encryption in addition to the messages. Encryption will therefore be successful in delivering the virus if mail is not inspected for malware elsewhere other than at the end points, such as a company's gateway. After decryption, the only way to fix this is to run virus scanning on end user stations. Other solutions do not offer end-to-end trust since they need a third party to share keys in order to detect malware. Compromises of this kind include, for instance:
  1. Solutions that keep private keys on the gateway server to enable decryption before a gateway malware scan. The end users are then given access to these unencrypted messages.
  2. Solutions that keep private keys on malware scanners allow them to inspect message content before relaying the encrypted message to its target.
- Because a certificate is necessary for implementation, not all users can benefit from S/MIME. For example, some users may want to encrypt a message using a public/private key pair in order to avoid the hassle or administrative burden of certificates.

If the relevant key pair's private key is unavailable or otherwise inoperable (for example, the certificate has been deleted or lost, or the private key's password has been forgotten), no message that a S/MIME email client stores encrypted may be decrypted. A certificate that has expired, been revoked, or is untrusted, however, will still work for cryptographic operations. With some email clients, it might not be possible to index the clear text of encrypted messages. Both possible issues do not apply to S/MIME communications that are only signed and not encrypted because they are not exclusive to S/MIME but rather to cypher text in general. The signature information is typically "separated" from the text being signed in S/MIME signatures.

4.8.2   PGP

The encryption application Pretty Good Privacy (PGP) offers cryptographic privacy and authentication for data transfer. PGP is used to sign, encrypt, and decrypt files, directories, entire disc partitions, as well as to strengthen the security of e-mail exchanges.

In 1991, Phil Zimmermann created PGP. PGP and comparable programs encrypt and decrypt data in accordance with the OpenPGP standard (RFC 4880), which is an open standard for PGP encryption software.

Design of PGP

PGP encryption employs a series of supported techniques for hashing, data compression, symmetric-key cryptography, and finally public-key cryptography. Each public key has a username or email address associated with it. To contrast with the X.509 system, which utilizes a hierarchical method based on certificate authority and which was later included to PGP implementations, the earliest version of this system was commonly characterized as a web of trust. Options through an automated key management server are available in current versions of PGP encryption.

PGP Fingerprint

A compressed form of a public key is called a public key fingerprint. Someone can verify the correct associated public key from a fingerprint. A business card can be printed with a fingerprint that looks like C3A6 5E46 7B54 77DF 3C4C 9790 4D22 B3CA 5B32 FF66.

Compatibility

As PGP develops, later versions that support them can encrypt messages that older PGP systems cannot decipher, even with a working private key. Therefore, it's crucial for PGP communication partners to be aware of each other's capabilities or at the very least to agree on PGP settings.

Confidentiality

PGP can be used to send private messages. PGP accomplishes this via a hybrid cryptosystem that combines symmetric-key and public-key encryption. A symmetric encryption algorithm is used to encrypt the communication, and it needs a symmetric key that the sender has created. The symmetric key, which is also known as a session key, is only ever used once. The receiver receives the message together with its session key. It is necessary for the receiver to get the session key for them to be able to decrypt the message, but in order to safeguard it during transmission, it is encrypted using the recipient's public key. Only the receiver's private key has the ability to decrypt the session key, which may then be used to symmetrically decode the message.

Digital Signatures

Message integrity testing and authentication are supported by PGP. The message integrity property of the latter is used to determine whether a message has been altered after it was sent, while the sender authenticity property of the former is used to confirm that the message was sent by the person or entity claimed to be the sender (a digital signature). Any changes to the message will prevent the decryption with the right key from working because the information is encrypted. Either the RSA or DSA algorithms are used by the sender to provide a digital signature for the message using PGP. PGP does this by computing a hash from the plaintext (also known as a message digest) and then producing the digital signature from that hash using the sender's private key.

Web of Trust

It is crucial that the public key used to send messages to someone or some entity genuinely does 'belong' to the intended receiver. This is true for both message encryption and signature verification. An affiliation cannot be reliably verified by merely obtaining a public key; it is possible to impersonate someone on purpose or accidentally. Since the beginning, PGP has featured options for providing users' public keys in an "identity certification" that is also built cryptographically to make any tampering (or unintentional jumble) easy to see. Simply creating a certificate that cannot be altered without being noticed, however, is insufficient because this can only stop corruption once the certificate has been created, not before. The public key in a certificate must also belong to the person or organization claiming it, and users must verify this by some other way. A third-party user can digitally sign a given public key to confirm that a certain person (or more precisely, information connecting a user name to a key) is connected to it. Such signatures can have a variety of levels of confidence. Few (if any) programs take into account this degree of certification when determining whether to trust a key, despite the fact that numerous programs can read and write this data.

The web of trust system, which has not been widely adopted, provides advantages over a public key infrastructure scheme that is centrally administered, like the one employed by S/MIME. Users must be willing to accept certificates, either without manually verifying their validity or after accepting them. The fundamental issue has yet to have a good remedy established.

Certificates

Trust signatures can be used to assist the formation of certificate authority in the (more modern) OpenPGP protocol. A trust signature certifies that the key is legitimately owned by the claimant as well as the claimant's reliability in signing keys that are one level below their own. Since just the key's authenticity is validated, a level 0 signature is like a web of trust signature. Because a key certified to level 1 can generate an infinite number of level 0 signatures, it is comparable to the confidence one has in a certificate authority. A level 2 signature permits the owner of the key to make other keys certificate authorities, which is very similar to the trust assumption users must rely on anytime they use the default certificate authority list (such as those included in web browsers).

Public key certificates can always be revoked (cancelled) in PGP versions. If the user wants to keep their communication security, they will need to replace a lost or compromised private key. This is somewhat analogous to the lists of certificates that have been revoked in centralized PKI schemes. Certificate expiration dates are now supported in more recent versions of PGP.

PGP is not the only encryption protocol that has difficulty correctly recognizing a public key as belonging to a certain user. All public key/private key cryptosystems face the same issue, albeit under slightly different guises, and there is currently no totally workable solution. Most other PKI schemes do not allow users to choose whether to use their endorsement/vetting system; instead, they demand that every certificate attested to by a central certificate authority be accepted as accurate. At least PGP's original scheme gives users the option of using its endorsement/vetting system.

4.8.3   IPSec

Internet Protocol Security (IPsec) is a set of secure network protocols used in computing that authenticates and encrypts data packets for communication between two computers over an IP network. Virtual private networks employ it (VPNs).

IPsec protocols include those for negotiating the cryptographic keys to be used throughout a session and for establishing mutual authentication between agents at the start of one. IPsec can secure data transfers from one host to another, from one security gateway to another, or from one security gateway to a host (network-to-host). To secure communications across Internet Protocol (IP) networks, IPsec uses cryptographic security services. It supports replay protection, data origin authentication, network-level peer authentication, data integrity, and data confidentiality (encryption) (protection from replay attacks).

There were not many security features included in the original IPv4 suite. IPsec is a layer 3 OSI model or internet layer end-to-end security scheme that is a part of the IPv4 improvement. Contrarily, IPsec can automatically secure applications at the internet layer while some other Internet security systems in use operate above the network layer, such as Transport Layer Security (TLS), which operates above the transport layer, and Secure Shell (SSH), which operates at the application layer.

Security Architecture
The IPv4 suite includes the open standard IPsec. The following protocols are used by IPsec to carry out a variety of tasks:

- For IP datagrams, Authentication Headers (AH) offers connectionless data integrity, data origin authentication, and defense against replay attacks.
- Confidentiality, connectionless data integrity, data origin authentication, an anti-replay service (a type of partial sequence integrity), and limited traffic-flow confidentiality are all features of Encapsulating Security Payloads (ESP).
- A framework for authentication and key sharing is given by the Internet Security Association and Key Management Protocol (ISAKMP), with actual authenticated keying material provided either manually configured with pre-shared keys

or via Internet Key Exchange. To create the security associations (SA) with the collection of parameters and algorithms required for AH and/or ESP operations.

Authentication Header

The Security Authentication Header (AH), which was created at the US Naval Research Laboratory in the early 1990s, was partly inspired by earlier IETF work on the Simple Network Management Protocol (SNMP) version 2 authentication standard. The IPsec protocol family includes the authentication header (AH). By utilizing a hash function and a private shared key in the AH algorithm, connectionless integrity is guaranteed. In addition, AH ensures the source of the data by authenticating IP packets. With the use of the sliding window approach, an optional sequence number helps defend the IPsec packet's contents from replay assaults.

AH inhibits option-insertion attacks in IPv4. AH in IPv6 defends against both option insertion attacks and header insertion attacks.

The IP payload and all header fields of an IP datagram are protected by the AH in IPv4 apart from mutable fields (i.e., those that could be changed in transit) and IP choices like the IP Security Option.

Most of the IPv6 base header, the AH, the non-mutable extension headers that follow the AH, and the IP payload are all protected by the AH in IPv6. DSCP, ECN, Flow Label, and Hop Limit are among the modifiable fields that are not covered by IPv6 header protection. AH utilizes IP protocol number 51 and runs directly on top of IP.

Description of fields of AH given below:

Next Header (8 bits): Type of the next header, indicating what upper-layer protocol was protected. The value is taken from the list of IP protocol numbers.

Payload Len (8 bits): The length of this Authentication Header in 4-octet units, minus 2. For example, an AH value of 4 equals $3 \times$ (32-bit fixed-length AH fields) $+ 3 \times$ (32-bit ICV fields) $- 2$ and thus an AH value of 4 means 24 octets. Although the size is measured in 4-octet units, the length of this header needs to be a multiple of 8 octets if carried in an IPv6 packet. This restriction does not apply to an Authentication Header carried in an IPv4 packet.

Reserved (16 bits): Reserved for future use (all zeroes until then).

Security Parameters Index (32 bits): Arbitrary value which is used (together with the destination IP address) to identify the security association of the receiving party.

Sequence Number (32 bits): A monotonic strictly increasing sequence number (incremented by 1 for every packet sent) to prevent replay attacks. When replay detection is enabled, sequence numbers are never reused, because a new security association must be renegotiated before an attempt to increment the sequence number beyond its maximum value.

Integrity Check Value (multiple of 32 bits): Variable length check value. It may contain padding to align the field to an 8-octet boundary for IPv6, or a 4-octet boundary for IPv4.

Encapsulating Security Payload

IPsec's family of protocols includes Encapsulating Security Payload (ESP). It offers source authentication to ensure the originality of IP packets, hashing to ensure data integrity, and encryption to provide packet confidentiality. It is generally advised against utilizing encryption without authentication because it is insecure, while ESP does allow these settings as well.

The integrity and authentication of an IP packet are not provided for the full IP packet by ESP in transport mode, in contrast to Authentication Header (AH).

The entire inner IP packet (including the inner header) is protected by ESP in tunnel mode, in contrast, while the outer header (including any outer IPv4 options or IPv6 extension headers) is left unprotected. Tunnel mode encapsulates the entire original IP packet with a new packet header. Utilizing IP protocol 50, ESP runs directly on top of IP.

Description of fields of ESP are as follows:

Security Parameters Index (32 bits): Arbitrary value used (together with the destination IP address) to identify the security association of the receiving party.

Sequence Number (32 bits): A monotonically increasing sequence number (incremented by 1 for every packet sent) to protect against replay attacks. There is a separate counter kept for every security association.

Payload data (variable): The protected contents of the original IP packet, including any data used to protect the contents (e.g., an Initialization Vector for the cryptographic algorithm). The type of content that was protected is indicated by the Next Header field.

Padding (0–255 octets): Padding for encryption, to extend the payload data to a size that fits the encryption's cipher block size, and to align the next field.

Pad Length (8 bits): Size of the padding (in octets).

Next Header (8 bits): Type of the next header. The value is taken from the list of IP protocol numbers.

Integrity Check Value (multiple of 32 bits): Variable length check value. It may contain padding to align the field to an 8-octet boundary for IPv6, or a 4-octet boundary for IPv4.

Modes of Operation

There are two types of modes, description given below:

Transport mode

Only the IP packet's payload is typically encrypted or authenticated in transport mode. However, when the authentication header is utilized, the IP addresses cannot be changed via network address translation because doing so always invalidates the hash value. As a result, the routing is unaffected. The transport and application layers are always protected by hashes, making it impossible for them to be altered in any way, such as by changing the port numbers. RFC publications outlining the NAT-T method have defined a way to encapsulate IPsec packets for NAT traversal.

Tunnel mode

The entire IP packet is encrypted and authenticated in tunnel mode. After that, it is enclosed in a fresh IP packet with a fresh IP header. For network-to-network communications (such as those between routers to link sites), host-to-network communications (such as those involving remote user access), and host-to-host communications, virtual private networks are created using the tunnel mode (e.g., private chat). NAT traversal is supported in tunnel mode.

Algorithms
Symmetric Encryption Algorithms
   Cryptographic algorithms defined for use with IPsec include:

- HMAC-SHA1/SHA2 for integrity protection and authenticity.
- Triple DES-CBC for confidentiality
- AES-CBC and AES-CTR for confidentiality.
- AES-GCM providing confidentiality and authentication together efficiently.

Key Exchange Algorithms

- Diffie–Hellman

   Authentication Algorithms

- RSA

   The IP stack of an operating system can implement IPsec. Using this manner of implementation, hosts and security gateways are put into use.

4.8.4   Secure Shell (SSH)

A cryptographic network protocol called Secure Shell (SSH) is used to operate network services over insecure networks safely. Remote login and command-line execution are two of its most noteworthy applications. Client-server architecture is the foundation of SSH applications, which link an SSH client instance with an SSH server.

   SSH functions as a layered protocol suite with three main hierarchical components:

- The user authentication protocol verifies the user to the server; the connection protocol multiplexes the encrypted tunnel into multiple logical communication channels; and
- The transport layer provides server authentication, confidentiality, and integrity.

The protocol suite's later development took place in many developer groups, leading to various implementation iterations. The protocol specification distinguishes between SSH-1 and SSH-2, which are the two main versions.

Authentication
Public-key cryptography is used by SSH to authenticate the remote computer and, if necessary, to allow it to authenticate the user.

- SSH can be applied in several different ways. In the simplest case, a network connection is encrypted at both ends using automatically produced public-private key pairs, and the user is then authenticated using a password.
- When a user manually generates a public-private key pair, authentication is virtually completed at the time the key pair is created, allowing a session to be opened instantly without a password prompt.
- In this case, the corresponding private key is kept secret by the owner and the public key is installed on all computers that must grant access to the owner. Although the private key serves as the foundation for authentication, the key is never sent over the network when performing authentication.
- SSH simply confirms that the public key's provider also holds the corresponding private key.
- It is crucial to validate unknown public keys in all SSH versions, i.e., link the public keys to identities, before accepting them as legitimate. Accepting a public key from an attacker without validating it will accept an untrusted attacker as a legitimate user.
- The authorized public key list is commonly kept on Unix-like systems in the file /.ssh/authorized keys in the user's home directory who has remote login privileges. SSH only respects this file if it cannot be modified by anyone other than the owner and root.
- The password is no longer necessary when both the remote end's public key and the local end's matching private key are present. But a passphrase can be used to lock the private key itself for much more security.
- Additionally, the private key can be in the usual locations, and a command line option can be used to specify its whole path. The public and private keys are always generated in pairs by the SSH-keygen utility.
- SSH further provides automated key generation-encrypted password-based authentication. The attacker in this scenario may impersonate the trustworthy server side, request the password, and gain it (man-in-the-middle attack).
- SSH, however, remembers the key that the server side previously used, therefore this is only feasible if the two sides have never authenticated before. Before accepting the key of a new, previously unidentified server, the SSH client issues a warning. On the server side, password authentication can be turned off.

Uses

SSH is a protocol that can be used for many applications across many platforms including most Unix variants, as well as Microsoft Windows. Some of the applications below may require features that are only available or compatible with specific SSH clients or servers.

For example, using the SSH protocol to implement a VPN is possible, but presently only with the OpenSSH server and client implementation.

- For login to a shell on a remote host (replacing Telnet and rlogin).
- For executing a single command on a remote host (replacing rsh).
- For setting up automatic (password less) login to a remote server (for example, using OpenSSH.

- In combination with rsync to back up, copy and mirror files efficiently and securely.
- For forwarding a port.
- For tunneling (not to be confused with a VPN, which routes packets between different networks, or bridges two broadcast domains into one).
- For using as a full-fledged encrypted VPN. Note that only OpenSSH server and client supports this feature.
- For forwarding X from a remote host (possible through multiple intermediate hosts)
- For browsing the web through an encrypted proxy connection with SSH clients that support the SOCKS protocol.
- For securely mounting a directory on a remote server as a filesystem on a local computer using SSHFS.
- For automated remote monitoring and management of servers through one or more of the mechanisms discussed above.
- For development on a mobile or embedded device that supports SSH.
- For securing file transfer protocols.

File Transfer Protocols The Secure Shell protocols are used in several file transfer mechanisms.

- Secure copy (SCP), which evolved from RCP protocol over SSH
- rsync, intended to be more efficient than SCP. Generally, runs over an SSH connection.
- SSH File Transfer Protocol (SFTP), a secure alternative to FTP (not to be confused with FTP over SSH or FTPS)
- Files transferred over shell protocol (FISH), released in 1998, which evolved from Unix shell commands over SSH
- Fast and Secure Protocol (FASP), aka Aspera, uses SSH for control and UDP ports for data transfer.

Architecture
Three distinct components make up the layered architecture of the SSH protocol:

- The Transmission Control Protocol (TCP) of TCP/IP is commonly used by the transport layer, and port number 22 is set aside as a server listening port. This layer implements encryption, compression, and integrity verification as well as initial key exchange and server authentication. Although each implementation may allow for more, it exposes to the higher layer an interface for transmitting and receiving plaintext packets of up to 32,768 bytes each. Usually after 1 GB of data has been transported or after an hour has passed, whichever comes first, the transport layer arranges for key re-exchange.
- Client authentication is handled by the user authentication layer, which also offers a number of authentication algorithms. Client-driven authentication means that the SSH client, and not the server, may ask the user for a password. Only the client's requests for authentication receive a response from the server. The following user-authentication techniques are frequently used:

- **Password:** a method for straightforward password authentication, including a facility allowing a password to be changed. Not all programs implement this method.
- **Public key:** a method for public-key-based authentication, usually supporting at least DSA, ECDSA or RSA keypairs, with other implementations also supporting X.509 certificates.
- **Keyboard-interactive:** a versatile method where the server sends one or more prompts to enter information and the client displays them and sends back responses keyed-in by the user. Used to provide one-time password authentication such as S/Key or SecurID. Used by some OpenSSH configurations when PAM is the underlying host-authentication provider to effectively provide password authentication, sometimes leading to inability to log in with a client that supports just the plain password authentication method.
- GSSAPI authentication methods which provide an extensible scheme to perform SSH authentication using external mechanisms such as Kerberos 5 or NTLM, providing single sign-on capability to SSH sessions. These methods are usually implemented by commercial SSH implementations for use in organizations, though OpenSSH does have a working GSSAPI implementation.
- The concept of channels, channel requests, and global requests, which describe the SSH services offered, are defined by the connection layer. A single SSH connection can be multiplexed into numerous logical channels that can all transport data in both directions at the same time. Channel requests are used to transmit out-of-band data particular to a given channel, such as the exit code of a server-side process or the size change of a terminal window. Additionally, using the receive window size, each channel controls its own flow. Using a global request, the SSH client asks for a server-side port to be forwarded. Channel types that are common include:
- shell for terminal shells, SFTP and exec requests (including SCP transfers)
- direct-tcpip for client-to-server forwarded connections
- forwarded-tcpip for server-to-client forwarded connections

Public host key fingerprints are made available by the SSHFP DNS record, which helps validate the host's legitimacy.

In addition to serving as a secure shell, SSH may be used for a variety of other applications thanks to its open architecture, which offers a great deal of flexibility. The user-authentication layer is highly extensible with custom authentication methods; the connection layer offers the ability to multiplex many secondary sessions into a single SSH connection, a feature comparable to BEEP and absent from TLS. The functionality of the transport layer alone is comparable to Transport Layer Security (TLS); the user-authentication layer is also comparable to TLS in functionality.

Algorithms
- RSA and DSA for public-key cryptography.
- Diffie–Hellman for key exchange.
- HMAC, AEAD and UMAC for MAC.

- AES for symmetric encryption.
- AES-GCM.
- SHA for key fingerprint.

Vulnerabilities
SSH-1

Due to inadequate data integrity protection provided by the CRC-32 employed in this version of the protocol, a vulnerability in SSH 1.5 that permitted the unauthorized insertion of material into an encrypted SSH stream was described in 1998. Most implementations included a patch called SSH Compensation Attack Detector. A new integer overflow vulnerability was included in many these modified implementations, allowing attackers to run arbitrary code with root capabilities on the SSH daemon. A flaw was found in January 2001 that enables attackers to change the final block of an IDEA-encrypted session. In the same month, a different flaw that allowed a hostile server to pass on a client authentication to another server was found. SSH-1 is now generally regarded as being out of date and should be avoided by explicitly disabling fallback to SSH-2. This is because SSH-1 has intrinsic design problems that render it susceptible. Most current servers and clients are SSH-2 compatible.

CBC Plaintext Recovery

A theoretical flaw was found in all versions of SSH in November 2008 that permitted the recovery of up to 32 bits of plaintext from a block of ciphertext that had been encrypted using the then-current default encryption technique, CBC. The simplest fix is to switch to CTR, counter mode, instead of CBC mode, which makes SSH immune to the attack.

4.8.5   Transport Layer Security (TLS) and its Predecessor Secure Socket Layer (SSL)

The TLS protocol is used by client-server applications to interact over networks in a way that guards against listening in and tampering.

The client must ask the server to establish a TLS connection because apps can communicate with or without TLS (or SSL). Using a separate port number for TLS sessions is one of the key strategies for accomplishing this. While port 443 is frequently used for encrypted HTTPS transmission, port 80 is commonly utilized for unencrypted HTTP traffic. Another method is to use a protocol-specific STARTTLS request to the server, such as when utilizing the mail or news protocols, to switch the connection to TLS.

Once both the client and the server have consented to use TLS, they engage in a handshaking process (see TLS handshake) to negotiate a stateful connection. The protocols create cypher parameters and a session-specific shared key during a handshake with an asymmetric cypher, after which all subsequent communication is encrypted with a symmetric cypher. The client and server agree on several parameters during this handshake that are used to establish the security of the connection:

- When a client requests a secure connection from a TLS-enabled server and offers a list of supported cypher suites, the handshake starts (ciphers and hash functions).
- The server selects an encryption and hash function from this list that it also supports, notifying the client of its choice.
- A digital certificate is typically then provided as identification by the server. The certificate includes the server's name, the trusted certificate authority (CA) that attests to the certificate's authenticity, and the public encryption key for the server.
- Before continuing, the client verifies the certificate's validity.
- The client either: encrypts a random number (Pre-Master-Secret) with the server's public key and sends the result to the server (which only the server should be able to decrypt with its private key); both parties then use the random number to generate a unique session key for further encryption and decryption of data during the session; or uses Diffie-Hellman key exchange (or its variant elliptic-curve DH) to generate the session keys used for the secured connection, which is encrypted and decrypted using the session key until the connection shuts, starts after the handshake is over.

The TLS handshake will fail and the connection will not be established if any of the steps are unsuccessful.

The OSI model and the TCP/IP paradigm's various layers do not all cleanly suit TLS and SSL. TLS is supposedly above the transport layer because it runs "on top of some dependable transport protocol (e.g., TCP)". The presentation layer often performs the role of serving encryption to higher layers. Although applications employing TLS must actively control starting TLS handshakes and managing exchanged authentication certificates, apps often use TLS as if it were a transport layer.

Connections between a client (like a web browser) and a server (like wikipedia. org), when secured by TLS, should have one or more of the following characteristics:

- Because the transmitted data is encrypted using a symmetric-key technique, the connection is private (or secure). Based on a shared secret that was negotiated at the beginning of the session, the keys for this symmetric encryption are produced uniquely for each connection. Before the first byte of data is transferred, the server and client discuss the specifics of which encryption algorithm and cryptographic keys to employ (see below). The negotiation of a shared secret is dependable and secure (the negotiated secret cannot be accessed by an attacker who inserts themselves during the connection or by eavesdroppers) (no attacker can modify the communications during the negotiation without being detected).
- Public-key cryptography allows the communication between parties to be authenticated. For the server, this authentication is necessary; however, for the client, it is not.

- Because every message sent contains a message integrity check utilizing a message authentication code to avoid undetected data loss or alteration during transmission, the connection is dependable.

TLS offers a wide range of techniques for key exchange, data encryption, and message integrity authentication. Because of this, safe TLS configuration involves many customizable parameters, and not all options offer all the privacy-related characteristics listed above.

TLS has undergone multiple revisions to address security threats that have been developed to undermine some features of the communications security that it aims to provide. Web browser creators frequently make changes to their products to guard against potential security flaws that are later found.

Datagram Transport Layer Security
A related communications protocol called Datagram Transport Layer Security, or DTLS for short, gives datagram-based applications security by enabling them to communicate in a way that guards against eavesdropping, tampering, or message forgery. Based on the stream-oriented Transport Layer Security (TLS) protocol, the DTLS protocol aims to offer comparable security assurances. Contrary to TLS, it can be used with many datagram-oriented protocols, such as Secure Real-time Transport Protocol (SRTP), User Datagram Protocol (UDP), Datagram Congestion Control Protocol (DCCP), Control and Provisioning of Wireless Access Points (CAPWAP), and Stream Control Transmission Protocol (SCTP) encapsulation.

The application does not experience the delays brought on by stream protocols because the DTLS protocol datagram preserves the semantics of the underlying transport; however, the application must deal with packet reordering, datagram loss, and data that is larger than the size of a datagram network packet. When used to construct a VPN tunnel, DTLS overcomes the "TCP meltdown problem" by using UDP or SCTP instead of TCP.

Digital Certificates
A digital certificate confirms that the identified subject of the certificate is the owner of a public key and specifies some intended uses for that key. This enables other parties (relying parties) to trust assertions or signatures made by the private key that is associated with the certified public key. Key-stores and trust stores are available in a variety of file extensions, including .pem, .crt, .pfx, and .jks.

To verify the validity of certificates, TLS normally uses a group of reputable third-party certificate authority. Trust is typically rooted in a list of certificates provided with user agent software, and the relying party can alter this list.

Since the start of their poll, Symantec has been the market-leading certificate authority (CA), according to Net-craft, who keeps track of current TLS certificates. As of 2015, according to Net-count, craft's Symantec was responsible for little under one-third of all certificates and 44% of the valid certificates used by the one million busiest websites. Digi-Cert purchased the TLS/SSL division Symantec had previously sold. IdenTrust, DigiCert, and Sectigo are the top 3 certificate authority in terms of market share as of May 2019, according to an updated analysis.

In order to generate, sign, and manage the validity of certificates, as well as to verify the relationship between a certificate and its owner, certificate authorities and a public key infrastructure are required when using X.509 certificates. The 2013 mass surveillance disclosures made it more widely known that certificate authorities are a weak point from a security standpoint, allowing man-in-the-middle attacks (MITM) if the certificate authority cooperates. While this can sometimes be more convenient than verifying the identities via a web of trust (or is compromised).

Algorithms
Key exchange
An encryption key and cypher must be safely exchanged or agreed upon before a client and server may start exchanging information that is secured by TLS.

- Public and private keys generated with RSA (referred to as TLS-RSA in the TLS handshake protocol) are among the methods used for key exchange/agreement.
- Other methods include Diffie-Hellman (TLS-DH), ephemeral Diffie-Hellman (TLS-DHE), elliptic-curve Diffie-Hellman (TLS-ECDH), ephemeral elliptic-curve Diffie-Hell (TLS-SRP).

Because they are susceptible to man-in-the-middle attacks, the TLS-DH-anon and TLS-ECDH-anon key agreement methods are rarely utilized because they do not authenticate the server or the user. Forward secrecy is only provided by TLS-DHE and TLS-ECDHE. The size of the public/private encryption keys used during exchange and agreement differs between public key certificates, which also affects how solid the security is. Because the strength of the TLS encryption is closely correlated with the key size, Google said in July 2013 that it will stop using 1024-bit public keys and would instead convert to 2048-bit keys to strengthen the security of the TLS encryption it offers to its users.

Ciphers
Both stream cipher like – ChaCha20-Poly-1305 and RC4, and block ciphers with mode of operations like – AES-GCM, AES-CCM, AES-CBC, RC2-CBC, etc.

Data Integrity
A message authentication code (MAC) is used for data integrity. HMAC is used for CBC mode of block ciphers. Authenticated encryption (AEAD) such as GCM and CCM mode uses AEAD-integrated MAC and does not use HMAC. HMAC-based PRF, or HKDF is used for TLS handshake.

Note
GCM: Galois/Counter Mode (GCM), which is popular due to its performance, is a mode of operation for symmetric-key cryptographic block cyphers. With minimal hardware resources, GCM throughput rates for modern, high-speed communication channels can be reached. The process uses an authenticated encryption technique to guarantee both the integrity and secrecy of the data. For block cyphers with 128-bit blocks, GCM is defined. An incremental message authentication code can be created using the Galois Message Authentication Code (GMAC), a variation of the

GCM that only allows authentication. The initialization vectors for GCM and GMAC can be of any length.

Even when utilized with the same block cypher, several block cypher modes of operation can exhibit noticeably different performance and efficiency traits. GCM may fully utilize parallel processing, and GCM implementation can utilize an instruction pipeline or a hardware pipeline effectively. The efficiency and performance of the cypher block chaining (CBC) method of operation are hindered by pipeline stalls.

Like in normal counter mode, blocks are numbered sequentially, and then this block number is combined with an initialization vector (IV) and encrypted with a block cipher E, usually AES. The result of this encryption is then XORed with the plaintext to produce the ciphertext. Like all counter modes, this is essentially a stream cipher, and so it is essential that a different IV is used for each stream that is encrypted.

CCM mode: Cryptographic block cyphers can operate in CCM mode, also known as counter with cypher block chaining message authentication code or counter with CBC-MAC. It is a verified encryption algorithm created to offer both confidentiality and authenticity. Only block cyphers with 128-bit blocks are defined for CCM mode. To ensure that a given key is never used more than once, the CCM nonce must be carefully chosen. This is so because counter (CTR) mode, from which CCM is derived, is essentially a stream cypher.

As the name suggests, CCM mode combines counter (CTR) mode for confidentiality with cipher block chaining message authentication code (CBC-MAC) for authentication. These two primitives are applied in an "authenticate-then-encrypt" manner: CBC-MAC is first computed on the message to obtain a message authentication code (MAC), then the message and the MAC are encrypted using counter mode. The main insight is that the same encryption key can be used for both, provided that the counter values used in the encryption do not collide with the (pre-) initialization vector used in the authentication. A proof of security exists for this combination, based on the security of the underlying block cipher. The proof also applies to a generalization of CCM for any block size, and for any size of cryptographically strong pseudo-random function.

4.8.5.1 Applications

In applications design, TLS is usually implemented on top of Transport Layer protocols, encrypting all the protocol-related data of protocols such as HTTP, FTP, SMTP, NNTP and XMPP. Historically, TLS has been used primarily with reliable transport protocols such as the Transmission Control Protocol (TCP). However, it has also been implemented with datagram-oriented transport protocols, such as the User Datagram Protocol (UDP) and the Datagram Congestion Control Protocol (DCCP), usage of which has been standardized independently using the term Datagram Transport Layer Security (DTLS).

Websites

A primary use of TLS is to secure World Wide Web traffic between a website and a web browser encoded with the HTTP protocol. This use of TLS to secure HTTP traffic constitutes the HTTPS protocol.

Web Browser

The latest versions of all major web browsers support TLS 1.0, 1.1, and 1.2, and have them enabled by default. However, not all supported Microsoft operating systems support the latest version of IE. Additionally, many Microsoft operating systems currently support multiple versions of IE, but this has changed according to Microsoft's Internet Explorer Support Lifecycle Policy FAQ, "beginning January 12, 2016, only the most current version of Internet Explorer available for a supported operating system will receive technical support and security updates." The page then goes on to list the latest supported version of IE at date for each operating system. The next critical date would be when an operating system reaches the end-of-life stage. Since June 15, 2022, Internet Explorer 11 dropped support for Windows 10 editions which follow Microsoft's Modern Lifecycle Policy.

Security

Below is a list of significant TLS/SSL attacks.

Renegotiation Attack

A vulnerability of the renegotiation procedure was discovered in August 2009 that can lead to plaintext injection attacks against SSL 3.0 and all current versions of TLS. For example, it allows an attacker who can hijack an https connection to splice their own requests into the beginning of the conversation the client has with the web server. The attacker cannot actually decrypt the client–server communication, so it is different from a typical man-in-the-middle attack. A short-term fix is for web servers to stop allowing renegotiation, which typically will not require other changes unless client certificate authentication is used. To fix the vulnerability, a renegotiation indication extension was proposed for TLS. It will require the client and server to include and verify information about previous handshakes in any renegotiation handshakes.

Downgrade Attacks: FREAK Attack and Logjam Attack

A protocol downgrade attack (also called a version rollback attack) tricks a web server into negotiating connections with previous versions of TLS that have long since been abandoned as insecure.

Previous modifications to the original protocols, like False Start or Snap Start, reportedly introduced limited TLS protocol downgrade attacks, or allowed modifications to the cipher suite list sent by the client to the server. In doing so, an attacker might succeed in influencing the cipher suite selection to downgrade the cipher suite negotiated to use either a weaker symmetric encryption algorithm or a weaker key exchange. Encryption downgrade attacks can force servers and clients to negotiate a connection using cryptographically weak keys. A man-in-the-middle attack called FREAK was discovered affecting the OpenSSL stack, the default Android web

browser, and some Safari browsers. The attack involved tricking servers into negotiating a TLS connection using cryptographically weak 512-bit encryption keys.

Cross-Protocol Attacks: DROWN

The DROWN attack is an exploit that attacks servers supporting contemporary SSL/
TLS protocol suites by exploiting their support for the obsolete, insecure, SSLv2
protocol to leverage an attack on connections using up-to-date protocols that would
otherwise be secure. DROWN exploits a vulnerability in the protocols used and the
configuration of the server, rather than any specific implementation error. Full
details of DROWN were announced in March 2016, together with a patch for the
exploit. At that time, more than 81,000 of the top one million most popular websites
were among the TLS protected websites that were vulnerable to the DROWN attack.

Protocol Details

The TLS protocol exchanges records, which encapsulate the data to be exchanged
in a specific format. Each record can be compressed, padded, appended with a message authentication code (MAC), or encrypted, all depending on the state of the
connection. Each record has a content type field that designates the type of data
encapsulated, a length field and a TLS version field. The data encapsulated may be
control or procedural messages of the TLS itself, or simply the application data
needed to be transferred by TLS. The specifications required to exchange application data by TLS, are agreed upon in the "TLS handshake" between the client
requesting the data and the server responding to requests. The protocol therefore
defines both the structure of payloads transferred in TLS and the procedure to establish and monitor the transfer.

TLS Handshake

When the connection starts, the record encapsulates a "control" protocol – the handshake messaging protocol. This protocol is used to exchange all the information
required by both sides for the exchange of the actual application data by TLS. It
defines the format of messages and the order of their exchange. These may vary
according to the demands of the client and server – i.e., there are several possible
procedures to set up the connection. This initial exchange results in a successful
TLS connection (both parties ready to transfer application data with TLS) or an alert
message.

Basic TLS Handshake

A typical connection example follows, illustrating a handshake where the server
(but not the client) is authenticated by its certificate:
  Negotiation phase:

- A client sends a Client-Hello message specifying the highest TLS protocol version it supports, a random number, a list of suggested cipher suites and suggested
  compression methods. If the client is attempting to perform a resumed handshake, it may send a session ID. If the client can use Application-Layer Protocol
  Negotiation, it may include a list of supported application protocols, such
  as HTTP/2.

- The server responds with a Server-Hello message, containing the chosen proto-col version, a random number, cipher suite and compression method from the choices offered by the client. To confirm or allow resumed handshakes the server may send a session ID. The chosen protocol version should be the highest that both the client and server support. For example, if the client supports TLS version 1.1 and the server supports version 1.2, version 1.1 should be selected; version 1.2 should not be selected.
- The server sends its Certificate message (depending on the selected cipher suite, this may be omitted by the server).
- The server sends its Server-Key-Exchange message (depending on the selected cipher suite, this may be omitted by the server). This message is sent for all DHE, ECDHE and DH-anon cipher suites.
- The server sends a Server-Hello-Done message, indicating it is done with hand-shake negotiation.
- The client responds with a Client-Key-Exchange message, which may contain a Pre-Master-Secret, public key, or nothing. (Again, this depends on the selected cipher.) This Pre-Master-Secret is encrypted using the public key of the server certificate.
- The client and server then use the random numbers and Pre-Master-Secret to compute a common secret, called the "master secret". All other key data (session keys such as IV, symmetric encryption key, MAC key) for this connection is derived from this master secret (and the client- and server-generated random values), which is passed through a carefully designed pseudorandom function.

The client now sends a Change-Cipher-Spec record, essentially telling the server, "Everything I tell you from now on will be authenticated (and encrypted if encryp-tion parameters were present in the server certificate). "The Change-Cipher-Spec is itself a record-level protocol with content type of 20.

- The client sends an authenticated and encrypted Finished message, containing a hash and MAC over the previous handshake messages.
- The server will attempt to decrypt the client's Finished message and verify the hash and MAC. If the decryption or verification fails, the handshake is consid-ered to have failed and the connection should be torn down.

Finally, the server sends a Change-Cipher-Spec, telling the client, "Everything I tell you from now on will be authenticated (and encrypted, if encryption was negotiated)."

- The server sends its authenticated and encrypted Finished message.
- The client performs the same decryption and verification procedure as the server did in the previous step.

Application phase: at this point, the "handshake" is complete and the application protocol is enabled, with content type of 23. Application messages exchanged between client and server will also be authenticated and optionally encrypted exactly like in their Finished message. Otherwise, the content type will return 25 and the client will not authenticate.

Client-Authenticated TLS Handshake

The following full example shows a client being authenticated (in addition to the server as in the example above; see mutual authentication) via TLS using certificates exchanged between both peers.

Negotiation Phase:

- A client sends a Client-Hello message specifying the highest TLS protocol version it supports, a random number, a list of suggested cipher suites and compression methods.
- The server responds with a Server-Hello message, containing the chosen protocol version, a random number, cipher suite and compression method from the choices offered by the client. The server may also send a session id as part of the message to perform a resumed handshake.
- The server sends its Certificate message (depending on the selected cipher suite, this may be omitted by the server).
- The server sends its Server-Key-Exchange message (depending on the selected cipher suite, this may be omitted by the server). This message is sent for all DHE, ECDHE and DH-anon cipher suites.
- The server sends a Certificate-Request message, to request a certificate from the client.
- The server sends a Server-Hello-Done message, indicating it is done with handshake negotiation.
- The client responds with a Certificate message, which contains the client's certificate, but not its private key.
- The client sends a Client-Key-Exchange message, which may contain a Pre-Master-Secret, public key, or nothing. (Again, this depends on the selected cipher.) This Pre-Master-Secret is encrypted using the public key of the server certificate.
- The client sends a Certificate-Verify message, which is a signature over the previous handshake messages using the client's certificate's private key. This signature can be verified by using the client's certificate's public key. This lets the server know that the client has access to the private key of the certificate and thus owns the certificate.
- The client and server then use the random numbers and Pre-Master-Secret to compute a common secret, called the "master secret". All other key data ("session keys") for this connection is derived from this master secret (and the client- and server-generated random values), which is passed through a carefully designed pseudorandom function.

The client now sends a Change-Cipher-Spec record, essentially telling the server, "Everything I tell you from now on will be authenticated (and encrypted if encryption was negotiated). "The Change-Cipher-Spec is itself a record-level protocol and has type 20 and not 22.

- Finally, the client sends an encrypted Finished message, containing a hash and MAC over the previous handshake messages.
- The server will attempt to decrypt the client's Finished message and verify the hash and MAC. If the decryption or verification fails, the handshake is considered to have failed and the connection should be torn down.

Finally, the server sends a Change-Cipher-Spec, telling the client, "Everything I tell you from now on will be authenticated (and encrypted if encryption was negotiated)."

- The server sends its own encrypted Finished message.
- The client performs the same decryption and verification procedure as the server did in the previous step.

Application phase: at this point, the "handshake" is complete and the application protocol is enabled, with content type of 23. Application messages exchanged between client and server will also be encrypted exactly like in their Finished message.

TLS 1.3 Handshake

The TLS 1.3 handshake was condensed to only one round trip compared to the two round trips required in previous versions of TLS/SSL.

First the client sends a client-Hello message to the server that contains a list of supported ciphers in order of the client's preference and makes a guess on what key algorithm will be used so that it can send a secret key to share if needed. By making a guess at what key algorithm will be used, the server eliminates a round trip. After receiving the client-Hello, the server sends a server-Hello with its key, a certificate, the chosen cipher suite, and the finished message. After the client receives the server's finished message, it now is coordinated with the server on which cipher suite to use.

Session IDs

In an ordinary full handshake, the server sends a session id as part of the Server-Hello message. The client associates this session id with the server's IP address and TCP port, so that when the client connects again to that server, it can use the session id to shortcut the handshake. In the server, the session id maps to the cryptographic parameters previously negotiated, specifically the "master secret". Both sides must have the same "master secret" or the resumed handshake will fail (this prevents an eavesdropper from using a session id). The random data in the Client-Hello and Server-Hello messages virtually guarantee that the generated connection keys will be different from in the previous connection. In the RFCs, this type of handshake is called an abbreviated handshake. It is also described in the literature as a restart handshake.

Negotiation phase:

- A client sends a Client-Hello message specifying the highest TLS protocol version it supports, a random number, a list of suggested cipher suites and compression methods. Included in the message is the session id from the previous TLS connection.

- The server responds with a Server-Hello message, containing the chosen protocol version, a random number, cipher suite and compression method from the choices offered by the client. If the server recognizes the session id sent by the client, it responds with the same session id. The client uses this to recognize that a resumed handshake is being performed. If the server does not recognize the session id sent by the client, it sends a different value for its session id. This tells the client that a resumed handshake will not be performed. At this point, both the client and server have the "master secret" and random data to generate the key data to be used for this connection.

The server now sends a Change-Cipher-Spec record, essentially telling the client, "Everything I tell you from now on will be encrypted." The Change-Cipher-Spec is itself a record-level protocol and has type 20 and not 22.

- Finally, the server sends an encrypted Finished message, containing a hash and MAC over the previous handshake messages.
- The client will attempt to decrypt the server's Finished message and verify the hash and MAC. If the decryption or verification fails, the handshake is considered to have failed and the connection should be torn down.

Finally, the client sends a Change-Cipher-Spec, telling the server, "Everything I tell you from now on will be encrypted."

- The client sends its own encrypted Finished message.
- The server performs the same decryption and verification procedure as the client did in the previous step.

Application phase: at this point, the "handshake" is complete and the application protocol is enabled, with content type of 23. Application messages exchanged between client and server will also be encrypted exactly like in their Finished message.

Session Tickets
RFC 5077 extends TLS via use of session tickets, instead of session IDs. It defines a way to resume a TLS session without requiring that session-specific state is stored at the TLS server.

When using session tickets, the TLS server stores its session-specific state in a session ticket and sends the session ticket to the TLS client for storing. The client resumes a TLS session by sending the session ticket to the server, and the server resumes the TLS session according to the session-specific state in the ticket. The session ticket is encrypted and authenticated by the server, and the server verifies its validity before using its contents.

Bibliography

1. Stallings, William. *Cryptography and network security, 4/E*. Pearson Education India, 2006.
2. Karate, Atul. *Cryptography and network security*. Tata McGraw-Hill Education, 2013.
3. Frozen, Behrouz A., and Debdeep Mukhopadhyay. *Cryptography and network security*. Vol. 12. New York, NY, USA: McGraw Hill Education (India) Private Limited, 2015.
4. Easttom, C. (2015). Modern cryptography. *Applied mathematics for encryption and information security. McGraw-Hill Publishing.*
5. Katz, J., & Lindell, Y. (2020). *Introduction to modern cryptography*. CRC press.
6. Bellare, M., & Rogaway, P. (2005). Introduction to modern cryptography. *Ucsd Cse, 207*, 207.
7. Zheng, Z. (2022). Modern Cryptography Volume 1: A Classical Introduction to Informational and Mathematical Principle.
8. Shemanske, T. R. (2017). *Modern Cryptography and Elliptic Curves* (Vol. 83). American Mathematical Soc..
9. Bhat, Bawna, Abdul Wahid Ali, and Apurva Gupta. "DES and AES performance evaluation." *International Conference on Computing, Communication & Automation*. IEEE, 2015.
10. Rihan, Shaza D., Ahmed Khalid, and Saife Eldin F. Osman. "A performance comparison of encryption algorithms AES and DES." *International Journal of Engineering Research & Technology (IJERT)* 4.12 (2015): 151-154.
11. Mahajan, Prerna, and Abhishek Sachdeva. "A study of encryption algorithms AES, DES and RSA for security." *Global Journal of Computer Science and Technology* (2013).
12. Mao, Wenbo. *Modern cryptography: theory and practice*. Pearson Education India, 2003.
13. B Rajkumar "Vulnerability Analysis and Defense Against Attacks: Implications of Trust – Based Cross – Layer Security Protocol for Mobile Adhoc Networks "presented at the International" Conference on IT FWP 09, Andhra Pradesh, India. in 2009.
14. B Rajkumar, G Arunakranthi, "Implementation and Mitigation for Cyber Attacks with proposed OCR Process Model" in Int.J. of Natural Volatiles & Essential Oils, 2021; vol.8(5): 2149-2160.
15. Daemen, J., & Rijmen, V. (1999). AES proposal: Rijndael.
16. Zodpe, H., & Shaikh, A. (2021). A Survey on Various Cryptanalytic Attacks on the AES Algorithm. *International Journal of Next-Generation Computing*, 115-123.
17. Sharma, N. (2017). A Review of Information Security using Cryptography Technique. *International Journal of Advanced Research in Computer Science*, 8(4).
18. Gupta, A., & Walia, N. K. (2014). Cryptography Algorithms: a review.
19. Amalraj, A. J., & Jose, J. J. R. (2016). A survey paper on cryptography techniques. *International Journal of Computer Science and mobile computing*, 5(8), 55-59.
20. Pachghare, V. K. (2019). *Cryptography and information security*. PHI Learning Pvt. Ltd.
21. Koblitz, N., Menezes, A., & Vanstone, S. (2000). The state of elliptic curve cryptography. *Designs, codes and cryptography*, 19(2), 173-193.
22. Hankerson, D., Menezes, A. J., & Vanstone, S. (2006). *Guide to elliptic curve cryptography*. Springer Science & Business Media.
23. Kapoor, V., Abraham, V. S., & Singh, R. (2008). Elliptic curve cryptography. *Ubiquity, 2008*(May), 1-8.
24. Amara, M., & Siad, A. (2011, May). Elliptic curve cryptography and its applications. In *International workshop on systems, signal processing and their applications, WOSSPA* (pp. 247-250). IEEE.
25. Cilardo, A., Coppolino, L., Mazzocca, N., & Romano, L. (2006). Elliptic curve cryptography engineering. *Proceedings of the IEEE*, 94(2), 395-406.

Chapter 5
Modern Cryptanalysis Methods, Advanced Network Attacks and Cloud Security

5.1 Overview

Combining the two words "cryptogram" and "analysis," we get "cryptanalysis." The term "cryptogram" refers to a figure or representation with a hidden meaning used in cipher or code communication. A direct evaluation of the cryptosystem being used is a common component of cryptanalysis, which is essentially an advanced, focused mathematical attempt at decryption using knowledge of the encryption scheme that is already known. They can use information (encrypted or original) that is known to be used adaptively in later trials, as well as intercepted entire, partial, likely, or similar original messages (plaintext) and encrypted messages that have been decrypted. Mainly there are two types of cryptanalysis systems:

1. Linear Cryptanalysis
2. Differential Cryptanalysis

Any action taken to maintain the integrity and usefulness of your network and data is considered network security. It employs a combination of hardware and software technologies, focuses on a range of threats, prevents them from getting into or spreading throughout your network, and offers effective security access to the network. The prevention and security of network devices and software rely on cryptographic algorithms.

Online IP, services, applications, and other data are protected from cyberthreats and malicious behavior using a variety of technologies, policies, and apps called "cloud security." The cloud security maximally relies on asymmetric encryption mechanism.

Technology based on blockchain is significant because of what it promises to achieve: global trust. The distributed ledger of a blockchain is a centralized, automated means to record transactions or events in a way that is transparent and unchangeable. It is a beautiful method that does away with the complicated intermediates that so many of the trust mechanisms of today rely on. A blockchain network secures data using two different levels of cryptography. The key-encryption technique is one, while hashing is another.

It clear that network security, cloud security and blockchain incorporates phenomenon of modern cryptography. Thus, network security, cloud security and blockchain also covered in this chapter.

5.1.1   Cryptanalysis

The two components of cryptology are **cryptanalysis**, which is the study of the cryptographic technique, and cryptography, which focuses on constructing secret codes.

Cryptanalysis is the science of attempting to "**break the system**," or to obtain the message **M** directly from the cypher text **C**, by first obtaining the key. An attack is a failed attempt at cryptanalysis. A **brute-force attack** is one that tries every key that might be used. This requires testing only approximately half of the key-space. All potential communications (i.e., plain texts), cypher texts, and keys make up a cryptosystem, along with the encryption and decryption algorithms. The term "**Kerchoff's principle**" refers to a basic, if speculative, cryptographic notion. It states that the key alone must determine a cryptosystem's security. In other words, it is necessary to assume that any potential intrusion or **eavesdropper** is fully aware of the cryptosystem and how it is implemented when evaluating the security of a cryptosystem.

We can summarize the encryption procedure in the following equation:

$$d\left(e\left(M\right)\right) = M$$

says that we get the original message **M** back, if we first encrypt the message **M** and then decrypt the encrypted message, where **e** is the encryption transformation which scrambles the message **M** to give the cipher text **C**, so that **e(M) = C**. Further, **d** is the decryption algorithm, so that **d(C) = d(e(M)) = M**. An important mathematical consequence of above notation is:

$$e\left(d\left(M\right)\right) = M$$

In above case the order is reversed. In other words, if we first perform the decryption algorithm on the message itself and then perform the encryption algorithm on the result, we also end up with the message **M**. We are tacitly assuming here that the message set equals the set of cipher texts, i.e., **e** and **d** are defined on the same set.

5.2   Types of Cryptanalysis Systems

The two main types of cryptanalyses are:

Linear Cryptanalysis: In order to decipher how a cypher operates in cryptography, linear cryptanalysis seeks to find affine approximations to that action. Attacks have been made against both block cyphers and stream cyphers. One of the two most frequent attacks against block cyphers is linear cryptanalysis, with differential cryptanalysis coming in a close second.

Differential Cryptanalysis: A type of cryptanalysis known as differential cryptanalysis can be used to break both block and stream cyphers as well as cryptographic hash functions. It is the study of how variations in information intake may affect the subsequent difference at the output, taken in its broadest sense. In the context of a block cypher, it alludes to a set of techniques for spotting differences in a web of transformations, identifying instances in which the cypher exhibits non-random behavior, and exploiting those characteristics to discover the secret key (cryptography key).

5.2.1   Linear Cryptanalysis

A general type of cryptanalysis used in cryptography; linear cryptanalysis seeks affine approximations to a cipher's operation. For both block cyphers and stream cyphers, attacks have been created. One of the two most common attacks against block cyphers is linear cryptanalysis, with differential cryptanalysis coming in second.

Linear cryptanalysis consists of two steps:

The **first step** is to create linear equations between plaintext, ciphertext, and key bits that have a high bias, or whose probabilities of holding (across the space of all possible values of their variables) are as close to **0** or **1**.

The **second step** is to derive key bits using these linear equations along with well-known plaintext-ciphertext combinations.

Step 1: Constructing Linear Eqs

A linear equation expresses the equality of two expressions that combine binary variables with the exclusive-or (XOR) operation for the purposes of linear cryptanalysis. As an illustration, the XOR sum of the first and third plaintext bits (as in a block cipher's block) and the first ciphertext bit are equal to the second bit of the key in the following equation from a hypothetical cypher:

$$P_1 \oplus P_2 \oplus C_1 = K_2$$

Any linear equation linking the plaintext, ciphertext, and key bits would hold with probability 1/2 in a perfect cypher. The equations used in linear cryptanalysis will have different probabilities, hence it is more accurate to call them linear approximations.

Each cypher has a unique process for creating approximations. Analysis of the simplest type of block cypher, a substitution-permutation network, is primarily focused on the S-boxes, the encryption's lone nonlinear component (i.e., the operation of an S-box cannot be encoded in a linear equation). It is possible to list every conceivable linear equation connecting an S-input boxes and output bits, calculate their biases, and select the best ones for small enough S-boxes. The remaining operations of the cypher, such as key mixing and permutation, must then be added to the linear approximations for S-boxes to produce linear approximations for the full cypher. This combining step benefits from the usage of the piling-up lemma. Additionally, there are methods for iteratively enhancing linear approximations.

Step 2: Deriving Key Bits
After obtaining an approximate linear representation of the form:

$$P_{i1} \oplus P_{i2} \oplus \ldots \oplus C_{j1} \oplus C_{j2} \oplus \ldots = K_{k1} \oplus K_{k2} \oplus \ldots$$

The values of the key bits used in the approximation can then be determined by applying a simple method to known plaintext-ciphertext combinations.

Count how many times the approximation holds true over all of the known plaintext-ciphertext combinations for each set of values of the key bits on the right-hand side (referred to as a partial key); label this count T. The set of values for those key bits that is considered to be the most likely is the partial key whose T has the largest absolute deviation from half the number of plaintext-ciphertext pairs. This is so that the approximation will hold with a strong bias, as it is presumable that the proper partial key will produce. Instead of the actual probability's magnitude, the magnitude of the bias is important in this situation.

When there are no longer many unknown key bits, brute force can be used to attack them. This technique can be repeated with further linear approximations to acquire guesses at the values of key bits.

Lemma 1: Piling-up Lemma
The piling-up lemma is a notion in cryptanalysis that is applied to linear cryptanalysis to create linear approximations to block cipher behavior. It was first presented as a tool for linear cryptanalysis by Mitsuru Matsui. The lemma asserts that the sum of the input biases determines the bias (deviation of the anticipated value from 1/2) of a linear Boolean function (XOR-clause) of independent binary random variables:

$$\epsilon(X1 \oplus X2 \oplus \ldots \oplus Xn) = 2^{n-1} \prod_{(i=1)}^{n} \epsilon(Xi)?,$$ For n independent, random binary

variables, X1, X2, …Xn.
    or

$$I(X1 \oplus X2 \oplus \ldots \oplus Xn) = \prod_{i=1}^{n} I(Xi)$$

Where $\epsilon \in [-1/2, 1/2]$ is bias and $\mathbf{I} \in [-1, 1]$ is the imbalance.

The lemma states that the bias is always reduced (or at least is not increased) when independent binary variables are XORed; additionally, the output is unbiased if and only if there is at least one unbiased input variable.

5.2.2   Differential Cryptanalysis

Differential cryptanalysis is a general type of cryptanalysis that can be used to decrypt data using cryptographic hash functions, stream cyphers, and block cyphers. It is, in the broadest sense, the study of how variations in information input might influence the final difference. In the context of a block cypher, it alludes to a collection of methods for identifying variances throughout the network of transformations, identifying instances in which the cypher displays non-random behavior, and taking use of these characteristics to uncover the secret key.

Differential cryptanalysis is frequently a chosen plaintext attack, which necessitates the attacker's ability to acquire ciphertexts for a particular selection of plaintexts. Extensions do exist, though, that could be used to launch a known plaintext or even ciphertext-only attack. The fundamental approach makes use of plaintext pairings connected by a fixed difference.

There are other techniques to define difference, but the most common one is the exclusive OR (XOR) operation. To identify statistical trends in their distribution, the attacker then computes the differences of the related ciphertexts. A differential is the resultant pair of differences.

The type of S-boxes used for encryption determines their statistical characteristics, so the attacker analyses differentials (Δ_x, Δ_y),

$$\Delta_y = S(x \oplus \Delta_x) \oplus S(x)$$

One specific ciphertext difference is anticipated to occur frequently in the basic attack. The cipher can be recognized from random in this way. The key can be located more quickly than with a thorough search thanks to more complex variations.

The simplest method of recovering a key by differential cryptanalysis involves an attacker requesting the ciphertexts for a large number of plaintext pairs, then assuming that the differential will hold for at least r 1 rounds, where r is the total number of rounds. After assuming that the difference between the blocks prior to the final round is fixed, the attacker determines which round keys (for the final round) are feasible. This can be accomplished when round keys are few by merely thoroughly decrypting the ciphertext pairs once with each potential round key. One round key is taken to be the right round key if it has been identified as a prospective round key a lot more often than any other key.

The input difference for each given cypher must be properly chosen for the attack to succeed. An internal study of the algorithm is performed; the conventional approach is to identify a differential feature, which is a path of very likely differences through the various phases of encryption. Differential cryptanalysis has been a primary worry for cypher designers since it became widely known.

The Advanced Encryption Standard is one algorithm that has been shown to be secure against the attack, and new designs are anticipated to be accompanied with proof that the algorithm is resistant to this attack.

I. Higher-order Differential Cryptanalysis

Higher-order differential cryptanalysis, a technique used to attack block cyphers, is a generalization of differential cryptanalysis in the field of cryptography. Higher-order differential cryptanalysis examines the propagation of a set of differences between a broader group of texts as opposed to normal differential cryptanalysis, which uses the difference between just two texts. Notably, the KN-Cipher, which had previously been shown to be resistant to normal differential cryptanalysis, has been broken using higher-order differential cryptanalysis.

In the field of cryptography, Kaisa Nyberg and Lars Knudsen developed the encryption algorithm known as KN-Cipher in 1995. The KN-Cipher, one of the earliest cyphers made to be provably secure against simple differential cryptanalysis, was later broken by higher order differential cryptanalysis.

II. Truncated Differential Cryptanalysis

Truncated differential cryptanalysis is a generalization of differential cryptanalysis, a block cypher attack, in the field of cryptography. In 1994, Lars Knudsen invented the method. The whole difference between two texts is analyzed by standard differential cryptanalysis, whereas the partial difference is considered by the abbreviated variant. In other words, the attack does not predict the entire block, just some of the bits. This functioned in several stream cyphers and block cyphers.

III. Impossible Differential Cryptanalysis

A type of differential cryptanalysis for block cyphers in cryptography is known as impossible differential cryptanalysis. A difference that is impossible (with probability 0) at some intermediate state of the cypher algorithm is exploited by impossible differential cryptanalysis, which tracks differences that propagate through the cypher with a probability greater than predicted.

5.3   Difference Between Linear and Differential Cryptanalysis

- In 1992, Matsui and Yamagishi essentially devised linear cryptanalysis. Eli Biham and Adi Shamir originally outlined differential cryptanalysis in 1990.
- A single bit is always used in linear cryptanalysis (one bit at a time). Multiple bits can be analyzed simultaneously using differential cryptanalysis.

- The ciphertext attack is a significant drawback for linear cryptanalysis. Plain text assault is a very significant disadvantage in the context of differential cryptanalysis.
- Linear cryptanalysis can be used to quickly determine the linear relationship between some plaintext, ciphertext, and unknown key bits. Differential cryptanalysis is used to uncover information about some crucial bits, obviating the necessity for a thorough search.
- Input attribute subsets refer to the internal organization of a single input. Since the input qualities differ, the underlying structure of each individual input is irrelevant in this situation.
- The cryptanalyst uses all the available subkeys to decrypt each ciphertext, then examines the intermediate ciphertext to find the random result for one encryption cycle. Cryptanalyst examines the changes in the obtained intermediate ciphertext following numerous encryption rounds. Differential linear cryptanalysis is the process of combining attacks.

5.4   Types of Cryptanalytic Attacks

(i) **Known-Plaintext Analysis (KPA)**

   In this type of attack, some plaintext-ciphertext pairs are already known. Attacker maps them in order to find the encryption key. This attack is easier to use as a lot of information is already available.

(ii) **Chosen-Plaintext Analysis (CPA)**

   In this type of attack, the attacker chooses random plaintexts and obtains the corresponding ciphertexts and tries to find the encryption key. It's very simple to implement like KPA but the success rate is quite low.

(iii) **Ciphertext-Only Analysis (COA)**

   In this type of attack, only some cipher-text is known and the attacker tries to find the corresponding encryption key and plaintext. It's the hardest to implement but is the most probable attack as only ciphertext is required.

(iv) **Adaptive Chosen-Plaintext Analysis (ACPA)**

   This attack is similar CPA. Here, the attacker requests the cipher texts of additional plaintexts after they have ciphertexts for some texts.

(i) **Known Plaintext Attack**

The known-plaintext attack (KPA) or crib is an attack model for cryptanalysis where the attacker has samples of both the plaintext and its encrypted version (ciphertext), and is at liberty to make use of them to reveal further secret information such as secret keys and code books. The term "crib" originated at Bletchley Park, the British World War II decryption operation.

History

The usage "**crib**" was adapted from a slang term referring to cheating—thus, "**I cribbed my answer from your test paper.**" A "**crib**" originally was a literal or interlinear translation of a foreign-language text—usually a Latin or Greek text—that students might be assigned to translate from the original language. The idea behind a crib is that cryptologists were looking at **incomprehensible ciphertext**, but if they had a clue about some word or phrase that might be expected to be in the ciphertext, they would have a **"wedge"**—a test to break into it. If their otherwise random attacks on the cipher managed to sometimes produce those words or (preferably) phrases, they would know they might be on the right track. When those words or phrases appeared, they would feed the settings they had used to reveal them back into the whole encrypted message, to good effect.

In the case of **Enigma**, the German High Command was very meticulous about the overall security of the Enigma system, but nonetheless understood the possible problem of cribs. The day-to-day trench operators, on the other hand, were less careful. The **Bletchley Park** team would guess some of the plaintext based upon when the message was sent. For instance, a daily weather report was transmitted by the Germans, at the same time every day.

Due to the regimented style of military reports, it would contain the word "**Wetter**" (German for "weather") at the same location in every message, and knowing the local weather conditions helped Bletchley Park guess other parts of the plaintext as well. For example, an officer in the Africa Corps helped greatly by constantly sending: "**Nothing to report**." Other operators too would send standard salutations or introductions. Standardized weather reports were also particularly helpful.

At **Bletchley Park in World War II**, strenuous efforts were made to use and even force the Germans to produce messages with known plaintext; schemes to force the Germans to produce them were called "**gardening**".

For example, when cribs were lacking, Bletchley Park would sometimes ask the Royal Air Force to "seed" a particular area in the North Sea with mines (a process that came to be known as gardening, by obvious reference). The Enigma messages that were shortly sent out would most likely contain the name of the area, or the harbour threatened by the mines. When a captured German revealed under interrogation that Enigma operators had been instructed to encode numbers by spelling them out, **Alan Turing** reviewed decrypted messages, and determined that the number "eins" ("1") appeared in 90% of messages.

He automated the crib process, creating the Eins Catalogue, which assumed that "eins" was encoded at all positions in the plaintext. The catalogue included every possible position of the various rotors, starting positions, and key settings of the Enigma. The Polish Cipher Bureau had likewise exploited "**cribs**" in the "**ANX method**" before World War II. Classical ciphers are typically vulnerable to known-plaintext attack.

For example, a **Caesar cipher** can be solved using a single letter of corresponding plaintext and ciphertext to decrypt entirely. A general monoalphabetic substitution cipher needs several character pairs and some guessing if there are fewer than 26 distinct pairs.

Present Day

Modern ciphers such as **Advanced Encryption Standard** are not susceptible to known-plaintext attacks. Encrypted file archives such as ZIP are prone to this attack.

For example, an attacker with an encrypted ZIP file needs only one unencrypted file from the archive which forms the "**known-plaintext**". Then using some publicly available software they can quickly calculate the key required to decrypt the entire archive. To obtain this unencrypted file the attacker could search the website for a suitable file, find it from another archive they can open, or manually try to reconstruct a plaintext file armed with the knowledge of the filename from the encrypted archive.

(ii) **Chosen-Plaintext Analysis (CPA)**

A **chosen-plaintext attack** (CPA) is an attack model for **cryptanalysis** which presumes that the attacker has the capability to choose arbitrary plaintexts to be encrypted and obtain the corresponding ciphertexts. The goal of the attack is to gain some further information which reduces the security of the encryption scheme. In the worst case, a chosen-plaintext attack could reveal the scheme's secret key.

This appears, at first glance, to be an unrealistic model; it would certainly be unlikely that an attacker could persuade a human cryptographer to encrypt large amounts of plaintexts of the attacker's choosing. Modern cryptography, on the other hand, is implemented in software or hardware and is used for a diverse range of applications; for many cases, a chosen-plaintext attack is often very feasible. Chosen-plaintext attacks become extremely important in the context of public key cryptography, where the encryption key is public and attackers can encrypt any plaintext, they choose.

Any cipher that can prevent **chosen-plaintext** attacks is then also guaranteed to be secure **against known-plaintext and ciphertext-only attacks**; this is a conservative approach to security.

Two forms of chosen-plaintext attack can be distinguished:

- **Batch chosen-plaintext attack**, where the cryptanalyst chooses all plaintexts before any of them are encrypted. This is often the meaning of an unqualified use of "chosen-plaintext attack".
- **Adaptive chosen-plaintext attack**, where the cryptanalyst makes a series of interactive queries, choosing subsequent plaintexts based on the information from the previous encryptions.

Non-randomized (deterministic) public key encryption algorithms are vulnerable to simple "**dictionary**"-type attacks, where the attacker builds a table of likely messages and their corresponding ciphertexts. To find the decryption of some observed ciphertext, the attacker simply looks the ciphertext up in the table. As a result, public-key definitions of security under chosen-plaintext attack require **probabilistic encryption** (i.e., randomized encryption). **Conventional symmetric ciphers**, in which the same key is used to encrypt and decrypt a text, may also be vulnerable to other forms of chosen-plaintext attack, for example, differential cryptanalysis of block ciphers.

A technique termed **Gardening** was used by Allied codebreakers in World War II who were solving messages encrypted on the **Enigma machine**. Gardening can be viewed as a chosen-plaintext attack.

(iii) Ciphertext-Only Attack (COA)

In cryptography, a **ciphertext-only attack (COA)** or known ciphertext attack is an attack model for cryptanalysis where the attacker is assumed to have access only to a set of ciphertexts.

The attack is completely successful if the corresponding plaintexts can be deduced, or even better, the key. The ability to obtain any information at all about the underlying plaintext is still considered a success. **For example**, if an adversary is sending ciphertext continuously to maintain traffic-flow security, it would be very useful to be able to distinguish real messages from nulls. Even making an informed guess of the existence of real messages would facilitate traffic analysis.

In the history of cryptography, early ciphers, implemented using pen-and-paper, were routinely broken using ciphertexts alone. Cryptographers developed statistical techniques for attacking ciphertext, such as frequency analysis. Mechanical encryption devices such as Enigma made these attacks much more difficult (although, historically, Polish cryptographers were able to mount a successful ciphertext-only cryptanalysis of the Enigma by exploiting an insecure protocol for indicating the message settings).

Every modern cipher attempt to provide protection against ciphertext-only attacks. The vetting process for a new cipher design standard usually takes many years and includes exhaustive testing of large quantities of ciphertext for any statistical departure from random noise.

See: Advanced Encryption Standard process. Also, the field of steganography evolved, in part, to develop methods like mimic functions that allow one piece of data to adopt the statistical profile of another. Nonetheless poor cipher usage or reliance on home-grown proprietary algorithms that have not been subject to thorough scrutiny has resulted in many computer-age encryption systems that are still subject to ciphertext-only attack. Examples include:

- Early versions of Microsoft's PPTP virtual private network software used the same RC4 key for the sender and the receiver (later versions had other problems). In any case where a stream cipher like RC4 is used twice with the same key it is open to ciphertext-only attack. See: stream cipher attack.
- Wired Equivalent Privacy (WEP), the first security protocol for Wi-Fi, proved vulnerable to several attacks, most of them ciphertext-only.
- Some modern cipher designs have later been shown to be vulnerable to ciphertext-only attacks.
- **For example**, Akelarre. A cipher whose key space is too small is subject to brute force attack with access to nothing but ciphertext by simply trying all possible keys. All that is needed is some way to distinguish valid plaintext from random noise, which is easily done for natural.

Languages when the ciphertext is longer than the unicity distance. One example is DES, which only has 56-bit keys. All too common current examples are commercial security products that derive keys for otherwise impregnable ciphers like AES from a user-selected password. Since users rarely employ passwords with anything close to the entropy of the cipher's key space, such systems are often quite easy to break in practice using only ciphertext.

(iv) **Adaptive Chosen-Plaintext Analysis (ACPA)**

A (full) adaptive chosen-ciphertext attack is an attack in which ciphertexts may be chosen adaptively before and after a challenge ciphertext is given to the attacker, with only the stipulation that the challenge ciphertext may not itself be queried. This is a stronger attack notion than the lunchtime attack, and is commonly referred to as a CCA2 attack, as compared to a CCA1 (lunchtime) attack. Few practical attacks are of this form. Rather, this model is important for its use in proofs of security against chosen-ciphertext attacks. A proof that attacks in this model are impossible implies that any realistic chosen-ciphertext attack cannot be performed.

A practical adaptive chosen-ciphertext attack is the Bleichenbacher attack against PKCS#1.

Cryptosystems proven secure against adaptive chosen-ciphertext attacks include the Cramer-Shoup system and RSA-OAEP. An adaptive chosen-ciphertext attack (abbreviated as CCA2) is an interactive form of chosen-ciphertext attack in which an attacker sends a number of ciphertexts to be decrypted, then uses the results of these decryptions to select subsequent ciphertexts. It is to be distinguished from an indifferent chosen-ciphertext attack (CCA1).

The goal of this attack is to gradually reveal information about an encrypted message, or about the decryption key itself. For public-key systems, adaptive-chosen-ciphertexts are generally applicable only when they have the property of ciphertext malleability—that is, a ciphertext can be modified in specific ways that will have a predictable effect on the decryption of that message.

Practical Attacks
Adaptive-chosen-ciphertext attacks were largely considered to be a theoretical concern until 1998, when Daniel Bleichenbacher of Bell Laboratories demonstrated a practical attack against systems using RSA encryption in concert with the PKCS#1 v1 encoding function, including a version of the Secure Socket Layer (SSL) protocol used by thousands of web servers at the time. The Bleichenbacher attacks took advantage of flaws within the PKCS #1 function to gradually reveal the content of an RSA encrypted message. Doing this requires sending several million test ciphertexts to the decryption device (e.g., SSL-equipped web server.) In practical terms, this means that an SSL session key can be exposed in a reasonable amount of time, perhaps a day or less.

Preventing Attacks
In order to prevent adaptive-chosen-ciphertext attacks, it is necessary to use an encryption or encoding scheme that limits ciphertext malleability. A number of encoding schemes have been proposed; the most common standard for RSA

encryption is Optimal Asymmetric Encryption Padding (OAEP). Unlike ad-hoc schemes such as the padding used in the early versions of PKCS#1, OAEP has been proven secure in the random oracle model. OAEP was incorporated into PKCS#1 as of version 2.0 published in 1998 as the now-recommended encoding scheme, with the older scheme still supported but not recommended for new applications.

5.5   Network Security: Common and Advanced Network Attacks

Any action intended to safeguard your network's usability and data integrity is considered a form of network security.

- Both hardware and software technologies are included.
- It takes aim at several hazards.
- It prevents them from getting on your network or spreading there.
- Access to the network is controlled by effective network security.

Network security comprises numerous levels of protection both inside the network and at the edge. Policies and controls are implemented by each network security layer. Access to network resources is granted to authorized users, but malicious actors are prevented from posing threats and vulnerabilities.

Digitization has changed the way we live. Living, working, playing, and learning have all altered. Every company must safeguard its network if it hopes to provide the services that both consumers and employee's demand. Additionally, network security enables you to defend against threats to confidential data. In the end, it safeguards your reputation.

In this section we are going to discuss the security measures of network. And we also discuss following common and advanced network attacks:

1. Reconnaissance Attacks
2. Access Attacks
3. Social Engineering Attacks
4. DoS and DDoS Attacks
5. Common IPv4 and IPv6 Attacks
6. TCP and UDP Vulnerabilities
7. IP Services
8. DNS attacks

Security Measures for Networks
Firewalls

Your trustworthy internal network and shady external networks, like the Internet, are separated by firewalls. To permit or prohibit traffic, they employ a set of predetermined regulations. A firewall may be composed of both software and hardware.

Cisco provides threat-focused next-generation firewalls and unified threat management (UTM) devices.

Email Security

The main threat to a security compromise comes from email gateways. Attackers create complex phishing campaigns to trick recipients and direct them to malicious websites using personal information and social engineering techniques. To stop the loss of critical information, an email security solution regulates outbound communications and inhibits incoming threats.

Anti-virus and Anti-malware Software

Viruses, worms, Trojan horses, ransomware, and spyware are all examples of "malware," which is short for "malicious software." Malware can sometimes infect a network and then remain inactive for days or even weeks. The finest antimalware applications continually monitor files after they have been opened to detect anomalies, eliminate malware, and repair damage in addition to scanning for malware at the point of entry.

Network Segmentation

Network traffic is divided into multiple categories by software-defined segmentation, which also makes applying security controls simpler. The classifications should ideally be based on endpoint identity rather than just IP addresses. In order to ensure that the appropriate degree of access is granted to the proper people and that suspicious devices are contained and remedied, access permissions can be assigned based on role, location, and other factors.

Access Control

Your network should not be accessible to every user. You must be able to identify each person and each device in order to keep out possible attackers. You can then put your security policies into effect. Non-compliant endpoint devices can be blocked or given restricted access. This process is network access control (NAC).

Application Security

Regardless of whether your IT team created it or you purchased it, all software you use to run your business needs to be secured. Sadly, any application may have flaws or vulnerabilities that hackers could use to get access to your network. Application security includes the tools, programs, and procedures you employ to plug those gaps.

Behavioral analytics

You must be familiar with typical network behavior in order to spot anomalous behavior. Tools for behavioral analytics automatically identify actions that differ from the usual. As a result, your security team will be better able to spot possible trouble indicators of compromise and promptly eliminate risks.

Data loss prevention

Businesses must take precautions to prevent employees from sending private information outside of the network. Data loss prevention solutions, often known as DLP, can prevent people from unsafely uploading, sending, or even printing sensitive information.

Intrusion prevention systems

In order to actively stop attacks, an intrusion prevention system (IPS) monitors network traffic. In order to avoid outbreaks and reinfection, Cisco Next-Generation IPS (NGIPS) appliances combine vast amounts of global threat intelligence to trace the movement of questionable files and malware across the network as well as block harmful behavior.

Mobile device security

Mobile apps and gadgets are increasingly being targeted by cybercriminals. 90% of IT businesses may support corporate applications on personal mobile devices during the next 3 years. You must, of course, regulate which devices have access to your network. Additionally, you will have to set up their connections to protect the privacy of network traffic.

Security information and event management

The information that your security staff needs to recognize risks and take appropriate action is collected by SIEM systems. These goods are available as server software, physical and virtual appliances, and other formats.

VPN

The link between an endpoint and a network, frequently through the Internet, is encrypted using a virtual private network. A remote-access VPN often employs Secure Sockets Layer or IPsec to authenticate communication between the device and the network.

Web Security

Your staff's internet usage can be managed by a web security solution, which can also limit online dangers and prevent access to dangerous websites. It will safeguard your on-site or cloud-based web gateway. The measures you take to safeguard your own website are frequently referred to as "web security."

Wireless-security

Compared to wired networks, wireless ones are less secure. Adding a wireless LAN without taking strict security precautions can be equivalent to installing Ethernet connections all over the place, including in the parking lot. You need products made expressly to safeguard wireless networks if you want to stop an attack from spreading.

Network Level Encryption

You can establish secure communications via unsecure routes thanks to encryption. Privacy and authentication are two helpful guarantees that are provided by network traffic encryption. It goes without saying that encryption protects your data from being accessed by unauthorized parties when it is transferred over an unsecured network and decrypted at the receiving end. Although less noticeable, authentication is very beneficial. In essence, if the receiving end can correctly decode the data, it may be certain that the data truly came from the sending end. Why? since only the transmitting end was capable to correctly encrypting the data. Naturally, all of this is predicated on the secret keys being kept that way; someone who has your keys can compromise both your authentication and privacy.

At What Level Do You Encrypt?
The most frequent levels of encryption on the Internet are those at the application, connection, and network levels. All the programs (clients and servers) you intend to employ must support application-level encryption. Because you can install specialized, encrypted clients and servers on those devices, this might be a good strategy if you have one or two programs that you use often across the Internet among a small number of machines. However, it does not scale well for broad use, and you might not even have access to the source code for all the programs you want to run encrypted. Application-level encryption is offered by certain applications using PGP. Prior to transmitting email via the Internet, senders use PGP to encrypt it, and recipients use PGP to decrypt it. (PGP is also often used outside of apps, which is incredibly flexible but less user-friendly.)

It takes too much time and effort to integrate support for application-level encryption into too many distinct clients, servers, and processes for it to be helpful as a general kind of network link protection. Application-level encryption, however, can be advantageous if you simply require a single application to function safely.

One network link is the only one protected by link-level encryption. For instance, encryption in the modems at each end of a leased line will safeguard your data while it travels over that leased line, but not while it travels over other lines, goes through routers, or visits other intermediary hosts. Link-level encryption is carried out at a too low level to be of general utility. Most of the time, it is impossible to guarantee that link-level encryption is being carried out correctly (or at all) at each of the points along the untrusted network between the source and the destination.

An acceptable compromise between link-level encryption and application-level encryption appears to be network-level encryption. All network communication between two trusted sites is encrypted at one end, routed via the unreliable intermediary network, and then decrypted at the other end with network-level encryption. Routers or other network devices are used to encrypt and decode data at each trustworthy site's perimeter. Since all traffic must pass through a firewall, network-level encryption makes sense there. Traffic to machines within either trusted site is not encrypted, so those machines can take use of the encryption without the need for special software or configuration. Traffic to machines within either trusted site is not encrypted, so those machines can take use of the encryption without the need for special software or configuration. The packets are encrypted for machines outside of the trusted sites, making them private (unintelligible to anyone without the keys) and authenticated (could only have been sent by a key-holder).

What Do You Encrypt?

- How much of the packet do you want to encrypt when implementing network-level encryption? Just the TCP, UDP, or ICMP data segments, leaving the IP headers and other TCP, UDP, or ICMP headers unencrypted?
- The entire TCP, UDP, or ICMP packet, which is part of the IP data segment?
- A complete IP packet?

Encrypting only the TCP, UDP, or ICMP data segments will make your packet filtering system's job easier while also preventing the data itself from being compromised by an attacker (it can still see all the headers it needs to for normal packet filtering). A snooper can still observe which machines are communicating with which other machines using which protocols.

You can prevent a snooper from discovering what protocols you are using by encrypting the IP data segment, which implies that the entire UDP, TCP, or ICMP packet, headers, and all, is encrypted. However, you may complicate matters for your own packet filtering system. TCP, UDP, and ICMP headers are encrypted as part of the IP data segment, thus they are no longer visible to packet filtering systems unless they are situated between the encryption unit and the internal network. If your packet filtering system is separate from the encryption unit, it would be forced to base every choice just on IP source and destination addresses, which is extremely infrequently sufficient.

Encrypting the entire IP packet shields it from prying eyes, but depending on how close it is to the encryption unit, it may also shield your packet filtering system from prying eyes as well. To properly encrypt an IP packet between two sites, encapsulation "tunnel" must be provided, such as a straightforward TCP connection, between the encryption units at the two sites. Because the IP headers are no longer present for the intermediary routers to view, the tunnel is required. An attacker can only observe that the two encryption units are communicating with one another. Such "virtual private networks" can be built using some commercial routers, such Morning Star Express routers. As a result, your original packet is enclosed in an encrypted PPP packet, which is then encapsulated in a TCP packet from one Morning Star box to the other. This is how Morning Star accomplishes this.

The majority of websites that employ network-level encryption don't care if hackers can identify the machines that are communicating with one another or even the protocols they're employing (this attack is commonly called traffic analysis). For their own ease in processing the packets, such sites often simply encrypt the TCP, UDP, or ICMP data portions of packets. It is faster for a router to find the start of the IP data segment than it is for it to find the start of the IP data segment and, within that, the start of the TCP, UDP, or ICMP data segment, so websites that encrypt the entire TCP, UDP, or ICMP packet (the IP data segment) typically do so for performance reasons rather than for security.

Where Do You Encrypt?

The location of the encryption and decryption in relation to your packet filtering is a crucial consideration if you are planning to implement network-level encryption. The filters only need to permit the encrypted packets to enter and exit if encryption and decryption are performed inside the packet filtering boundary. Since all tunneled packets are addressed to the same remote address and port number at the other end of the tunnel, this is especially simple if tunnelling is being used. However, when encryption and decryption take place inside your filtering perimeter, packets that arrive encrypted are not examined by the packet filters. If the other site has been compromised, this makes you open to attack from it.

The packets entering from the other site can be thoroughly examined by your packet filtering system if the encryption and decryption are performed outside the packet filtering boundary. However, they can also be the target of intense examination by anyone who has accessed a device on your perimeter network, such as your bastion host.

Some commercial router solutions are starting to include encryption as a feature, and numerous vendors have declared their plan to do so. Over the coming years, this trend is likely to continue. However, there are currently either few or no standards for IP network-level encryption, which makes it difficult for the devices to work together. Everyone assumes that the other end is holding another one of their goods. As encryption becomes increasingly prevalent, we hope that this will improve and that standards will develop.

Key Distributions

Key distribution for network-level encryption can be a very challenging issue, just like with any encryption scheme. In order for the two ends to be able to encrypt and decrypt data transferred to and from each other, everything of the discussion up to this point has assumed that they share a key. Key distribution is "out of band," according to most systems currently in use, and according to their manufacturers, "key distribution is your concern, not ours." Customers must manually set keys on each participating system (by voice over phone, floppy disc, or through some other secure, private technique). This means that sites with whom you often share information can benefit from the use of network-level encryption (e.g., partners, key clients, or other branches of your own organization). Due to the setup time and effort, it is not suitable for ad hoc or temporary connections. Some systems can handle ad hoc or temporary connections more quickly and efficiently by using public key technologies or key distribution systems.

Common and Advanced Network Attacks

When malware is delivered and installed, the payload can be used to cause a variety of network related attacks. To mitigate attacks, it is useful to understand the types of attacks. By categorizing network attacks, it is possible to address types of attacks rather than individual attacks (Fig. 5.1).

Networks are susceptible to the following types of attacks:

- Reconnaissance Attacks
- Access Attacks
- DoS Attacks

5.5.1   Reconnaissance Attacks

Reconnaissance is information gathering. It is analogous to a thief surveying a neighborhood by going door-to-door pretending to sell something. What the thief is doing is looking for vulnerable homes to break into, such as unoccupied residences, residences with easy-to-open doors or windows, and those residences without security systems or security cameras. Threat actors use reconnaissance (or recon) attacks to do unauthorized discovery and mapping of systems, services, or vulnerabilities. Recon attacks precede access attacks or DoS attacks (Table 5.1).

5.5.2   Access Attacks

Access attacks exploit known vulnerabilities in authentication services, FTP services, and web services. The purpose of these types of attacks is to gain entry to web accounts, confidential databases, and other sensitive information.

Threat actors use access attacks on network devices and computers to retrieve data, gain access, or to escalate access privileges to administrator status.

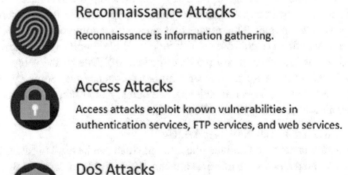

Reconnaissance Attacks

Reconnaissance is information gathering.

Access Attacks

Access attacks exploit known vulnerabilities in authentication services, FTP services, and web services.

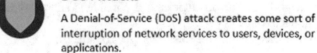

DoS Attacks

A Denial-of-Service (DoS) attack creates some sort of interruption of network services to users, devices, or applications.

Fig. 5.1 Types of network attacks

Table 5.1 Detailed description of reconnaissance attack

Technique	Description
Perform an information query of a target	The threat actor is looking for initial information about a target. Various tools can be used, including the Google search, organizations website, whois, and more.
Initiate a ping sweep of the target network	The information query usually reveals the target's network address. The threat actor can now initiate a ping sweep to determine which IP addresses are active.
Initiate a port scan of active IP addresses	This is used to determine which ports or services are available. Examples of port scanners include Nmap, SuperScan, Angry IP Scanner, and NetScanTools.
Run vulnerability scanners	This is to query the identified ports to determine the type and version of the application and operating system that is running on the host. Examples of tools include Nipper, Secuna PSI, Core Impact, Nessus v6, SAINT, and Open VAS.
Run exploitation tools	The threat actor now attempts to discover vulnerable services that can be exploited. A variety of vulnerability exploitation tools exist including Metasploit, Core Impact, Sqlmap, Social Engineer Toolkit, and Netsparker.

Password Attacks: In a password attack, the threat actor attempts to discover critical system passwords using various methods. Password attacks are very common and can be launched using a variety of password cracking tools.

Spoofing Attacks: In spoofing attacks, the threat actor device attempts to pose as another device by falsifying data. Common spoofing attacks include IP spoofing, MAC spoofing, and DHCP spoofing. These spoofing attacks will be discussed in more detail later in this module.

Other Access attacks include: Trust exploitations, Port redirections, Man-in-the-middle attacks, and Buffer overflow attacks (Fig. 5.2).

In a **trust exploitation attack**, a threat actor uses unauthorized privileges to gain access to a system, possibly compromising the target (Fig. 5.3).

In a **port redirection attack**, a threat actor uses a compromised system as a base for attacks against other targets. The example in the figure shows a threat actor using SSH (port 22) to connect to a compromised Host A. Host A is trusted by Host B and, therefore, the threat actor can use Telnet (port 23) to access it (Fig. 5.4).

In a **man-in-the-middle attack**, the threat actor is positioned in between two legitimate entities in order to read or modify the data that passes between the two parties. The figure displays an example of a man-in-the-middle attack (Fig. 5.5).

In a **buffer overflow attack**, the threat actor exploits the buffer memory and overwhelms it with unexpected values. This usually renders the system inoperable, creating a DoS attack. The figure shows that the threat actor is sending many packets to the victim in an attempt to overflow the victim's buffer (Fig. 5.6).

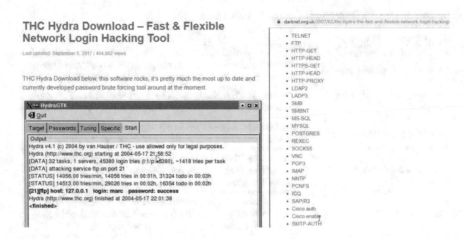

Fig. 5.2 Access attack tool

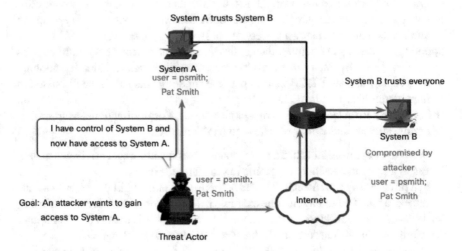

Fig. 5.3 Trust exploitation: access attack

5.5.3   Social Engineering Attack

Social engineering is an access attack that attempts to manipulate individuals into performing actions or divulging confidential information. Some social engineering techniques are performed in-person while others may use the telephone or internet.

Social engineers often rely on people's willingness to be helpful. They also prey on people's weaknesses. For example, a threat actor could call an authorized employee with an urgent problem that requires immediate network access. The threat actor could appeal to the employee's vanity, invoke authority using name-dropping techniques, or appeal to the employee's greed.

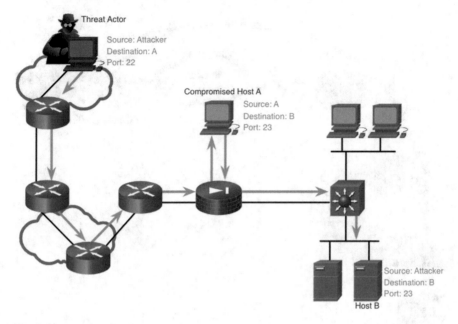

Fig. 5.4 Port redirection access attack

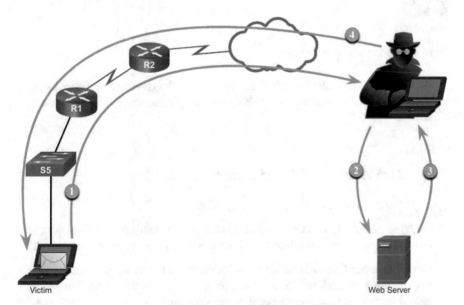

Fig. 5.5 Man-in-the-middle access attack

The Social Engineering Toolkit (SET) was designed to help white hat hackers and other network security professionals create social engineering attacks to test their own networks.

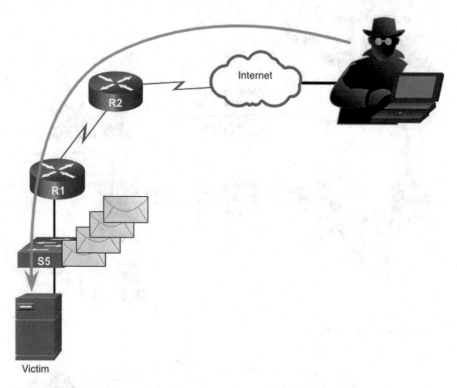

Fig. 5.6 Buffer overflow access attack

Enterprises must educate their users about the risks of social engineering, and develop strategies to validate identities over the phone, via email, or in person (Table 5.2; Fig. 5.7).

5.5.4   DoS Attack and DDoS Attack

DoS Attack

A Denial of Service (DoS) attack creates some sort of interruption of network services to users, devices, or applications. There are two major types of DoS attacks:

- **Overwhelming Quantity of Traffic**—The threat actor sends an enormous quantity of data at a rate that the network, host, or application cannot handle. This causes transmission and response times to slow down. It can also crash a device or service.
- **Maliciously Formatted Packets**—The threat actor sends a maliciously formatted packet to a host or application and the receiver is unable to handle it. This causes the receiving device to run very slowly or crash.

Table 5.2 Description of social engineering attack

Social Engineering Attack	Description
Pretexting	A threat actor pretends to need personal or financial data to confirm the identity of the recipient.
Phishing	A threat actor sends fraudulent email which is disguised as being from a legitimate, trusted source to trick the recipient into installing malware on their device, or to share personal or financial information.
Spear phishing	A threat actor creates a targeted phishing attack tailored for a specific individual or organization.
Spam	Also known as junk mail, this is unsolicited email which often contains harmful links, malware, or deceptive content.
Something for Something	Sometimes called "Quid pro quo", this is when a threat actor requests personal information from a party in exchange for something such as a gift.
Baiting	A threat actor leaves a malware infected flash drive in a public location. A victim finds the drive and unsuspectingly inserts it into their laptop, unintentionally installing malware.
Impersonation	This type of attack is where a threat actor pretends to be someone they are not to gain the trust of a victim.
Tailgating	This is where a threat actor quickly follows an authorized person into a secure location to gain access to a secure area.
Shoulder surfing	This is where a threat actor inconspicuously looks over someone's shoulder to steal their passwords or other information.
Dumpster diving	This is where a threat actor rummages through trash bins to discover confidential documents.

- DoS attacks are a major risk because they interrupt communication and cause significant loss of time and money. These attacks are relatively simple to conduct, even by an unskilled threat actor (Fig. 5.8).

DDoS Attack
A Distributed DoS Attack (DDoS) is like a DoS attack, but it originates from multiple, coordinated sources. For example, A threat actor builds a network of infected hosts, known as zombies. The threat actor uses a command-and-control system to send control messages to the zombies. The zombies constantly scan and infect more hosts with bot malware. The bot malware is designed to infect a host, making it a zombie that can communicate with the command-and-control system. The collection of zombies is called a botnet. When ready, the threat actor instructs the command-and-control system to make the botnet of zombies carry out a DDoS attack (Fig. 5.9).

5.5.5   Common IPv4 and IPv6 Attacks

IP does not validate whether the source IP address contained in a packet actually came from that source. For this reason, threat actors can send packets using a spoofed source IP address. Threat actors can also tamper with the other fields in the IP header to carry out their attacks. Security analysts must understand the different fields in both the IPv4 and IPv6 headers.

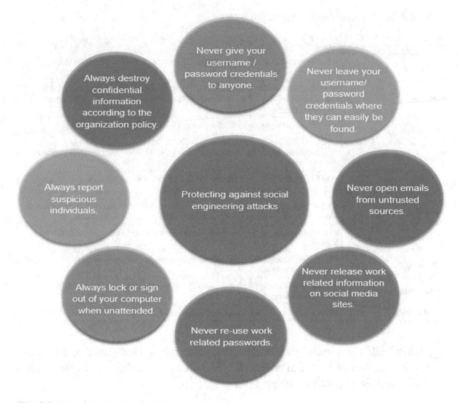

Fig. 5.7 Social engineering attacks

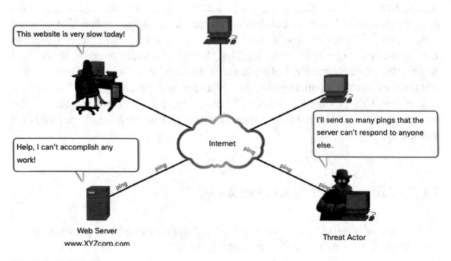

Fig. 5.8 DoS attack

Fig. 5.9 Example of
step-by-step DDoS attack

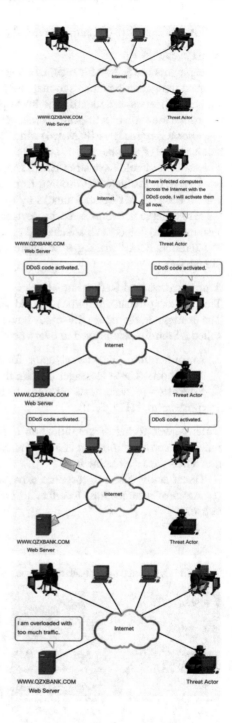

Some of the more common IP related attacks are shown in the table (Table 5.3).

ICMP Attacks

Threat actors use ICMP for reconnaissance and scanning attacks. They can launch information-gathering attacks to map out a network topology, discover which hosts are active (reachable), identify the host operating system (OS fingerprinting), and determine the state of a firewall. Threat actors also use ICMP for DoS attacks.

Note: ICMP for IPv4 (ICMPv4) and ICMP for IPv6 (ICMPv6) are susceptible to similar types of attacks.

Networks should have strict ICMP access control list (ACL) filtering on the network edge to avoid ICMP probing from the internet. Security analysts should be able to detect ICMP-related attacks by looking at captured traffic and log files. In the case of large networks, security devices such as firewalls and intrusion detection systems (IDS) detect such attacks and generate alerts to the security analysts.

Common ICMP messages of interest to threat actors are listed in the table (Table 5.4).

Amplification and Reflection Attacks

Threat actors often use amplification and reflection techniques to create DoS attacks. The example in the figure illustrates how an amplification and reflection technique called a Smurf attack is used to overwhelm a target host.

1. **Amplification**—The threat actor forwards ICMP echo request messages to many hosts. These messages contain the source IP address of the victim.
2. **Reflection**—These hosts all reply to the spoofed IP address of the victim to overwhelm it (Fig. 5.10).

Note: Newer forms of amplification and reflection attacks such as DNS-based reflection and amplification attacks and Network Time Protocol (NTP) amplification attacks are now being used.

Threat actors also use resource exhaustion attacks. These attacks consume the resources of a target host to either to crash it or to consume the resources of a network.

Table 5.3 Description of IP attack techniques

IP Attack Techniques	Description
ICMP attacks	Threat actors use Internet Control Message Protocol (ICMP) echo packets (pings) to discover subnets and hosts on a protected network, to generate DoS flood attacks, and to alter host routing tables.
Amplification and reflection attacks	Threat actors attempt to prevent legitimate users from accessing information or services using DoS and DDoS attacks.
Address spoofing attacks	Threat actors spoof the source IP address in an IP packet to perform blind spoofing or non-blind spoofing.
Man-in-the-middle attack (MITM)	Threat actors position themselves between a source and destination to transparently monitor, capture, and control the communication. They could eavesdrop by inspecting captured packets, or alter packets and forward them to their original destination.
Session hijacking	Threat actors gain access to the physical network, and then use an MITM attack to hijack a session.

Table 5.4 Common ICMP messages

ICMP Messages used by Hackers	Description
ICMP echo request and echo reply	This is used to perform host verification and DoS attacks.
ICMP unreachable	This is used to perform network reconnaissance and scanning attacks.
ICMP mask reply	This is used to map an internal IP network.
ICMP redirects	This is used to lure a target host into sending all traffic through a compromised device and create a MITM attack.
ICMP router discovery	This is used to inject bogus route entries into the routing table of a target host.

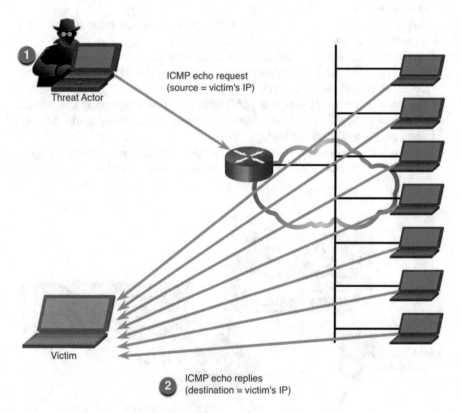

Fig. 5.10 Amplification and reflection attack

Address Spoofing Attacks

IP address spoofing attacks occur when a threat actor creates packets with false source IP address information to either hide the identity of the sender, or to pose as another legitimate user. The threat actor can then gain access to otherwise inaccessible data or circumvent security configurations. Spoofing is usually incorporated into another attack such as a Smurf attack.

Spoofing attacks can be non-blind or blind:

Non-blind spoofing—The threat actor can see the traffic that is being sent between the host and the target. The threat actor uses non-blind spoofing to inspect the reply packet from the target victim. Non-blind spoofing determines the state of a firewall and sequence-number prediction. It can also hijack an authorized session.

Blind spoofing—The threat actor cannot see the traffic that is being sent between the host and the target. Blind spoofing is used in DoS attacks.

Steps of MAC Address Spoofing

- MAC address spoofing attacks are used when threat actors have access to the internal network.
- Threat actors alter the MAC address of their host to match another known MAC address of a target host, as shown in the figure.
- The attacking host then sends a frame throughout the network with the newly-configured MAC address. When the switch receives the frame, it examines the source MAC address (Fig. 5.11).
- The switch overwrites the current MAC table entry and assigns the MAC address to the new port, as shown in the figure. It then forwards frames destined for the target host to the attacking host.
- Application or service spoofing is another spoofing example. A threat actor can connect a rogue DHCP server to create an MITM condition (Fig. 5.12).

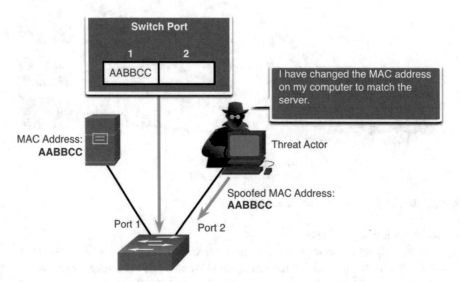

Fig. 5.11 Address spoofing attack

5.5.6 TCP and UDP Vulnerabilities

TCP Segment Header

While some attacks target IP, this topic discusses attacks that target TCP and UDP. TCP segment information appears immediately after the IP header. The fields of the TCP segment and the flags for the Control Bits field are displayed in the figure (Fig. 5.13).

The following are the six control bits of the TCP segment:

URG—Urgent pointer field significant
ACK—Acknowledgment field significant
PSH—Push function
RST—Reset the connection
SYN—Synchronize sequence numbers
FIN—No more data from sender

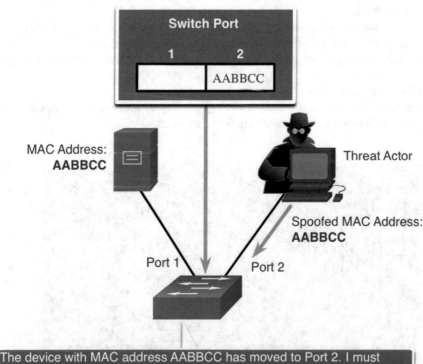

Fig. 5.12 Switch updates CAM table with spoofed address

TCP Services

TCP provides these services:

- **Reliable delivery**—TCP incorporates acknowledgments to guarantee delivery, instead of relying on upper-layer protocols to detect and resolve errors. If a timely acknowledgment is not received, the sender retransmits the data. Requiring acknowledgments of received data can cause substantial delays. Examples of application layer protocols that make use of TCP reliability include HTTP, SSL/TLS, FTP, DNS zone transfers, and others.
- **Flow control**—TCP implements flow control to address this issue. Rather than acknowledge one segment at a time, multiple segments can be acknowledged with a single acknowledgment segment.
- **Stateful communication**—TCP stateful communication between two parties occurs during the TCP three-way handshake. Before data can be transferred using TCP, a three-way handshake opens the TCP connection. If both sides agree to the TCP connection, data can be sent and received by both parties using TCP. A **TCP connection is established in three steps:**

1. The initiating client requests a client-to-server communication session with the server.
2. The server acknowledges the client-to-server communication session and requests a server-to-client communication session (Fig. 5.14).
3. The initiating client acknowledges the server-to-client communication session.

TCP Attacks

Network applications use TCP or UDP ports. Threat actors conduct port scans of target devices to discover which services they offer.

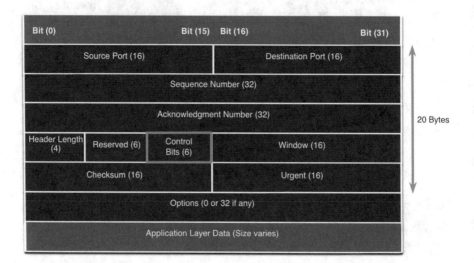

Fig. 5.13 TCP header

TCP SYN Flood Attack

- The TCP SYN Flood attack exploits the TCP three-way handshake. The figure shows a threat actor continually sending TCP SYN session request packets with a randomly spoofed source IP address to a target.
- The target device replies with a TCP SYN-ACK packet to the spoofed IP address and waits for a TCP ACK packet. Those responses never arrive.
- Eventually the target host is overwhelmed with half-open TCP connections, and TCP services are denied to legitimate users.

Step-by-Step TCP SYN Flood Attack

1. The threat actor sends multiple SYN requests to a web server.
2. The web server replies with SYN-ACKs for each SYN request and waits to complete the three-way handshake. The threat actor does not respond to the SYN-ACKs.
3. A valid user cannot access the web server because the web server has too many half-opened TCP connections (Fig. 5.15).

TCP Reset Attack

A TCP reset attack can be used to terminate TCP communications between two hosts. TCP can terminate a connection in a civilized (i.e., normal) manner and uncivilized (i.e., abrupt) manner. The figure displays the civilized manner when TCP uses a four-way exchange consisting of a pair of FIN and ACK segments from each TCP endpoint to close the TCP connection.

Terminating a TCP session uses the following four-way exchange process:

1. When the client has no more data to send in the stream, it sends a segment with the FIN flag set.

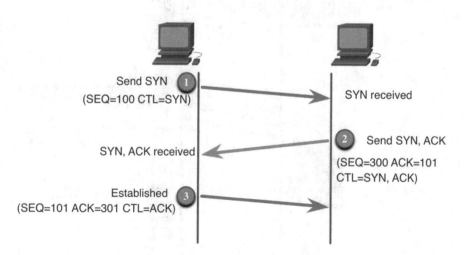

Fig. 5.14 TCP three way handshaking

2. The server sends an ACK to acknowledge the receipt of the FIN to terminate the session from client to server.
3. The server sends a FIN to the client to terminate the server-to-client session.
4. The client responds with an ACK to acknowledge the FIN from the server (Fig. 5.16).

TCP Session Hijacking
TCP session hijacking is another TCP vulnerability.

1. Although difficult to conduct, a threat actor takes over an already-authenticated host as it communicates with the target.
2. The threat actor must spoof the IP address of one host, predict the next sequence number, and send an ACK to the other host.
3. If successful, the threat actor could send, but not receive, data from the target device.

UDP Segment Header and Operation
UDP is commonly used by DNS, TFTP, NFS, and SNMP. It is also used with real-time applications such as media streaming or VoIP. UDP is a connectionless transport layer protocol. It has much lower overhead than TCP because it is not connection-oriented and does not offer the sophisticated retransmission, sequencing, and flow control mechanisms that provide reliability. The UDP segment structure, shown in the figure, is much smaller than TCP's segment structure (Fig. 5.17).

Although UPD is normally called unreliable, in contrast to TCP's reliability, this does not mean that applications that use UDP are always unreliable, nor does it

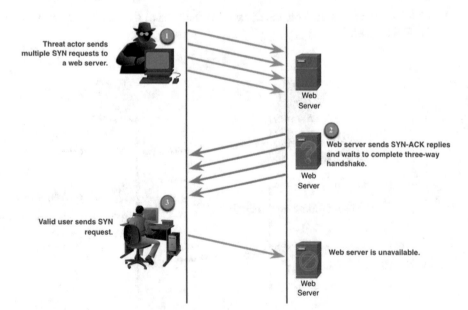

Fig. 5.15 Step-by-step TCP SYN flood attack

mean that UDP is an inferior protocol. It means that these functions are not provided by the transport layer protocol and must be implemented elsewhere if required. The low overhead of UDP makes it very desirable for protocols that make simple request and reply transactions.

For example, using TCP for DHCP would introduce unnecessary network traffic. If no response is received, the device resends the request.

UDP Attacks
- UDP is not protected by any encryption. You can add encryption to UDP, but it is not available by default.
- The lack of encryption means that anyone can see the traffic, change it, and send it on to its destination.
- Changing the data in the traffic will alter the 16-bit checksum, but the checksum is optional and is not always used.
- When the checksum is used, the threat actor can create a new checksum based on the new data payload, and then record it in the header as a new checksum.
- The destination device will find that the checksum matches the data without knowing that the data has been altered. This type of attack is not widely used.

UDP Flood Attacks
- You are more likely to see a UDP flood attack. In a UDP flood attack, all the resources on a network are consumed.
- The threat actor must use a tool like UDP Unicorn or Low Orbit Ion Cannon. These tools send a flood of UDP packets, often from a spoofed host, to a server on the subnet.

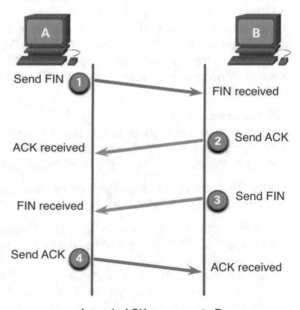

Fig. 5.16 Terminating TCP connection

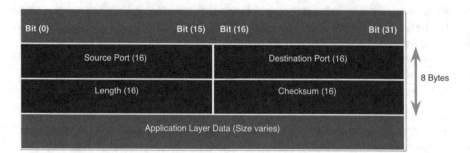

Fig. 5.17 UDP header

- The program will sweep through all the known ports trying to find closed ports. This will cause the server to reply with an ICMP port unreachable message.
- Because there are many closed ports on the server, this creates a lot of traffic on the segment, which uses up most of the bandwidth. The result is very similar to a DoS attack.

5.5.7 IP Services Vulnerabilities

ARP Vulnerabilities

The TCP/IP protocol suite was never built for security.

Therefore, the services that IP uses for addressing functions such as ARP, DNS, and DHCP, are also not secure (Fig. 5.18a).

Hosts broadcast an ARP Request to other hosts on the segment to determine the MAC address of a host with a particular IP address (Fig. 5.18b).

All hosts on the subnet receive and process the ARP Request. The host with the matching IP address in the ARP Request sends an ARP Reply (Fig. 5.18c, 5.18d, and 5.18e).

ARP Cache Poisoning

1. ARP cache poisoning can be used to launch various man-in-the-middle attacks.
2. PC-A requires the MAC address of its default gateway (R1); therefore, it sends an ARP Request for the MAC address of 192.168.10.1 (Fig. 5.19a).

Note: There are many tools available on the internet to create ARP MITM attacks including dsniff, Cain & Abel, ettercap, Yersinia, and others.

- R1 updates its ARP cache with the IP and MAC addresses of PC-A. R1 sends an ARP Reply to PC-A, which then updates its ARP cache with the IP and MAC addresses of R1 (Fig. 5.19b).
- The threat actor sends two spoofed gratuitous ARP Replies using its own MAC address for the indicated destination IP addresses. PC-A updates its ARP cache with its default gateway which is now pointing to the threat actor's host MAC

address. R1 also updates its ARP cache with the IP address of PC-A pointing to the threat actor's MAC address.

- The threat actor's host is executing an ARP poisoning attack. The ARP poisoning attack can be passive or active. Passive ARP poisoning is where threat actors steal confidential information. Active ARP poisoning is where threat actors modify data in transit, or inject malicious data (Fig. 5.19c).

5.5.8   DNS Attacks

The Domain Name System (DNS) protocol defines an automated service that matches resource names, such as www.cisco.com, with the required numeric network address, such as the IPv4 or IPv6 address. It includes the format for queries, responses, and data and uses resource records (RR) to identify the type of DNS response.

Securing DNS is often overlooked. However, it is crucial to the operation of a network and should be secured accordingly. DNS attacks include the following:

- DNS open resolver attacks
- DNS stealth attacks
- DNS domain shadowing attacks
- DNS tunnelling attacks

DNS Open Resolver Attacks
Many organizations use the services of publicly open DNS servers such as GoogleDNS (8.8.8.8) to provide responses to queries. This type of DNS server is called an open resolver. A DNS open resolver answers queries from clients outside

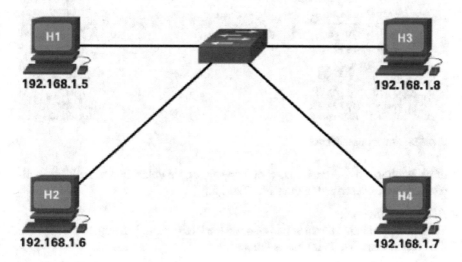

Fig. 5.18a ARP vulnerabilities

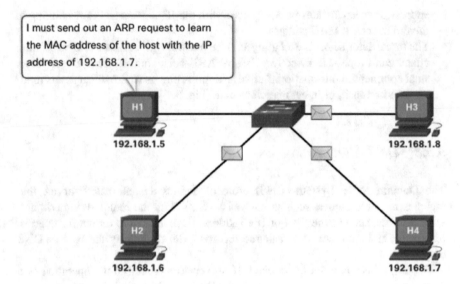

Fig. 5.18b ARP vulnerabilities

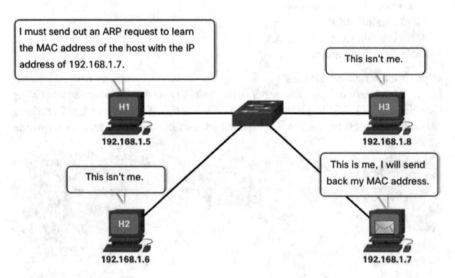

Fig. 5.18c ARP vulnerabilities

of its administrative domain. DNS open resolvers are vulnerable to multiple malicious activities described in the table (Table 5.5).

DNS Stealth Attacks

To hide their identity, threat actors also use the DNS stealth techniques described in the table to carry out their attacks (Table 5.6).

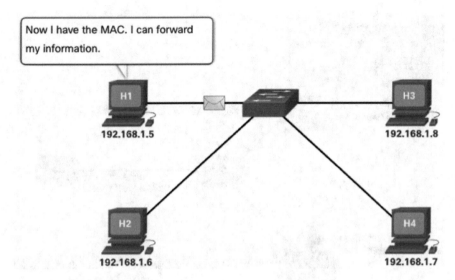

Fig. 5.18d ARP vulnerabilities

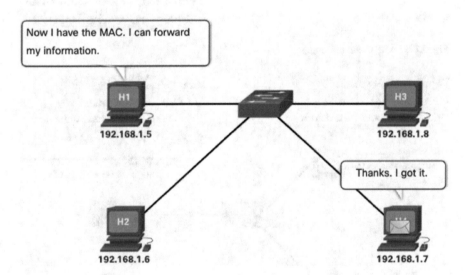

Fig. 5.18e ARP vulnerabilities

DNS Domain Shadowing Attacks

Domain shadowing involves the threat actor gathering domain account credentials in order to silently create multiple sub-domains to be used during the attacks. These subdomains typically point to malicious servers without alerting the actual owner of the parent domain.

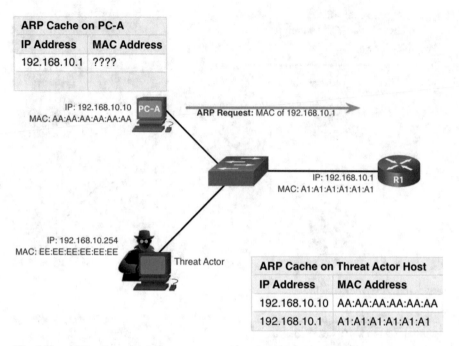

Fig. 5.19a ARP cache poisoning

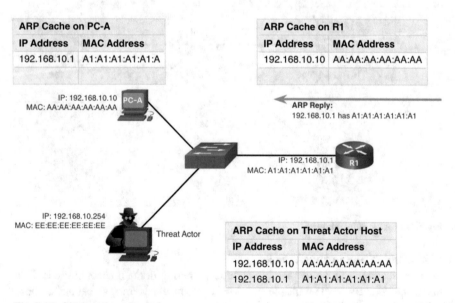

Fig. 5.19b ARP cache poisoning

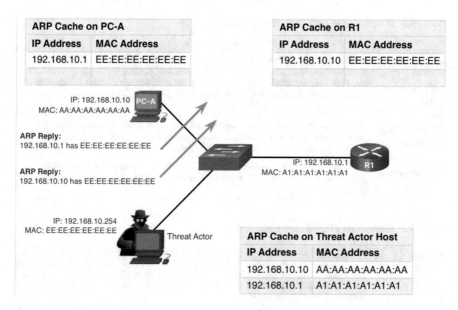

Fig. 5.19c ARP cache poisoning

DNS Tunneling

Threat actors who use DNS tunnelling place non-DNS traffic within DNS traffic. This method often circumvents security solutions when a threat actor wishes to communicate with bots inside a protected network, or exfiltrate data from the organization, such as a password database. When the threat actor uses DNS tunnelling, the different types of DNS records are altered.

This is how DNS tunnelling works for CnC commands sent to a botnet:

- The command data is split into multiple encoded chunks.
- Each chunk is placed into a lower-level domain name label of the DNS query.
- Because there is no response from the local or networked DNS for the query, the request is sent to the ISP's recursive DNS servers.
- The recursive DNS service will forward the query to the threat actor's authoritative name server.
- The process is repeated until all the queries containing the chunks of are sent.
- When the threat actor's authoritative name server receives the DNS queries from the infected devices, it sends responses for each DNS query, which contain the encapsulated, encoded CnC commands.
- The malware on the compromised host recombines the chunks and executes the commands hidden within the DNS record.

To stop DNS tunnelling, the network administrator must use a filter that inspects DNS traffic. Pay close attention to DNS queries that are longer than average, or those that have a suspicious domain name. DNS solutions, like Cisco OpenDNS, block much of the DNS tunnelling traffic by identifying suspicious domains.

Table 5.5 Description of DNS open resolver attack

DNS Resolver Vulnerabilities	Description
DNS cache poisoning attacks	Threat actors send spoofed, falsified record resource (RR) information to a DNS resolver to redirect users from legitimate sites to malicious sites. DNS cache poisoning attacks can all be used to inform the DNS resolver to use a malicious name server that is providing RR information for malicious activities.
DNS amplification and reflection attacks	Threat actors use DoS or DDoS attacks on DNS open resolvers to increase the volume of attacks and to hide the true source of an attack. Threat actors send DNS messages to the open resolvers using the IP address of a target host. These attacks are possible because the open resolver will respond to queries from anyone asking a question.
DNS resource utilization attacks	A DoS attack that consumes the resources of the DNS open resolvers. This DoS attack consumes all the available resources to negatively affect the operations of the DNS open resolver. The impact of this DoS attack may require the DNS open resolver to be rebooted or services to be stopped and restarted.

Table 5.6 Description of DNS stealth attack

DNS Stealth Techniques	Description
Fast Flux	Threat actors use this technique to hide their phishing and malware delivery sites behind a quickly-changing network of compromised DNS hosts. The DNS IP addresses are continuously changed within minutes. Botnets often employ Fast Flux techniques to effectively hide malicious servers from being detected.
Double IP Flux	Threat actors use this technique to rapidly change the hostname to IP address mappings and to also change the authoritative name server. This increases the difficulty of identifying the source of the attack.
Domain Generation Algorithms	Threat actors use this technique in malware to randomly generate domain names that can then be used as rendezvous points to their command and control (C&C) servers.

5.6   Cloud Security

Cloud security is a discipline of cyber security dedicated to securing cloud computing systems. This includes keeping data private and safe across online-based infrastructure, applications, and platforms. Securing these systems involves the efforts of cloud providers and the clients that use them, whether an individual, small to medium business, or enterprise uses. Cloud providers host services on their servers through always-on internet connections. Since their business relies on customer trust, cloud security methods are used to keep client data private and safely stored. However, cloud security also partially rests in the client's hands as well. Understanding both facets is pivotal to a healthy cloud security solution.

At its core, cloud security is composed of the following categories:

- Data security
- Identity and access management (IAM)
- Governance (policies on threat prevention, detection, and mitigation)
- Data retention (DR) and business continuity (BC) planning
- Legal compliance

Cloud security may appear like legacy IT security, but this framework demands a different approach. Before diving deeper, let us first look at what cloud security is.

Cloud security is the whole bundle of technology, protocols, and best practices that protect cloud computing environments, applications running in the cloud, and data held in the cloud. Securing cloud services begins with understanding what exactly is being secured, as well as, the system aspects that must be managed.

As an overview, backend development against security vulnerabilities is largely within the hands of cloud service providers. Aside from choosing a security-conscious provider, clients must focus mostly on proper service configuration and safe use habits. Additionally, clients should be sure that any end-user hardware and networks are properly secured.

The full scope of cloud security is designed to protect the following, regardless of your responsibilities:

- **Physical networks**—routers, electrical power, cabling, climate controls, etc.
- **Data storage**—hard drives, etc.
- **Data servers**—core network computing hardware and software.
- **Computer virtualization frameworks**—virtual machine software, host machines, and guest machines.
- **Operating systems (OS)**—software that houses.
- **Middleware**—application programming interface (API) management.
- **Runtime environments**—execution and upkeep of a running program.
- **Data**—all the information stored, modified, and accessed.
- **Applications**—traditional software services (email, tax software, productivity suites, etc.).
- **End-user hardware** –computers, mobile devices, Internet of Things (IoT) devices, etc.

With cloud computing, ownership over these components can vary widely. This can make the scope of client security responsibilities unclear. Since securing the cloud can look different based on who has authority over each component, it is important to understand how these are commonly grouped.

To simplify, cloud computing components are secured from two main viewpoints:

- **Cloud service types** are offered by third-party providers as modules used to create the cloud environment. Depending on the type of service, you may manage a different degree of the components within the service:
- **The core of any third-party cloud service** involves the provider managing the physical network, data storage, data servers, and computer virtualization frameworks. The service is stored on the provider's servers and virtualized via their internally managed network to be delivered to clients to be accessed remotely. This offloads hardware and other infrastructure costs to give clients access to their computing needs from anywhere via internet connectivity
- **Software-as-a-Service (SaaS)** cloud services provide clients access to applications that are purely hosted and run on the provider's servers. Providers manage the applications, data, runtime, middleware, and operating system. Clients are only tasked with getting their applications. *SaaS examples include Google Drive, Slack, Salesforce, Microsoft 365, Cisco WebEx, Evernote.*

- **Platform-as-a-Service** cloud services provide clients a host for developing their own applications, which are run within a client's own "sandboxed" space on provider servers. Providers manage the runtime, middleware, operating system. Clients are tasked with managing their applications, data, user access, end-user devices, and end-user networks. *PaaS examples include Google App Engine, Windows Azure.*
- **Infrastructure-as-a-Service (IaaS)** cloud services offer clients the hardware and remote connectivity frameworks to house the bulk of their computing, down to the operating system. Providers only manage core cloud services. Clients are tasked with securing all that gets stacked atop an operating system, including applications, data, runtimes, middleware, and the OS itself. In addition, clients need to manage user access, end-user devices, and end-user networks. *IaaS examples include Microsoft Azure, Google Compute Engine (GCE), Amazon Web Services (AWS).*
- **Cloud environments** are deployment models in which one or more cloud services create a system for the end-users and organizations. These segments the management responsibilities—including security—between clients and providers. The currently used cloud environments are:

  - **Public cloud environments** are composed of multi-tenant cloud services where a client shares a provider's servers with other clients, like an office building or coworking space. These are third-party services run by the provider to give clients access via the web.
  - **Private third-party cloud environments** are based on the use of a cloud service that provides the client with exclusive use of their own cloud. These single-tenant environments are normally owned, managed, and operated off-site by an external provider.
  - **Private in-house cloud environments** also composed of single-tenant cloud service servers but operated from their own private data center. In this case, this cloud environment is run by the business themselves to allow full configuration and setup of every element.
  - **Multi-cloud environments** include the use of two or more cloud services from separate providers. These can be any blend of public and/or private cloud services.
  - **Hybrid cloud environments** consist of using a blend of private third-party cloud and/or onsite private cloud data center with one or more public clouds.

By framing it from this perspective, we can understand that cloud-based security can be a bit different based on the type of cloud space users are working in. But the effects are felt by both individual and organizational clients alike.

How Does Cloud Security Work?

Every cloud security measure works to accomplish one or more of the following:

- Enable data recovery in case of data loss
- Protect storage and networks against malicious data theft
- Deter human error or negligence that causes data leaks
- Reduce the impact of any data or system compromise

Data security is an aspect of cloud security that involves the technical end of threat prevention. Tools and technologies allow providers and clients to insert barriers between the access and visibility of sensitive data. Among these, *encryption* is one of the most powerful tools available. Encryption scrambles your data so that it's only readable by someone who has the encryption key. If your data is lost or stolen, it will be effectively unreadable and meaningless. *Data transit protections* like virtual private networks (VPNs) are also emphasized in cloud networks.

Identity and access management (IAM) pertains to the accessibility privileges offered to user accounts. Managing authentication and authorization of user accounts also apply here. *Access controls* are pivotal to restrict users—both legitimate and malicious—from entering and compromising sensitive data and systems. Password management, multi-factor authentication, and other methods fall in the scope of IAM.

Governance focuses on policies for threat prevention, detection, and mitigation. With SMB and enterprises, aspects like *threat intel* can help with tracking and prioritizing threats to keep essential systems guarded carefully. However, even individual cloud clients could benefit from valuing safe *user behavior policies and training*. These apply mostly in organizational environments, but rules for safe use and response to threats can be helpful to any user.

Data retention (DR) and business continuity (BC) planning involve technical disaster recovery measures in case of data loss. Central to any DR and BC plan are methods for *data redundancy* such as backups. Additionally, having technical systems for ensuring uninterrupted operations can help. Frameworks for *testing the validity of backups* and detailed employee recovery instructions are just as valuable for a thorough BC plan.

Legal compliance revolves around protecting user privacy as set by legislative bodies. Governments have taken up the importance of protecting private user information from being exploited for profit. As such, organizations must follow regulations to abide by these policies. One approach is the use of *data masking,* which obscures identity within data via encryption methods.

What Makes Cloud Security Different?

Traditional IT security has felt an immense evolution due to the shift to cloud-based computing. While cloud models allow for more convenience, always-on connectivity requires new considerations to keep them secure. Cloud security, as a modernized cyber security solution, stands out from legacy IT models in a few ways.

Data storage: The biggest distinction is that older models of IT relied heavily upon onsite data storage. Organizations have long found that building all IT frameworks in-house for detailed, custom security controls is costly and rigid. Cloud-based frameworks have helped offload costs of system development and upkeep, but also remove some control from users.

Scaling speed: On a similar note, cloud security demands unique attention when scaling organization IT systems. Cloud-centric infrastructure and apps are very modular and quick to mobilize. While this ability keeps systems uniformly adjusted to organizational changes, it does poses concerns when an organization's need for upgrades and convenience outpaces their ability to keep up with security.

End-user system interfacing: For organizations and individual users alike, cloud systems also interface with many other systems and services that must be secured. Access permissions must be maintained from the end-user device level to the software level and even the network level. Beyond this, providers and users must be attentive to vulnerabilities they might cause through unsafe setup and system access behaviors.

Proximity to other networked data and systems: Since cloud systems are a persistent connection between cloud providers and all their users, this substantial network can compromise even the provider themselves. In networking landscapes, a single weak device or component can be exploited to infect the rest. Cloud providers expose themselves to threats from many end-users that they interact with, whether they are providing data storage or other services. Additional network security responsibilities fall upon the providers who otherwise delivered products live purely on end-user systems instead of their own.

Solving most cloud security issues means that users and cloud providers—both in personal and business environments—must both remain proactive about their own roles in cyber security. This two-pronged approach means users and providers mutually must address:

- Secure system configuration and maintenance.
- User safety education—both behaviorally and technically.
- Ultimately, cloud providers and users must have transparency and accountability to ensure both parties stay safe.

Cloud Security Risks

What are the security issues in cloud computing? Because if you do not know them, then how are you supposed to put proper measures in place? After all, weak cloud security can expose users and providers to all types of cyber security threats. Some common cloud security threats include:

- **Risks of cloud-based infrastructure** including incompatible legacy IT frameworks, and third-party data storage service disruptions.
- **Internal threats due to human error** such as misconfiguration of user access controls.
- **External threats** caused almost exclusively by malicious actors, such as malware, phishing, and DDoS attacks.
- The biggest risk with the cloud is that there is no perimeter. Traditional cyber security focused on protecting the perimeter, but cloud environments are highly connected which means insecure APIs (Application Programming Interfaces) and account hijacks can pose real problems. Faced with cloud computing security risks, cyber security professionals need to shift to a data-centric approach.

- Interconnectedness also poses problems for networks. Malicious actors often breach networks through compromised or weak credentials. Once a hacker manages to make a landing, they can easily expand and use poorly protected interfaces in the cloud to locate data on different databases or nodes. They can even use their own cloud servers as a destination where they can export and store any stolen data. Security needs to be in the cloud—not just protecting access to your cloud data.
- Third-party storage of your data and access via the internet each pose their own threats as well. If for some reason those services are interrupted, your access to the data may be lost. For instance, a phone network outage could mean you cannot access the cloud at an essential time. Alternatively, a power outage could affect the data center where your data is stored, possibly with permanent data loss.
- Such interruptions could have long-term repercussions. A recent power outage at an Amazon cloud data facility resulted in data loss for some customers when servers incurred hardware damage. This is a good example of why you should have local backups of at least some of your data and applications.

Why Cloud Security Is Important?

In the 1990s, business and personal data lived locally—and security was local as well. Data would be located on a PC's internal storage at home, and on enterprise servers, if you worked for a company.

Introducing cloud technology has forced everyone to reevaluate cyber security. Your data and applications might be floating between local and remote systems - and always internet-accessible. If you are accessing Google Docs on your smartphone, or using Salesforce software to look after your customers, that data could be held anywhere. Therefore, protecting it becomes more difficult than when it was just a question of stopping unwanted users from gaining access to your network. Cloud security requires adjusting some previous IT practices, but it has become more essential for two key reasons:

- **Convenience over security.** Cloud computing is exponentially growing as a primary method for both workplace and individual use. Innovation has allowed new technology to be implemented quicker than industry security standards can keep up, putting more responsibility on users and providers to consider the risks of accessibility.
- **Centralization and multi-tenant storage.** Every component—from core infrastructure to small data like emails and documents—can now be located and accessed remotely on 24/7 web-based connections. All this data gathering in the servers of a few major service providers can be highly dangerous. Threat actors can now target large multi-organizational data centers and cause immense data breaches.
- Unfortunately, malicious actors realize the value of cloud-based targets and increasingly probe them for exploits. Despite cloud providers taking many security roles from clients, they do not manage everything. This leaves even non-technical users with the duty to self-educate on cloud security.

- That said, users are not alone in cloud security responsibilities. Being aware of the scope of your security duties will help the entire system stay much safer.

5.7 Introduction to Blockchain and Bitcoin

5.7.1 Blockchain

Blockchain cryptography is a complicated topic. However, you can achieve a better and simpler understanding of cryptography by reflecting on the fundamentals of its working. Take the example of radio signals that help you listen to broadcasts on your vehicle's radio. The broadcast is publicly available to everyone, and other people could also listen to the broadcast.

On the other hand, take the example of radio communications between two soldiers on a military mission. Such type of defense-level communications will be highly secure and encrypted, and only the intended participants can receive and know the information. You can find the applications of cryptography in blockchain in the exact same manner.

Basically, cryptography serves as a technique for the transmission of secure messages among two or more participants. The sender leverages a specific type of key and algorithm for encryption of a message before sending it to the receiver. Then, the receiver employs decryption for obtaining the original message. So, what is the important aspect in the operations of cryptography? The answer directly points out encryption keys.

Encryption keys ensure that unauthorized recipients or readers cannot read a message, data value, or transaction. They are the right tools for making sure that the intended recipients only are capable of reading and processing a specific message, data value, or transaction. Therefore, keys can bring 'crypto' traits to information.

The majority of blockchain applications do not involve explicit use of sending secret, encrypted messages, especially in the public blockchain. On the other hand, a new generation of blockchain applications utilizes different variants of cryptography encryption for ensuring security and complete anonymity of transaction details. Many new tools related to applications of cryptography in blockchain have emerged over the years with diverse functionalities. Some notable examples of the tools include hashing and digital signatures.

With a basic outline of details in blockchain cryptography explained properly, it is evident that cryptography refers to the practice of creating protocols for preventing third parties from accessing and viewing data. The modern applications of cryptography bring a combination of different disciplines such as physics, math, computer science, engineering, and others.

However, the focus of applications of blockchain cryptography primarily emphasizes terms such as encryption, decryption, cipher, and keys. Readers must have already come to terms with the applications of encryption and decryption in cryptography. Cipher is the algorithm that helps in performing the processes of encryption and decryption, generally by following a series of well-defined steps.

Keys refer to the trivial amount of information required to obtain output from the cryptography algorithm. Now, let us look at digital signatures and hashing, the two components that establish the significant role of cryptography in the blockchain.

Implications of Blockchain and Cryptography with Digital Signatures
Digital signature basically refers to a mathematical approach for creating digital codes that are utilized for verifying whether digital messages and documents are legible or not. Public-key encryption is suitable for producing and substantiating the codes. In addition, attaching digital signatures to an electronically disseminated document ensures verification of specifications of the content and the sender.

Before diving further into the implications of blockchain and cryptography with digital signatures, let us reflect back on security fundamentals. It is important to address the requirements of four significant traits in the online transmission of valuable data. The four important traits include confidentiality, non-repudiation, authentication, and integrity.

Generally, encryption algorithms such as AES can address the need for confidentiality. However, digital signatures are preferable alternatives for addressing the requirement of the other three traits of non-repudiation, integrity, and authentication. The effectiveness of blockchain cryptography with digital signatures depends a lot on two prominent methods of encryption.

5.7.2   Bitcoin

Encryption and Bitcoin
The Bitcoin network and database itself does not use any encryption. As an open, distributed database, the blockchain has no need to encrypt data. All data passed between Bitcoin nodes is unencrypted in order to allow total strangers to interact over the Bitcoin network.

However, some Bitcoin services require more security and privacy. In order to securely store private keys, most Bitcoin wallets encrypt their data using a variety of encryption schemes. For example, Bitcoin Core encrypts its wallet using the Advanced Encryption Standard (AES). This is the same encryption algorithm used by the NSA for its classified information, and AES is considered extremely secure. In order to decrypt a Bitcoin Core wallet, a user must enter their password, which is used as the decryption key.

Hashing and Bitcoin
The Bitcoin protocol mainly uses SHA-256 for all hashing operations. Most importantly, hashing is used to implement Bitcoin's Proof-of-Work mechanism. A hash is a large number, and for a miner to submit a block to the network, the hash of the block must be below a certain threshold. Because hashing is a random, unpredictable process, finding a valid hash can only be achieved through intensive guessing.

Digital Signatures and Bitcoin

Bitcoin implements a digital signature algorithm called ECDSA which is based on elliptic curve cryptography. While ECDSA allows a private key to sign any type of message, digital signatures are most frequently used to sign transactions and send bitcoin.

The Bitcoin protocol allows pieces of bitcoin called UTXOs to be sent to a public key, such that only a valid signature from the corresponding private key can unlock it. This signature is published to the blockchain so that any member of the Bitcoin network can verify that the signature, the public key, and the message match.

Bitcoin is a purely peer-to-peer system. A Bitcoin transaction can be sent from payer to payee without any third-party taking custody of the funds. Although miners process each transaction, they are unable to produce valid signatures for other people's bitcoin and thus unable to steal any bitcoin.

Bibliography

1. Cisco, networkingacademy, network security.
2. Stallings, William. *Cryptography and network security, 4/E*. Pearson Education India, 2006.
3. Karate, Atul. *Cryptography and network security*. Tata McGraw-Hill Education, 2013.
4. Frozen, Behrouz A., and Debdeep Mukhopadhyay. *Cryptography and network security*. Vol. 12. New York, NY, USA: McGraw Hill Education (India) Private Limited, 2015.
5. Easttom, C. (2015). Modern cryptography. *Applied mathematics for encryption and information security. McGraw-Hill Publishing*.
6. Katz, J., & Lindell, Y. (2020). *Introduction to modern cryptography*. CRC Press.
7. Bellare, M., & Rogaway, P. (2005). Introduction to modern cryptography. *Ucsd Cse, 207*, 207.
8. Zheng, Z. (2022). Modern Cryptography Volume 1: A Classical Introduction to Informational and Mathematical Principle.
9. Shemanske, T. R. (2017). *Modern Cryptography and Elliptic Curves* (Vol. 83). American Mathematical Soc.
10. Bhat, Bawna, Abdul Wahid Ali, and Apurva Gupta. "DES and AES performance evaluation." *International Conference on Computing, Communication & Automation*. IEEE, 2015.
11. Rihan, Shaza D., Ahmed Khalid, and Saife Eldin F. Osman. "A performance comparison of encryption algorithms AES and DES." *International Journal of Engineering Research & Technology (IJERT)* 4.12 (2015): 151–154.
12. Mahajan, Prerna, and Abhishek Sachdeva. "A study of encryption algorithms AES, DES and RSA for security." *Global Journal of Computer Science and Technology* (2013).
13. Mao, Wenbo. *Modern cryptography: theory and practice*. Pearson Education India, 2003.
14. B Rajkumar "Vulnerability Analysis and Defense Against Attacks: Implications of Trust – Based Cross – Layer Security Protocol for Mobile Adhoc Networks "presented at the International" Conference on IT FWP 09, Andhra Pradesh, India. in 2009.
15. B Rajkumar, G Arunakranthi, "Implementation and Mitigation for Cyber Attacks with proposed OCR Process Model" in Int. J. of Natural Volatiles & Essential Oils, 2021; vol. 8(5): 2149–2160.
16. Daemen, J., & Rijmen, V. (1999). AES proposal: Rijndael.
17. Zodpe, H., & Shaikh, A. (2021). A Survey on Various Cryptanalytic Attacks on the AES Algorithm. *International Journal of Next-Generation Computing*, 115–123.
18. Sharma, N. (2017). A Review of Information Security using Cryptography Technique. *International Journal of Advanced Research in Computer Science, 8*(4).

19. Gupta, A., & Walia, N. K. (2014). Cryptography Algorithms: a review.
20. Amalraj, A. J., & Jose, J. J. R. (2016). A survey paper on cryptography techniques. *International Journal of Computer Science and mobile computing*, *5*(8), 55–59.
21. Pachghare, V. K. (2019). *Cryptography and information security*. PHI Learning Pvt. Ltd.
22. Koblitz, N., Menezes, A., & Vanstone, S. (2000). The state of elliptic curve cryptography. *Designs, codes and cryptography*, *19*(2), 173–193.
23. Hankerson, D., Menezes, A. J., & Vanstone, S. (2006). *Guide to elliptic curve cryptography*. Springer Science & Business Media.
24. Kapoor, V., Abraham, V. S., & Singh, R. (2008). Elliptic curve cryptography. *Ubiquity*, *2008*(May), 1–8.
25. Amara, M., & Siad, A. (2011, May). Elliptic curve cryptography and its applications. In *International workshop on systems, signal processing and their applications, WOSSPA* (pp. 247–250). IEEE.
26. Cilardo, A., Coppolino, L., Mazzocca, N., & Romano, L. (2006). Elliptic curve cryptography engineering. *Proceedings of the IEEE*, *94*(2), 395–406.

Printed in the United States
by Baker & Taylor Publisher Services